MAKING
SPELLS
FOR GOOD
MAGIC

MAKING
SPELLS
FOR GOOD
MAGIC

a practical guide to white magic-making for personal empowerment, with over 60 nature charms, rituals, incantations and invocations, and over 280 photographs and illustrations

CONSULTANT EDITOR RAJE AIREY

southwater

This edition is published by Southwater

Southwater is an imprint of Anness Publishing Ltd
Hermes House, 88-89 Blackfriars Road, London SE1 8HA
tel. 020 7401 2077; fax 020 7633 9499
www.southwaterbooks.com; info@anness.com

© Anness Publishing Ltd 2005

UK agent: The Manning Partnership Ltd, 6 The Old Dairy, Melcombe Road, Bath BA2 3LR;
tel. 01225 478 444; fax 01225 478 440; sales@manning-partnership.co.uk

UK distributor: Grantham Book Services Ltd, Isaac Newton Way, Alma Park Industrial Estate,
Grantham, Lincs NG31 9SD; tel. 01476 541080; fax 01476 541061; orders@gbs.tbs-ltd.co.uk

North American agent/distributor: National Book Network, 4501 Forbes Boulevard, Suite 200, Lanham,
MD 20706; tel. 301 459 3366; fax 301 429 5746; www.nbnbooks.com

Australian agent/distributor: Pan Macmillan Australia, Level 18, St Martins Tower, 31 Market St, Sydney,
NSW 2000; tel. 1300 135 113; fax 1300 135 103; customer.service@macmillan.com.au

New Zealand agent/distributor: David Bateman Ltd, 30 Tarndale Grove, Off Bush Road, Albany,
Auckland; tel. (09) 415 7664; fax (09) 415 8892

Publisher: Joanna Lorenz
Editorial Director: Helen Sudell
Executive Editor: Joanne Rippin
Photographs: Michelle Garrett, Don Last, John Freeman
Designer: Anthony Cohen
Cover Design: Adelle Morris

The Publisher would like to thank The Bridgeman Art Library for the use of its images:
p20 *The Achievement by Sir Galahad* by Sir Edward Burne-Jones; 146 top *Odin* by Sir Edward Burne-Jones;
146 bottom *Ramesses IV* by Jean Francois Campollion; 147 *The Angel Gabriel* by Sir Edward Burne-Jones.

Previously published as part of a larger volume, *Natural Magic*

1 3 5 7 9 10 8 6 4 2

CONTENTS

INTRODUCTION

Essentially, magic is the art of making things happen by drawing on the powers of the natural world. But even if we are not yet able to influence events, most of us retain a sense of the magical, despite living in an urban, technological society and, for the most part, out of touch with the natural world and its powers. "Magic" is often the word we instinctively use to describe a stunning sunset, a leafy forest glade, or a wintry landscape transformed by a carpet of snow. It may also be how we refer to an idyllic time, or to one of life's very special moments, such as the birth of a child or an outstanding achievement. All of these experiences, however diverse, have something in common: they touch us at our deepest core, enchanting, surprising and delighting us.

We may also use the term "magic" to express our sense of wonder and awe at creation and our place in it: the feeling that for this moment at least, all is right with the world. Magic is what can happen when we step outside our everyday reality to connect with something precious and larger than our selves.

REDEFINING OUR VALUES

In modern western society, with its emphasis on reason, logic and scientific enquiry, a living relationship with the otherworld has largely been lost. Although we are materially wealthy, many people feel dissatisfied with their lives; there is the feeling that something is missing but we are not quite sure what. This condition has engendered a search for meaning and a spirituality that makes sense, and it is in this context that interest in magic is steadily growing.

Magic suggests that there is more to our world than can be seen with the naked eye, and that a rational and objective approach is not always the best way. In fact, to establish a relationship with the otherworld, it is necessary to put logic and reason aside, and to engage with the irrational, emotional and intuitive, or the forces of "unreason". Connecting with the world of magic means rediscovering the languages of dreams and visions, imagination and fantasy, myth and story, image and symbol and to be prepared to enter the unknown.

ABOUT THIS BOOK

The aim of this book is to give the reader enough information and practical techniques to enable them to establish their own unique relationship with the otherworld and learn how to use its powers for self-mastery. While there are many schools of magic, each with its own path and set of disciplines, this book does not adhere to any one particular way, but draws on material from a diversity of magical traditions, including shamanism, wicca and "high magic". An important central theme in the book is that to become a magic-worker involves responsibility – towards yourself and others – and teaches that magic powers should always be used for the greatest good of all.

The practical information in this book includes detailed instructions on how to work with specific spells and rituals and create and nurture sacred space. Information on divination, including tarot and astrology, is also given, while a special section shows how to develop your intuitive powers. As you turn the pages of this book and develop your skills, you will discover how to step outside your everyday self and enter into a magical world full of self-discovery and adventure.

Sharing rituals and ceremonies with a magical partner can be a source of strength and inspiration.

Using the four Elements in your magic is one of the most obvious ways to forge magical links to the natural world.

One of the most challenging and rewarding ways to practise magic is to use your mind to access other worlds and dimensions.

PLANNING AND PREPARATION

Before you undertake any piece of magic, there are certain set procedures that must be followed, more or less, all the time. For magic to be successful adequate preparation is essential, and putting in the effort during the initial stages will set the scene for the magic itself. It is worth making the time to track down all the correct ingredients and also to prepare yourself and your workspace so that you are in the right frame of mind for making magic. Contraindications to making magic would be when you feel tired or drained, or when your mind is busy and won't switch off.

This first chapter will give you a good grounding in all the practical information you need to start working magic, beginning with ethics and responsibilities. It goes on to explain how to consecrate yourself, your space and your equipment through bathing and cleansing rituals that include smudging and the use of herbs and oils. It also describes techniques for

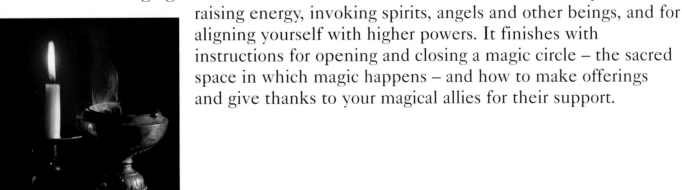

raising energy, invoking spirits, angels and other beings, and for aligning yourself with higher powers. It finishes with instructions for opening and closing a magic circle – the sacred space in which magic happens – and how to make offerings and give thanks to your magical allies for their support.

THE POWER OF MAGIC

When you work with magic you are working with powerful forces for change, and it is important to realize this before you begin to send wishes and weave spells. The energy you put into magic increases as it is released and what you give out returns to you threefold. So be careful with what you wish for, as you might have to live with the consequences for a long time. It is important not to be fearful of magic, however, but instead learn how to be humble and ask for the right things in the right way. When you ask with sincerity, and from the heart, you ask from the right place, and this is the way to exercise the true power that you hold within you.

ETHICS AND RESPONSIBILITIES

The witches' law states that "if you harm none, do what you will." At first, this may appear like a licence to do whatsoever you like, and magic-workers are often criticized for having no moral code. However, it actually means that as long as you cause no harm to any person, animal or thing, you may follow your True Will. True Will is not a personal choice or desire, but the purpose of your existence here on earth. The reason you are alive is to discover your True Will, or purpose, and work towards realizing it. Furthermore, it is a universal law that whatever we give out is reflected back, hence the biblical saying, "as you sow, so shall you reap".

Reaping the consequences of our actions – good or bad – is inevitable, if not in this life, then in another incarnation. Consequently, it is always a good idea to align yourself with the divine will of the universe before starting to perform a magical act. You may think of the divine will as the God or Goddess, your Higher Self, the ultimate source, or the One – whichever description best works for you.

The energy and concentration you devote to your magic making will return to you threefold.

MAKING THE PLEDGE

Before starting to weave magical spells or rituals, it is important that you pledge yourself and your actions to the light. This is a way of reminding yourself of your intentions and should be done simply and from the heart.

1 Place your hands upon your heart and ask that you be filled with the light of love. Imagine the golden light and feelings of love filling your heart and then your whole being.

2 Open your arms and raise them above your head, palms facing up towards the heavens, and say the pledge. Then bring your arms down to your sides.

When making the Spellweaver's Pledge imagine golden light filling your whole being.

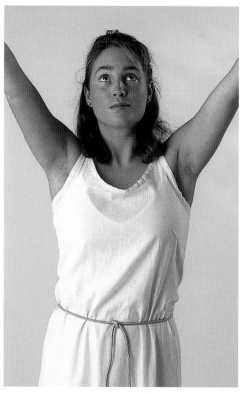

Raising your arms, as you say the pledge, links you with the heavens.

The Spellweaver's Pledge

I call upon the divine will of the universe to send a blessing upon my heart, so that I may be filled with the light of love and truth in all that I do. I pledge that from this day I will do my best to harm none with my thoughts, words or deeds. I pledge that any magic I perform will be for the highest good of all. So mote it be!

HEDGEWITCHES

Of course, it is not necessary to work with others or to belong to any recognized group in order to practise magic. A magical practitioner who works alone and according to his or her own individual style and belief is sometimes known as a hedgewitch. In days of old, the hedgewitch, or country witch, or wise woman, would have been called upon regularly by members of the community. They would have performed such things as house blessings and clearings, to help with the protection of vulnerable people, property and personal possessions, and also to act as an oracle for discovering the reasons behind particular problems or hindrances.

Hedgewitches, who live in harmony with nature, use their knowledge of herbs, flowers, roots and leaves to make up concoctions for such purposes as healing, protection or fertility. The country witches of today seldom write anything down, relying – as did their predecessors – on memory and inspiration for their workings, which are usually conducted in a sacred place. Their knowledge is passed on in the old way, by apprenticeship, whereby a newcomer is gradually taught magical rituals, healing spells, chants and movements, or else may be self-taught. A hedgewitch is so named because she is able to keep one foot in the material world and the other in the world of spirit, and the "hedge" represents the veil between the worlds.

COVENS AND LODGES

Many practitioners of magic like to work with others, either within a coven or group of witches, or in a magical lodge. Traditionally, these organizations have been kept secret, but one way of discovering other like-minded people is to look for announcements in popular occult magazines, which may list societies or training schools. Alternatively, seek out publications written by specialists in the area of magic that most interests you. It has never been easy to find a way into the Mysteries, but these basic steps are open to all.

Having found a suitable coven or lodge, the next step will be to undergo a ceremony of admission, or initiation. The word "initiation" means beginning, so this is a first step, rather than the conclusion of a magician's work. No one should accept initiation into a group unless they are certain that it is right for them, and that the group is trustworthy. If there are any doubts in your mind about a group, it is far better to wait than to rush into a situation.

COMMITMENT AND SECRECY

Although society is far more tolerant now than it was in the past, it is still best to keep some things secret and go about your magical work in privacy and silence, both of which will add to its power. Effective magicians never speak of some things, including who is working magic, when and where any magic or ritual is being done (unless it is some sort of public festival) and any magical names and mottos used. These are only ever known to the magicians and the gods. While you can read books on most techniques or activities, it is the practical experience of magic that makes it work, and that is a particular secret that cannot be shared.

Go about your magical work in quiet privacy: it is not a sideshow or something to do in public, but a personal commitment that you should take seriously.

TIME AND PLACE

Before you rush into any piece of magical work you need to consider timing and location. Timing is important because everything has a point of greatest power and therefore a right time and purpose. By utilizing the season, the correct phase of the moon, the four winds, the right planets, herbs, minerals and affirmations, you can increase the efficacy of your magic. Similarly, every place has a certain energy field, or spirit of place, that will be naturally better suited to some types of magic than others.

An offering on an outside altar can be as simple as a few flowers on a tree branch.

TIMING

To plan the best time for your magic you need to use your knowledge of the phases of the moon, the time of day and the season. Current positions of the planets and the kind of "energetic pattern" they are creating are also worth noting. You can consult an ephemeris, a table showing the movements of the planets, for this kind of astronomical information.

Consider whether the purpose of your magic is to attract or create something, or to reflect or dissolve something. The waxing phases of the sun or moon are for the former, while their waning phases are associated with the latter. The moon's cycles last roughly 28 days, while the solar cycle takes 365 days, or a calendar year; the sun is waxing, or growing in strength, from the winter to the summer solstice, and waning thereafter. To find out about the phases of the moon you can consult a diary or almanac.

PATIENCE

Modern society is fast-paced and based on instant gratification. We are not accustomed to having to wait for things and even the length of time it takes to cook our food is getting shorter and shorter. Yet magic does not work in this way. It takes time for things to manifest on the material plane, and we must resist the temptation to think it is not working if, once we have set magic in motion, we don't see an immediate result.

One of the golden rules for every magic worker is patience. Just as it takes time for a sown seed to germinate and develop into a healthy plant, so it is with magic – and the bigger the plant you are trying to grow, the longer it may take to come to fruition. So once you have set your magic in motion, leave it alone. Do not keep repeating the spell or ritual without need as this shows a lack of faith in its original power. Another thing to remember is that magic can move in mysterious ways, so try not to be cynical or disappointed if the results are not exactly what you had planned or envisioned; they will be exactly what your inner self called for to meet your true needs at this particular time.

INSIDE OR OUTSIDE

You have two choices about where to perform your magic – indoors or outdoors. Traditionally, spells are cast outside. Some covens meet out of doors, in woods or high hills, in all weathers. These outdoor witches use whatever is around them for their symbols: water in a seashell from rain or a spring, a small

One of the most important elements of your magic work is patience. If you are naturally impatient then you will need to work on your ability to wait.

Woodland clearings, or the tops of hills, are traditionally places where magic is made, but anywhere outside will do, so long as it is quiet and secluded and you can be sure you will not be interrupted.

bonfire, a tree branch for a wand and their hand for a sword. If you want to work outside it is helpful to find a natural beauty spot that is peaceful and secluded, where you won't be disturbed. Such a place could be part of a garden, near a particular rock or tree, or in meadowland. It will be somewhere that inspires a feeling of being part of creation and where you feel safe. You may also want to set up a natural altar in your chosen spot, using "found" objects that you come across, such as stones, feathers, nuts, flowers, leaves, pine cones etc.

If you do not have access to an appropriate place outside, you can use a room in your home. If you have the space, it should be a room or section of a room that is primarily dedicated to making magic. If this is not possible, you will need to create a magical space each time you work, but in any case, it is important to keep the atmosphere clean and balanced. This can be done by cleaning it regularly with salt and burning purifying herbs.

Visualizing sacred space

Sometimes it is not possible to travel physically to a special place for magic work. However, everyone has the ability to create an inner sacred space that can become a sanctuary or temple, a retreat from the everyday world where magic can happen.

Your inner sacred space can be any kind of place in which your spirit feels happy and at home – a woodland clearing, a cave, a deserted beach, even a corner of your own garden. Concentrate on creating the place and remembering it in detail. You will need a candle and some incense.

1 Take five deep breaths to centre yourself and focus your mind on what you are about to do. Voice your intent out loud. Light a candle and burn some incense, holding your intention in your mind. Contemplate the candle flame for a while, imagining it lighting up the recesses inside you, so that you may find a way to the place you seek more easily.

2 When you feel ready, sit in a comfortable position and focus on your breathing. With closed eyes, take deep, slow, relaxing breaths from your diaphragm. Now picture an opening, a natural doorway such as a hole in the ground or the mouth of a cave. This will lead you to the sacred space you seek.

3 When you pass through the doorway, and enter your sacred space, pay attention to details that will make the place seem more real. Notice what you are standing on: is it grass or stone, sand or pebbles? Pause to smell the fragrance of a flower, reach out and touch trees or rocks, hear the sound of birdsong and the sighing of the wind, sit by a freshwater spring and drink its water.

4 When you feel it is time to leave your sacred space, give thanks and promise to return. Retrace your steps through the entrance and come back to your physical body.

Natural objects or representations of them are good for working magic outside.

PREPARATION RITUALS

Taking the time to prepare yourself before you start working magic is an important part of the magic itself. If you work spells or rituals when you are feeling tired or when your mind is busy with other things, then you can't expect to achieve good results. In fact, because magic involves connecting with powerful energies, it is not recommended that you attempt to perform magic at all when you are like this. Wait instead until you have more vital energy and are able to switch off your thoughts and become like an empty vessel. Magical energies will then be able to flow through you without you becoming drained or too attached to the result of your work.

Add some essential oils to your bath and bathe by candlelight as preparation for magic work.

PREPARING YOURSELF

There is a saying that "cleanliness is next to godliness", and it is an esoteric belief that harmful negative energies will fasten on to any dirt on the body of an individual engaged in magic work. Traditionally, initiates fasted, refrained from sexual activity, bathed and anointed themselves with oils and herbs to prepare themselves for magic. While it is not necessary to go to such extreme lengths, some level of deliberate preparation will give your magic work more significance. Eating a light, plainly cooked meal rather than one that is rich in spices and sauces is preferable before you begin, for example. When we have sex our energies mingle with those of the other person, so make sure that any sexual contact is especially loving and nourishing as it can affect our magic – for better or worse, depending on the qualities of the relationship.

Bathing is highly recommended; an invigorating shower or a long soak in the bath are both appropriate. Water not only cleanses the physical body but also washes away psychic dirt from the subtle bodies. We pick up this psychic dirt all the time – from negative energies in the atmosphere created by our negative thoughts, anxieties, stresses and petty jealousies as well as from vibrations in the environment. If you do not wish to bathe, simply washing your hands and face is helpful.

While you are bathing, imagine that you are cleansing away all impurities from your body, mind and soul, and as the water drains away visualize all those impurities draining away from you. Using essential oils or herbs in the bath is

After your bath you might like to anoint yourself with rose water or an oil blend containing rose geranium essential oil before performing a ritual.

Cleansing herbal bath mix

The ingredients for this mix are associated with purification and cleansing. Use fresh herbs if possible.

You will need
7 basil leaves
3 bay leaves
3 sprigs oregano
1 sprig tarragon
small square of muslin (cheesecloth)
10 ml/2 tsp organic oats
pinch rock or sea salt
thread

Pile the herbs in the muslin, then add the oats and the salt. Tie the corners of the muslin with thread. Hang the sachet from the bath tap so that the running water is infused with the essence of the mixture.

Golden light breathing exercise

The more concentrated and positive effort you fill your magic with, the more potent it will be, so to be successful as a worker of magic you need to know how to raise or increase energy. Energetic breathing will help you build up your concentrated energy. This technique is cleansing and empowering; it increases energy in the body and gives you more resources to work with.

1 Stand with your feet hip-width apart and feel them make contact with the ground. Rest your hands on your stomach and take a few deep breaths into the stomach area.

2 Place your hands just below your sternum. Begin to breathe, not too deeply, but slowly and with concentration.

3 Breathe in through your nose and visualize drawing golden light into yourself. Hold the breath for a short time (do not strain) and imagine your heart opening. Breathe out through your mouth, letting the golden light circulate around your body.

4 Continue breathing in this way until you feel energized and wide awake. Then rest your hands on your heart for a few moments, letting the breath gradually return to normal.

Spend some time preparing yourself mentally, with a period of meditation, to achieve the right frame of mind before you begin your magic work.

also helpful: lavender, geranium or rose are good choices, or look for any others that are particularly purifying.

Next, choose what you are going to wear. A robe is ideal, otherwise select loose-fitting garments that do not constrict the flow of energy through your body. Don't worry about looking fashionable – comfort is much more important when making magic. In fact, many witches like to work "sky clad", or naked, as they feel much freer and closer to nature like this, but this is up to you.

MENTAL AND PSYCHIC PREPARATION

When undertaking any magic work it is important to be in the right frame of mind, so mental and psychic preparation is recommended. After you have bathed, a period of meditation immediately preceding the start of a ritual will help to achieve calm composure. Meditation can be accompanied by some quiet, spiritually inspiring music and the burning of a suitable incense. A light fragrance such as geranium or a head-clearing scent such as rosemary is best, leaving the heavier aromas for the ritual.

PREPARING THE TEMPLE

Whether or not you have an actual "temple" room in your home, you will need to create a sacred space for working magic. Again, this needs to be properly prepared. The first step is to create a "clean slate", as any psychic impurities or negative energies present when magic is performed can intrude and interfere, contaminating the result and perhaps changing it completely. As a modern analogy, we might think of such impure energy as a kind of occult computer virus, with a purifying and cleansing routine acting like an anti-virus program.

Every culture has its own favoured purifying and cleansing methods, many of which date back thousands of years. In Old Testament times, for instance, brooms made of hyssop were used to clean out temples and other sacred buildings. Today, many occultists like to use the Rose Cross ritual. This involves lighting an appropriate incense and carrying it around the room while wafting the smoke in a pattern from corner to corner in a cross shape, then making the shape of a circle in the middle of the cross. This shape represents a cross with a rose in its centre, which is the symbol of the Rosicrucian Brotherhood, a secret occult order that dates back to the fifteenth century.

A feather can be used in smudging, fanning the fragrant smoke around your body to cleanse your aura of any negative energies.

Smudge sticks are densely packed and can burn slowly for a long time.

SMUDGING

One of the most popular purifying and cleansing techniques, smudging is a shamanic practice that has enjoyed widespread revival in recent years. Its shamanic origin means it lends itself to just about any magical path without causing contention. It is very simple but extremely effective, and because it needs a little input from the practitioner, it encourages magical thought and activity while the basic tools for the ceremony – a smudge stick and a smudge fan – are being put together.

A smudge stick is a densely packed bundle of herbs, which usually includes sage – a plant that smoulders when lit, producing clouds of fragrant smoke. The fan should be made of feathers, or else a single feather can be used. The purpose of the fan is to waft the smoke all over the area being cleansed – over the walls, floor and ceiling and around the doors, windows and any other openings into the room, such as the fireplace or air vents. The nature of the herbs, the intention of the person who gathers and ties them together, and the action of the fan will drive away any negative thought-forms lingering in an area.

MAKING A SMUDGE STICK

It is very rewarding to grow and dry your own herbs, thus ensuring that their magical qualities are tended during all stages of growth, and that you honour the spirits of the herbs when cutting them. The three herbs suggested here are all for purification. The best variety of sage to use is American white, or mountain, sage (*Salvia apiana*). All the herbs must be thoroughly dried.

You will need
dried sage stalks
dried lavender flower stalks
dried thyme stalks
natural twine

Gather all the dried herb stalks together and arrange them in an intertwined bundle. Tie the stalks together at the end, and then wind both ends of twine upwards around the bundle until it is bound together. Light one end, extinguish the flame and let the smoke rise to fill the area. As you fan the smoke, strengthen the action by visualizing the herbs' cleansing qualities.

BLESSING YOUR EQUIPMENT

In the same way that you prepare yourself before performing magic, all equipment and materials that you intend to use should also be cleansed and consecrated beforehand. Once blessed, the items can be stored, ready for use. The blessing described here is for a cord, but you can adapt it for any other item. You can also perform this ceremony on an altar if you prefer.

You will need
compass
incense
candle
bowl of spring water
bowl of sea salt
cord

1 In a cleared space outside or on the floor, mark out a circle with the four points of the compass. Put the incense in the east quarter, the candle in the south, the bowl of water in the west and the bowl of salt in the north.

2 Begin with the east quarter. Light the incense and say the first line of the blessing. Pass the cord through the smoke rising up from the incense, while imagining a clear, cool breeze passing through the cord.

If you do not have a smudge stick or dried herbs, then you can use incense sticks for your cleansing and purification rituals.

3 Turn to the south quarter and say the second line of the blessing, passing the cord through the candle flame as you do so.

4 Turn to the west quarter and say the third line of the blessing, while sprinkling the cord with water.

5 Turn to the north quarter and say the fourth line of the blessing, sprinkling the cord with salt. Finish by saying the final lines of the blessing.

THE BLESSING
I cleanse, bless and consecrate this cord with the powers of Air.
I cleanse, bless and consecrate this cord with the powers of Fire.
I cleanse, bless and consecrate this cord with the powers of Water.
I cleanse, bless and consecrate this cord with the powers of Earth.
Finish with
May this cord now be cleansed and purified for the highest good of all.
And so mote it be!

Thought-forms

In occult terms, an atmosphere can contain "thought-forms". These subtle vibrational patterns are produced by the workings of the mind and are picked up at a subliminal level, rather like how a radio set receives broadcast messages. A received thought-form reflects the nature of the original broadcast: happy, sad, gloomy, cheerful, and so on. Thought-forms that are deliberately created by a magician can be extremely valuable and they form a major part of magic. But unconsciously produced thought-forms tend to be negative and can get in the way of making successful magic, which is why purification rituals are so important.

CASTING A MAGIC CIRCLE

The working place is a circle of light, whether visualized, or made with physical elements.

Whether you work inside or outdoors, it is traditional to create a magic circle before starting a ritual, spell or other piece of magic. The circle will help you concentrate on your work and will banish any unwanted thoughts or influences. With practice, you will come to know it is there, protective and empowering, each time you begin your ritual. You need to visualize the area within the circle as a place of stillness beyond normal time and space. It is a place where physical, social and spatial boundaries are redrawn, and represents the wholeness of the human, the natural and the divine. It is where the internal and external are connected and where all is incorporated into one – matter and spirit reunited. You may outline the circle using a wand or staff, and as you turn to draw the line in the air you may see it burning with golden fire.

MAKING YOUR CIRCLE MAGICAL

A legacy from ceremonial or high magic, the circle traditionally recognizes the four points of the compass. North is the place of Earth; west is the place of Water; south has the heat of Fire; and east possesses the breath of Air.

It is customary to open the circle in the east, which through its association with Air symbolizes intellect and rational thought. Its magical tool is the athame (dagger) or sword, although a feather may also be used. The next point on the circle is Fire in the south, the energy of the magical will that desires to create. Its magical tool is the wand, which can be a slender branch of wood; hazel is especially appropriate as it has the capacity to bend, although a candle may also be used to represent this point. The south is the quarter of the circle for energizing, for setting in motion a course of action. Through its association with Water, the west is associated with emotions and feelings. While the east separates and divides, the west flows and merges; beginnings are initiated in the east, while letting go is the theme of the west. The west's symbol is the cup or

---

Making a magic circle

You can make a magic circle in many different ways. It can be visualized in your mind's eye, drawn in the air with a wand, a dagger or just your hand, or created physically – with stones, candles, or other symbolic objects. One popular way is to use a length of white, silver or gold cord, laid out on the ground. This will need opening and closing down before and after the spell.

You will need

2.7 m/9 ft length, 5 mm/¹⁄₄ in thick white cord
salt water

The Light Invocation

By the powers of Heaven and Earth, I cast this circle in the name of love, wisdom and truth, for the highest good.

1 Place the cord in a circle with an opening in the east. Step through the opening with whatever items you are going to use for your spell or ritual. Place them in the centre of the circle. Close the circle behind you and seal it with a sprinkling of salt water.

2 Go clockwise around the circle, sprinkling salt water on the cord as you go. Visualize yourself surrounded in golden light and say the light invocation. The circle is now ready to work within. When you have finished your spell, close the circle as detailed on the opposite page.

chalice, or else a bowl of water. The north corresponds to darkness and winter, the polar opposite of the south's fiery heat. It is the quarter for containment and inner reflection and is represented by the pentacle or sometimes salt.

CASTING THE CIRCLE

There are many different ways of casting a magic circle. It may be drawn in the air with an athame or with your hand, visualized as a ring of fire, or you may prefer to create an actual, visible circle, such as a cord circle – if you are new to magic, you may find this easier to work with. If you are working outside, you could make one out of rocks, pebbles, pine cones, pieces of wood, or even flowers: choose objects that seem to "speak" to you in some way and are in harmony with your magic.

One of the most versatile circles is a basic cord circle, which can be used indoors or outside. Remember that a magic circle is always opened in the east and should be cast in a deosil (clockwise) direction. It should always be closed before any magic work takes place, and you should not step out of it until you have finished. When you are finished, you must ritually take the circle apart or dissolve it.

CLOSING THE CIRCLE

At the end of your magic it is important to take the circle apart. This is to keep the magical energy pure and contained, marking the boundary between magical and everyday activity. Doing so also acknowledges that endings are part of

life's cycles. Work "widdershins" (anticlockwise) until you end up where you began. For instance, if you started working a spell or ritual in the south, you would close the circle by beginning in the east and moving round through north and west until you reach the south. Gather up your tools from each quarter as you go round and as you do, say the following words:
I give thanks to all who have helped me and leave my magic with you.
And so mote it be.

Nature's circles

If you are creating a circle from natural objects, use 12 items. Ask permission to use each object in your magic before taking it. Purify each item with a pinch of salt and say:
I bless this stone/rock/flower or whatever with love, light, wisdom and truth.
Then sprinkle salt on the object, asking for a dedication to the light. Welcome it to the circle and explain what you are going to do.

One way of making a magic circle is using candles or tealights.

Some magicians and witches visualize a circle to create a place between the worlds, and trace it with their finger at the beginning of a ritual or spell.

INVOCATIONS AND OFFERINGS

Once you have created your magic circle, it is customary to invoke the spirit beings that you wish to call upon to assist you in your magic. Their subtle yet powerful presence will help to connect you with the otherworld and make your magic more effective. At the same time, every magic worker knows that magic is a give-and-take relationship, so will always give thanks to these unseen helpers as well as to the spirit or energies of the place and the equipment that has been used. In this way, you ensure that your magic is aligned to the highest good of all.

A sacred herb in the Native American Indian tradition, tobacco is often used as an offering.

GUARDIANS OF THE WATCHTOWERS

In casting a magic circle, great importance is attached to astral beings called the Guardians of the Watchtowers. The "watchtowers" are the four quarters of north, south, east and west. The purpose of the powerful guardians is to protect those who invoke their aid and ensure the security of the circle. They will be with you while you work and should be thanked at the end.

The guardians may be seen as angels, totem animals, gods and goddesses, holy living creatures, elementals or any other kind of otherworld beings – every tradition has its own set, but it's up to you what you choose to work with. Cabbalists, for instance, often invoke the four archangels: Raphael (Healer of God) in the east; Michael (Like unto God) in the south; Gabriel (Strength of God) in the west; and Uriel (Light of God) in the north. Some practitioners may prefer to work with the Arthurian legends: King Arthur, master of the mysteries, in the east; Gawain, defender of all that is good, in the south; the Lady of the Lake, guardian of the secrets, in the west; and Merlin, the archmage with the power of vision, in the north.

INVOKING THE GUARDIANS

There is no single right way to invoke your heavenly powers, what matters is the spirit with which you do it, so be creative. Just remember that you cannot command or order these powers to be with you, but only ask or invite them from a humble heart. The following invocation calls upon the Guardians of the Watchtowers (the four directions), but if you are working with a different

Angels and Arthurian heroes are both called upon in magical working as guardians and helpers. Here Sir Galahad achieves the Grail, a potent magical symbol, watched by other knights of the Round Table, and three archangels.

An offering of salt is made on a very simple and impromptu altar.

Leaving an offering outside

When you are taking something from the natural world, show your gratitude by leaving something behind. If you are taking something from the land, always ask its spirit for permission first. Remember it is illegal to pick wild flowers or disturb protected species.

1 To make an offering, hold your gift in your hand and present it up to the sky.

2 Present your offering to the earth to show appreciation to the Great Mother.

3 Hold it out to each of the four directions – north, south, east and west – keeping in mind the connection between all things.

4 As you leave the offering in your chosen place, voice your thanks and intention. Speaking the following words aloud will help to focus your attention and energy:
I offer this in gratitude for the gifts given, in honour of creation and my part in it.

set of guardians, then you may insert their name after "I call".

1 Stand inside your magic circle, close your eyes and take a couple of breaths to centre yourself.

2 Face north, raise your hand and say:
I call the Guardians of the North to protect this place from earthly wrath.

3 Turn to face the east and say:
I call the Guardians of the East to calm the airs and bring me peace.

4 Turn to the south and say:
I call the Guardians of the South to protect me from the fire's red mouth.

5 Finally, turn to the west and say:
I call the Guardians of the West to lay the stormy seas to rest.

6 When you have completed the circle and are again facing north, say the following words. As you do so, imagine the circle you have cast is spreading through the universe like ripples in a pool, bringing tranquillity and peace to its centre, which is you and your circle.
Let blessings be upon this place
And let my Circle clear this space
Of spirits wicked, cruel or fell,
So that in peace I may dwell.

GIVING THANKS
It is always advisable to give thanks to your unseen helpers. One way to do this is by making an offering to the spirits. This must be natural or biodegradable. Not only will this acknowledge them as important, it will also encourage a cooperative relationship, for when you make an offering you exchange energy as well as giving thanks. You may also make an offering if you need special help, or in gratitude when your magic bears fruit.

You can make offerings on your altar or shrine, in your magic circle, or outside. In the North American Indian tradition, tobacco is often used, while the Celtic tradition favours salt. The offering can be anything that has special meaning to you and is in harmony with your magic – flowers, stones or coins, or something made especially for the purpose, such as a loaf of bread you baked, or a cake.

Elementals

Archetypal spirit beings associated with each of the four elements are sometimes known as 'elementals'. Believed to inhabit the realm of Faerie, they are sylphs, salamanders, undines and gnomes. Sylphs are the fairies of Air in the east, and their name is taken from the Greek *silphe*, meaning 'butterfly'. Salamanders rule Fire in the south, and their name is from the Greek *salambe*, meaning 'fireplace'. Undines are the ruling spirits of Water in the west, and their name is derived from the Latin *unda*, meaning 'wave'. Finally, gnomes are the creatures of Earth in the north; their name comes from the Greek *gnoma*, meaning 'knowledge'.

RITUAL THROUGH LIFE

A ritual is a way of making contact and communicating with the otherworld, thereby bringing transformation – or magic – to the individual and to the wider cosmos. Traditionally, it is a way of honouring transitional states as we move from one stage of life to another, and it provides an opportunity to step outside routine ways of thinking and behaving in order to connect with the unseen forces of the cosmos that shape our lives. Major life events, such as birth, marriage and death, are usually acknowledged by some kind of ritual ceremony, while seasonal festivals are also acknowledged by ritual acts. It is also possible to transform everyday events into something special through ritual.

This chapter looks at the power and purpose of ritual, differentiating between rites, ritual and ceremony and the role they have to play in magic.

It includes a variety of rituals that can be performed to assist with many different aspects of life. These include the banishing ritual of the pentagram, a traditional magical ritual to clear psychic energies, as well as rituals for inner calm and healing. It looks at how we can use rituals for blessing ourselves and our homes and how to make rituals a part of our daily lives. It concludes with information on rites of passage and how magic is being used to create meaningful rituals for the modern world.

THE POWER OF RITUAL

Since ancient times, rituals have played an important part in magical and sacred ceremonies. Rituals are patterned acts, performed to bring about specific objectives. For our earliest ancestors, they were often accompanied by sacrifice and were an attempt to placate, if not to control, forces that were potentially life-threatening, such as wild animals or extreme climatic conditions for instance. In magic, rituals are a way of connecting with the otherworld to give thanks, make offerings, ask for guidance or make requests. The tools that are used in ritual, the elements and the powers that are invoked, all have particular meaning and significance and must be used with care.

Lighting a candle focuses the mind, and acts as a signal to all present that the ritual is beginning.

THE PATTERN OF RITUAL

A ritual is a patterned activity. This means that it follows a recognizable structure and sequence of steps, time after time. What is important is that you engage with it in mind, body and soul and do not just "go through the motions". The latter would make it an empty gesture devoid of meaning and therefore it would lack any real power to make magic happen.

To begin with, it is essential that a clear and precise objective is outlined and that everyone who is involved is fully aware of this purpose, which is often stated at the start of the work. Most magical rituals follow four basic stages: purifying mind, body and soul; getting dressed or robing; preparing the place; and creating the circle. Whether the ritual is for divination or a celebration, to consecrate a talisman or work for healing, its purpose is then said aloud so that all those taking part are clear about why they are there, and agree to its purpose.

WORKING THE RITUAL

Once you have made the necessary preparations, opened the sacred space and stated your purpose, you can proceed to magically do whatever you have decided upon. This could be creating a talisman, weaving a spell, sitting in meditation, enacting a traditional myth, or celebrating a special time of year. Towards the end of the ritual it is usual to have a sacred sharing, or communion, with the deities, angels

Preparation for a ritual often begins with cleansing or purification. This can be symbolic, such as passing round a bowl of warm water, scented with essential oil, and floating flowers.

Outdoors or indoors?

Old-fashioned village witches often performed their rites and rituals alone or else with a close group of family and friends, and as far as possible they would work outdoors. Modern-day magic workers tend to hold their rites, rituals and ceremonies indoors for the sake of convenience.

and otherworldly beings who have been called upon to help your magic, as well as with any other people who are enacting the ritual with you. Something to eat, which may be bread and salt, biscuits, fruit or any other sacred food, placed on a platter, is blessed, often in the name of the Earth Mother who provided it, and eaten. Then wine, water, milk or any other drink in the chalice is blessed in the name of the Sky Father, or by the power of the Sun God, before being drunk. The chalice is taken with both hands to show complete involvement.

After the communion there is often a pause to meditate on what has been begun by the ritual, or if you are with others, to discuss business or any other matters. Then it is customary to say "thank you" and release the higher powers that you summoned to your ritual and to unwind the circle widdershins (anticlockwise), the opposite direction to the one used at the beginning. You may feel a shift of energy and gentle return to ordinary awareness at this point. When you are clearing up, you might find it useful to discuss the ceremony, although if you are working for an ongoing

Food is often a part of a ritual, and preparing it – such as dividing up bread or pouring out glasses of wine – can become part of the ceremony.

If you are passing round a chalice, hold and take it with both hands to show involvement.

purpose it is best not to talk about it so that the magic has time to develop in the silence of secrecy. If it was a festival, then that has been completed and may be shared.

RITES, RITUALS AND CEREMONIES

There is sometimes confusion over the difference between rites, rituals and ceremonies. The words "rite" and "ritual" are often interchangeable, but rites tend to have shorter and simpler workings, and are often performed by someone working alone. Much less emphasis is placed on the preparation and the closing of a rite, with the concentration instead on the central stages. They come in many shapes and forms, which vary depending on their source or tradition and on their purpose. Simple rituals veer more towards a rite, while those that are more elaborate and complex could more accurately be described as a ceremony.

A ceremony usually involves several people, and has a more complicated pattern and more elaborate equipment. Ceremonies may be held in public or in front of an audience. They are used by many traditions worldwide to mark special times – to celebrate birth and naming, to join two people in marriage, or to lay the dead to rest. Some ceremonies are performed by a priest before a congregation, while others allow the wider participation of the faithful, in processions, public offerings, hymn singing or ritual dance.

STICK WITH IT

It can take time before you can perform rituals and ceremonies with ease and confidence and at first you may feel embarrassed and rather self-conscious, particularly if there are others present. However, most people feel like this when they start doing something new and out of the ordinary, so persevere. It is worth putting up with a few uncomfortable feelings in the beginning, as these will begin to subside once you start to reap the rewards of natural magic.

A BANISHING RITUAL

A highly respected ritual that has been used by a number of the main magical disciplines for hundreds of years is the Lesser Banishing Ritual of the Pentagram. It is called "lesser" only to distinguish it from its counterpart, the Greater Ritual of the Pentagram, which is used for magical invocation rather than for banishing or clearing. The Banishing Ritual involves invoking angelic powers for the purpose of purification and is often used to space clear a place of unwanted energies or create higher vibrations for magic.

CABBALISTIC INFLUENCES

Because the banishing ritual is Cabbalistic in origin, much of its wording is in Hebrew (including some words from the Lord's Prayer) and it calls upon the archangels of the Judaeo-Christian tradition. The ritual is divided into three sections: the Cabbalistic cross; the drawing of the pentagrams; and the invocation of the angels. To close the ritual, the first section – the Cabbalistic cross – is repeated.

THE HIGHER SELF

The main reason for performing the Cabbalistic cross as part of the Banishing Ritual is to enable the magic-worker to get in touch with his or her "higher self". This higher self is visualized as white light that is present above the head, and is drawn down by the ritual. The higher self is able to bridge the gap between the everyday world and the higher astral planes, the source of infinite knowledge and wisdom.

PERFORMING THE RITUAL

Before you begin, prepare yourself by bathing, drinking spring water and sitting quietly in meditation for a while. You should be dressed in clean, comfortable clothes. Make sure you will not be disturbed at any time. Unplug or switch off phones, close the curtains if you are overlooked. When you are ready to begin, place yourself in the middle of the space you are working in. Work through the following steps slowly with reverence and respect.

1 Visualize a sphere of pure, clear light, about the size of a football, a little way above your head. Reach up to it with the fingers of your right hand and visualize that you are drawing a shaft of

The first movement of the ritual is to reach up to an imagined sphere of light above your head.

The traditional gesture of the god Osiris completes the cabbalistic cross part of the ritual.

this light down to you by touching your forehead. Say:
Ahte (pronounced "Ach-tay" and meaning "Thou art").

2 Touch your fingers to the centre of your chest, visualizing the shaft of light travelling down to infinity through the floor, as you say:
Malkuth (pronounced "Mal-koot" and meaning "the Kingdom").

3 Touch your right shoulder, saying:
Ve-Geburah (pronounced "vay-Geboorah", meaning "the Power").

4 Touch your left shoulder, saying:
Ve-Gedulah (pronounced "vay-Gedoolah", meaning "and the Glory"). As you do this, visualize a shaft of light emanating from infinity to your right, crossing your body as you perform the action and plunging away into infinity again on your left.

5 Now cross your wrists at the centre of your chest with the right wrist outermost in the "Osiris risen" position. As you do this, say:
Le Olahm (pronounced "lay-Ola-chiem" and meaning "Forever").
Now bow your head and say:
Amen ("So be it").

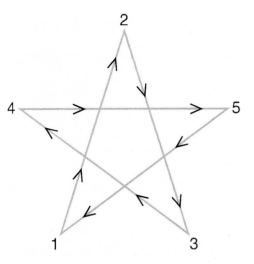

This diagram shows the order you should trace the pentagram. Begin at point number one.

DRAWING THE PENTAGRAMS

The next part of the ritual consists of drawing four pentagrams, one in each direction of the compass, starting with the east. The particular pentagram used here is called the "earth banishing pentagram". Each pentagram should stretch from about shoulder to knee height and is best drawn with the arm at full stretch if possible. As each one is completed, it should be "fixed" with a stabbing gesture of the fingers into the centre, accompanied by a Hebrew word.

1 Face the east to draw the first pentagram. When it is complete, fix it while saying the names of the letters that spell the name of God – Yahveh in Hebrew, or Jehovah in English: *Yod-He-Vau-He.*

2 Turn to face the south and draw the next pentagram. Fix it by saying: *Adonai* ("Lord").

3 Then draw the western pentagram, fixing it with the name by which God identified himself to Moses, pronounced Eeh-heh-yeh: *Eheieh* ("I am that I am").

4 Finally, draw the northern pentagram. The word to fix this with is pronounced "Ah-geh-lah". It is made up of the initial letters of the phrase Aith Gedol Leolam Adonai: *Agla* ("Thou art mighty forever Lord").

As you invoke the archangel Gabriel, turn your palms to face you.

THE INVOCATION OF THE ARCHANGELS

The third part of the ritual involves the invocation of the archangels.

1 Raise the palms of your hands to face forward and say:
Before me, Raphael (pronounce the angel's name "Raff-eye-ell").

2 Turn your palms to face behind you, saying:
Behind me, Gabriel (pronounced "Gab-rey-ell").

3 Lower your right hand, palm upwards, and say:
On my right hand, Michael (pronounced "Mick-eye-ell").

4 Lower your left hand the same way and say:

On my left hand Uriel (pronounced "Ur-eye-ell").

5 Finish by saying the following words. Raise your hands above your head and put them together as you utter the last line:
For about me flame the pentagrams. Above me shines the six-rayed star!

The Cabbalistic Cross

It should be noted that the hand makes the cross from right to left, not from left to right as in the Roman Catholic crossing gesture.

EVERYDAY RITUALS

Rituals help strengthen our connection with the universe. Just as vibrations spread across a spider's web or ripples radiate across water, a simple ritual can have far-reaching effects on you and those with whom you relate. By performing simple rituals based around your daily activities you can consciously choose to strengthen the connection between your everyday self and your higher self, and life itself becomes a ritual for living.

Ritual food can be chosen so that it embraces the essence of the four elements.

HABITUAL ACTIONS

In everyday life habitual actions such as cleaning our teeth or making a cup of tea are sometimes referred to as rituals, yet we do not generally associate them with magic. What differentiates habit from magical ritual is the consciousness we bring to the action. Performing an act with awareness has the effect of increasing the efficacy of that act. This is because the intent carries to other levels of our being: for instance, if you take a shower with the intent of cleansing your spirit as well as your body, the overall cleansing effect is greater. It will empower you and make you stronger. It will also "charge" your energy body with spiritual vibrations so that you will radiate a certain aura wherever you go and life becomes a magical experience.

FOOD AND DRINK

Preparing and eating food are powerfully symbolic activities and mealtimes provide a very good opportunity to incorporate ritual with day-to-day practicality. When you are preparing food, do it with love and appreciation of what has been supplied by Mother Earth to give you nourishment. Choose your ingredients carefully – ideally you should always use organic, locally grown and seasonal foods, and those that you have grown yourself are even more special.

Even the most ordinary activity can have ritual significance. Taking the time to buy and arrange some special flowers, for example, gives your home love as well as decoration.

Tea ceremony

Throughout the world, there are many customs associated with the brewing and serving of tea. The most notable of these comes from Japan, where the classic tea ceremony is a complex ritual that elevates drinking tea into a spiritual experience. The tea ceremony has many rules and set procedures and is presided over by a master of ceremonies. It is a good example of how a daily activity can be transformed into a magical experience.

Making food for rituals

Although for rituals many people just use commercial bread, broken into pieces, and any kind of wine, mead, cider or fruit juice as a drink, you may wish to try the old ways where special biscuits or scones and your own home-brewed wines or beer are made for rituals. Any type of food, or recipe will do, it is the act of making it that adds power to your ritual. As you become more experienced, you can adapt traditional recipes by adding favourite or appropriate ingredients. Although not everyone has the time to make wines for rituals, it is a pleasing skill to master. Country wines can be made with fruits, vegetables, herbs, berries and dried fruits. It is very important that you sterilize all the equipment before use.

Baking bread yourself for a specific magical purpose gives the ritual greater power.

Eating foods that are as close to their natural state as possible is not only beneficial for your body, but is also helpful from a spiritual point of view. Remember we are what we eat, and the plants and animals are all gifts of Mother Earth, so by sharing her bounty at mealtimes, we are also taking in some of the eternal blessings of creation.

In magical ritual, it is customary to bless our food or drink before taking it into our body. You can do this by holding your hands over the meal, closing your eyes and inwardly saying thank you to Mother Earth for her goodness. Make time to eat away from your normal activities, even if this is a quick snack. Take time to experience the different tastes, colours and textures of your meal. Don't work, read, watch TV or talk excessively to others while you are eating as this only takes energy away from eating. When you eat with awareness, even ordinary meals can become a ritual that nourishes body and soul.

FOOD FOR FESTIVALS

All over the world, special dishes are served at festival times throughout the year. These can range from a simple kind of special bread eaten occasionally to elaborate feasts with many courses to celebrate a major event such as a wedding or seasonal festival, like Yule.

But you may not want to wait for big occasions, and could make one meal a month (at new moon for example) an opportunity to share some simple dishes with others on your path, to discuss the arts of magic, and celebrate the passing seasons. It can be a time when you decorate your shrine with new flowers and symbols, and use that as the centrepiece of your gathering.

Home-brewed wine and mead are free from chemicals and full of goodness, and have the added value of having been made yourself, so adding to their magical purpose.

RITUAL THROUGH THE DAY

Just as everyday acts can be transformed into ritual, it is also possible to use rituals throughout the day to help strengthen your connection to your magical powers. Morning and evening are two especially potent times of day for ritual activity. Morning is the beginning of a new day and rituals performed at this time will set up a pattern of energy that you can take with you throughout the day. Evening is about endings and winding down; rituals performed at this time will help you come back home to yourself.

As you touch your forehead to begin, say clearly and firmly, "I am Spirit!"

MORNING RITUALS

Greeting the morning puts you in touch with the rhythms of nature and is a great way to start a new day. You can work out your own simple ritual involving a few stretches or breathing exercises to wake up the body, perhaps followed by a moment of quiet or meditation to collect yourself for the day. Taking a shower is also energizing and refreshing and changes your energy from sleep to awake; use fragrances such as rosemary, all the citrus scents, peppermint or eucalyptus in your shower products.

START-THE-DAY RITUAL

The following ritual summons a fresh charge of personal psychic energy to strengthen your being and encourage you to appreciate the joy of a new day.

1 Light your chosen incense or vaporize your essential oil. Stand facing a window, towards the east (during warm weather this ritual can also be performed outside facing the morning sun). Take some slow, deep breaths.

2 When you feel calm, make the sign of the pentagram on your body. Touch your forehead with the fingertips of your right hand, and say:
I am Spirit!
Then touch your left hip and say:
I am Earth!
Touch your right shoulder and say:
I am Water!
Touch your left shoulder and say
I am Air!
Touch your right hip and say:
I am Fire!
Finally, touch your forehead again to complete the figure of the pentagram and say:
Thus I seal my affirmation.

3 Inhale the fragrance of incense or oil for a few moments before beginning the new day.

It's good to make time for a period of quiet contemplation or meditation, accompanied by purifying incense, to prepare you for the day.

Wake-up herbs

For protection and purification: frankincense, juniper

For success: cinnamon, carnation, cloves

For a clear mind: rosemary, basil, peppermint

To dispel sluggishness: grapefruit, lemon, lime, bergamot

EVENING RITUALS

Just as you began with energizing and empowering rituals to greet the day, evening time is about winding down and relaxing and giving thanks for the day that has passed. It is a time of transition between wakefulness and sleep, and it is important that you allow yourself to slow down before going to bed. A simple night-time ritual is to make an offering on your altar last thing at night using incense and candles to give thanks and let go of the day that has passed. Useful herbs, incense or oils for encouraging peaceful sleep include lavender, marjoram, hops, camomile, rose and passion flower.

END-THE-DAY RITUAL

To end the day, you can use this specially modified version of a much more elaborate ritual known as the Middle Pillar Exercise, which has its origins in

Placing an amethyst under your pillow will help you achieve a deep and untroubled sleep.

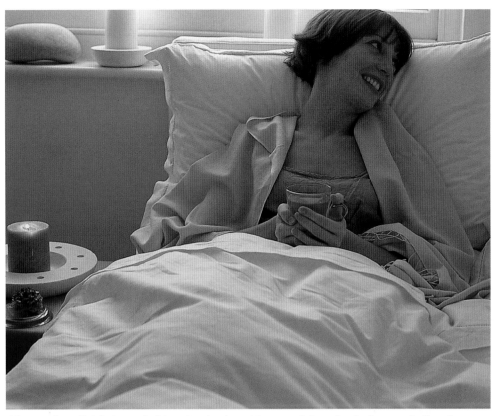

After you have finished your bedtime ritual, relax with a cup of dreaming herb tea and allow the tensions of the day to disperse.

the teachings of the Cabbala. To add to its effectiveness and enhance your ability to sleep, place an amethyst or clear quartz crystal under your pillow before you settle down to sleep.

1 Before you begin, calm and centre yourself. Stand facing west – the direction of the setting sun – and for a few moments focus on the sun setting on the horizon, whether it is actually still daylight or already dark.

2 Imagine a beam of brilliant white light shining down on you from an infinite height. As it touches your head and enters your body, it transforms your entire body into light-filled glass, like a clear bottle of human shape.

3 As the light courses down through your body, see it changing hue, moving through all the colours of the rainbow. As these colours flow down, imagine any dark areas of your body being cleansed by the rainbow light, pushing the blackness downwards and out through the soles of your feet.

4 As the rainbow-coloured light flows out of your body through your feet, imagine that it is forming a black pool or puddle, and that this pool is draining away into nothingness, leaving you clean and filled with brilliant opalescent, rainbow hues.

Dreaming tea

Mix the following herbs to make yourself a goodnight tea. It can help you to recall your dreams and have a restful night's sleep. (It is not advisable to drink this tea if you are pregnant.)

1 heaped tsp dried jasmine flowers
1 heaped tsp dried camomile flowers
2 sprigs fresh marjoram
a large cup or mug of freshly boiled spring water
honey (optional)

Place all the herbs in a jug and pour over the boiled water. Infuse for 5 minutes, strain into a cup and sweeten with honey if desired. Sip this tea about half an hour before you go to sleep.

A RITUAL FOR INNER CALM

When you are flooded with emotion, desires and restless thoughts it will be difficult to focus on making magic, as all you will be able to think about will be yourself. A magic-worker needs to be able to switch off from their personal concerns in order to connect with the higher self and the cosmos. This means being calm and still inside with your energies contained and focused. Methods to achieve this state form an essential part of Eastern sacred traditions, most notably Zen Buddhism, from which this ritual has been adapted.

Meditation is an ideal practice to help you move towards a clear-minded state.

ZEN PHILOSOPHY

The word Zen is derived from the Chinese *ch'an*, which in turn originates from the Sanskrit *dhyana*, meaning "meditation". A philosophy of Chinese origin that was adopted by the Japanese in the 12th century, Zen has its own unique identity within the wider practice of Buddhism. Its essential concept is that perfection (nirvana) can only be achieved when all is reduced (or expanded) to nothing. Zen rituals therefore tend toward simplicity, quiet, stillness and deep inner reflection to create an atmosphere of intense and almost tangible peace.

RITUAL FOR INNER CALM

This ritual is ideal when you are feeling stressed and anxious and are unable to settle yourself by your usual methods. To perform it, you will need as much silence and stillness as your surroundings permit. Ideally your space should be as empty and clutter-free as possible, as this will help to induce calm and composure. Remember to turn off your phones.

If possible, use a gong to mark the beginning and end of the ritual; otherwise find something else that will produce a similar clear, simple sound. You will also need a low table or altar covered with a plain black cloth and a few sticks of sandalwood incense in a suitable container. Set up the altar so that you can sit or kneel before it facing east.

THE RITUAL

Light the sandalwood incense. Kneel on a cushion or sit on a straight-backed chair before the altar. If you prefer, you may sit cross-legged in a half- or full-lotus position. When you are comfortable, perform the fourfold breath to still your thoughts. To do this, breathe in to an unhurried count of four, hold your breath for a count of four, breathe out for a count of four and hold your breath again

A simple sound is used to mark the beginning and ending of a Zen ritual.

The sound of Om

"Om" is spoken after taking as deep a breath as possible. It begins with the sound "ahh", moving into "oh" and ending with "mm" for as long as the out-breath lasts. All of these three sounds should merge into one. The sound of Om is said to symbolize all the sounds in the universe.

Zen koans

Koans are exercises in paradox, used in Zen teaching, and are designed to baffle the mind until it is defeated and reduced to nothingness. They take the form of questions that defy reason; perhaps the most famous is "What is the sound of one hand clapping?" When everything is reduced to its ultimate state of non-being, then the perfection of union with the higher spiritual forces of the cosmos becomes possible.

for a count of four. Take the next breath and repeat the sequence. Continue to practise the fourfold breath for a few minutes until you feel a state of great calm begins to unfold.

When you feel sufficiently calm and at ease with your surroundings, gently sound the gong once. As the sound fades, begin to chant the single word "Om" as slowly as possible. Keep your head bowed towards the altar. Repeat the chant 10–12 times, taking care throughout to avoid any feeling of "hurrying things along".

Once you have reached the end of the chanting, take two or three more fourfold breaths, then slowly bow towards the east, with your hands held at your chest in an attitude of prayer. In this position, repeat a single long "Om". Your mind should now be clear enough to concentrate your thoughts. Close your eyes and visualize a circular ripple of light in the centre of your abdomen, slowly spreading out horizontally, like the ripples from a stone tossed into a pool filmed in slow motion. As this circle of light reaches the horizon, it continues out into the universe and to infinity. Continue to observe this visualization for several minutes. As you do so, make your mental image as sharp as you can, ideally you are aiming for a reality equivalent to having your eyes open, but this takes a little practice.

To end the ritual, stand up, place your hands in the prayer position at your chest as before and bow deeply from the waist. Sound the gong one more time to close the meditation.

The Zen philosophy epitomizes simplicity, and ritual in the Zen style will therefore also be very simple and unadorned.

Incenses for inner calm

In the East, several incenses are particularly valued for their affinity with meditation, but two of the most noteworthy are sandalwood and agarwood (or "aloes"). Hindu temples were often made from sandalwood, while yogis (masters of yoga) use a yellow sandalwood paste to mark the "third eye" chakra. This paste is cooling and helps calm restless thoughts. Burning sandalwood incense has the same effect. Little known in the West, agarwood has been valued in Middle and Far Eastern countries for thousands of years. Its indescribable fragrance has been compared to a blend of sandalwood and ambergris and is reputedly one of the finest (and most costly) fragrances in the world. Agarwood is used in Japanese incense and is said to open up the heart to compassion while calming the mind.

A HEALING RITUAL

In many traditional societies, it is the medicine man or woman who performs healing rituals for the sick – whether this is a person, situation or even an environment. The healing ritual described here is based on traditional shamanic practices in its use of herbs, drums and chants to summon the assistance of the spirit world for the purpose of healing or rebalancing energies.

As you hold the stone to your heart, visualize the person you are working on.

THE ROLE OF THE SHAMAN

The word "shaman" comes from the Tungusic dialect of the Ural-Altaic tribes of Siberia. Shamans were the priest-doctors of the tribes, responsible for officiating at ceremonies and rituals, tending the sick and caring for all aspects of the spiritual wellbeing of the people. The term is now used more broadly to describe individuals who commune with the natural and supernatural world for the good of their community using traditional shamanic practices, such as drumming, journeying and dreaming.

A SHAMANIC HEALING RITUAL

The shamanic ritual outlined here calls upon the powers of the drum, of sacred herbs, and of the Inyan (the stone people of the Native American Indians) to summon dream spirits for healing, cleansing and purification. Have a representation (such as a picture) of the person, situation or place that you are doing this healing ritual for and place it on your altar or shrine. This ritual is best done in a fairly large open space so that you are able to move around, or if possible outside.

You will need
loose dried sage
heatproof bowl or shell
black or dark feather
large stone chosen for its individuality
tobacco
drum

1 Place the sage in the bowl and light it. Use the feather to fan the smoke around yourself and over the large stone. This is known as "smudging".

2 Take a pinch of tobacco and stand in the centre of your space facing north. Say the following words, then place the pinch of tobacco at the centre.
Great Spirit I honour you and humbly seek your presence within this grandfather rock.

3 Pick up the large stone and, holding it to your heart, ask it to help you clear any negative energies from the person, situation or place you are working on. Set the stone down on top of the tobacco saying the words:
Mitake oyasin ("For we are all related").

Sit for a moment in front of the burning sage, and breathe in its cleansing smoke.

The shaman's drum

The drum is one of the shaman's most powerful tools. Its primal sound touches the deepest recesses of mind, body and soul, connecting us with the heartbeat of Mother Nature and life itself. Before using a drum for a ceremony, it is customary to make an offering to the spirit of the drum. The spirit is made up of the essence of the animal that gave its hide, the tree that gave its wood and the maker who gave his or her skill and intent. The offering is given to honour the separate units that came together to make the whole. To make an offering, sprinkle a little tobacco over the drum before you begin to use it, saying thank you.

Drums play an important part in shamanic rituals. The sound of the drum is said to call healing spirits, while driving away sickness.

4 Take another pinch of tobacco and, still facing north, hold out your hand in that direction. With feeling and respect call out "Buffalo" and place the tobacco on the floor to the north.

5 Repeat the gestures for the east, south and west, calling out "Eagle", "Mouse" and "Bear" respectively.

6 Turn to the north again and say the following words, then stand the smudge bowl on the stone so that the smoke coils up through the room. *Guardians of the four winds, I, your brother/sister, do call your presence here.*

7 Take up the drum and, beginning at the edge of your space, walk deosil (clockwise) in a spiral until you reach the centre, drumming the atmosphere towards the stone. Drum over the stone into the herbs, visualizing any negative energies coiling away in the smoke. Thank the Great Spirit, grandfather rock, and the four totem animals for their help.

8 Repeat the words "Mitake oyasin" and then remove the smudge bowl from the stone. Take the stone outside to rest on the earth so that any remaining energy can be safely discharged into the ground.

RITUALS FOR BLESSING

One of the most essential arts in the witch's or magician's set of skills, is the ability to perform blessings. As well as blessing yourself, sometimes you may also need to bless places. You may sometimes have felt, when entering a place, that the atmosphere did not feel right or, when moving somewhere new, that it still had psychic disturbance caused by the previous occupants. Performing a blessing can change this and put the atmosphere right.

BLESSING YOURSELF WITH COLOUR

Before dealing with a difficult situation or if you need healing, or want to work a particularly powerful piece of magic, you might find the following ritual very helpful. It will help you to feel balanced, protected and able to deal with problems. Work through it slowly, really seeing or sensing the colours and their different energies. You can also use it to bless another.

1 Sit comfortably upright and close your eyes. Imagine that you are standing on a dark, black, curved surface. It is so intensely black that you could almost imagine it is the night sky, spangled with brilliant stars. Moving up your body from your feet, watch the colour changing to a dark, peaty brown, fading gradually as you move up your legs to a russet brown.

2 At the top of your legs, the colour is crimson red. Above that is a band of orange across your stomach, fading into a yellow band in the region of your solar plexus. Above the yellow, the colour changes to a rich leaf-green over

When you are performing a ritual to change an atmosphere it is important to use a new candle.

the heart region. At the top of your chest and throat, the colour changes through turquoise to a bright blue at your Adam's apple. From the bright blue, the colour changes to deep violet on the level of your "third eye", in the centre of your forehead, and finally there is a change to brilliant diamond white at the top of your head.

3 Allow these colours to become vivid and definite and try to discover a gradation of tone, from very dark at your feet to a brilliant white light above the top of your head.

4 See the vivid and shining white as a great ball above your head and then imagine drawing this force downwards through each colour band. It comes from beyond you, for it is the healing power of the creative force, or perhaps one of the healing angels.

5 As the light flows down through you, have a sense of it opening up like a rose unfolding. The chakra at the crown of your head is the link with your higher self through which you may work magic.

When blessing yourself with colour you need to be sitting comfortably before you begin the meditation.

Blessed colours

The colours that you visualize during the blessing have the following significance.

At the forehead the intense violet-purple represents your psychic faculty. As the brilliance flows downwards through your body, the blue rose of communication and speech flowers at the throat. Below that there is a green flower at the heart centre, from which the power of love and compassion flows to others. Next is the main healing centre of the solar plexus, through which the magical life force of the universe may be directed, in rays of golden sunlight, to those in need.

Across your abdomen is the orange-coloured flower that helps you cope with the mundane aspects of healing the sick, and will assist indigestion. Below that is the crimson blossom filled with the brilliance of white light that enlivens your most basic urges of sex and true unity. This can be used to heal and balance your own life, but you shouldn't use this healing power with others until you have fully mastered control of this centre of energy. Below that is a darker region of stability and strength. It is the strong base on which the blossoms of sacred light grow. This is a mysterious firmament, often envisioned as sprinkled with stars.

Traditional tools for changing an atmosphere: words recited from a book of power, the sound of a bell, and the cleansing power of a candle flame.

CHANGING THE ATMOSPHERE

When someone moves into a new home a common problem is that they feel disturbed by the atmosphere left by the previous occupants. You can deal with this matter fairly easily, if you are just changing the atmosphere to suit the new tenant, not trying to shift a ghost or a haunting – that is a job for the highly experienced.

You will need
twig of rowan wood
piece of red ribbon or thread
new white candle
candle holder

1 Bless yourself with colour as described in Blessing Yourself.

2 Tie the piece of red ribbon or thread around the rowan twig, and then carry it around the whole dwelling clockwise in every room and space, from top to bottom, mentally sweeping out old energies. Sweep these out of the front door as if they were dust.

3 Go outside, light the new white candle and carry it in. Carry the candle around all the rooms and spaces, clockwise, visualizing bright, new light entering.

4 When all feels well, stand in the centre of your home and stand quietly for a few moments. Before you snuff out your candle, you can recite this Navajo blessing:

This home will be a blessed home.
It will become the house of dawn.
Dawn light will live in beauty in it.
It will be a home of white corn,
It will be a home of soft goods,
It will be a home of crystal water,
It will be a home dusted with pollen,
It will be a home of life-long happiness,
It will be a home with beauty above it,
It will be a home of beauty all around.

Psychic upsets

Many psychic upsets are the result of people playing with the occult when they don't know what they are doing, such as using a Ouija board or attempting to set up a séance without knowing how. These actions can open a crack between the ordinary self and the inner one, and if people have fears or phobias, or repressed memories, these will be the first through the gap. These methods for contacting magical powers are not recommended for the novice, and should be left to trained witches and magicians.

A large number of candles placed in the corner of a room will dispel stagnant energies.

RITES OF PASSAGE: BEGINNINGS

Life is a journey with many milestones along the way. Different cultures around the world have many different ways of acknowledging these phases with ritual and celebration. Also known as "rites of passage", these rituals are designed to acknowledge the transition from one stage of life to another, and usually involve not only the individual but also their family and sometimes the wider community. For instance, most traditions have a way of naming a baby, others have rites at puberty or first menses, while marriage is almost universally acknowledged as one of life's major stepping stones. These rites of passage are usually embedded in the established religion of the society, although many customs also have their roots in magic.

A ring is an excellent symbol of commitment, as it is the unbroken circle without beginning or end.

WEDDING RITUALS

Although a traditional church "white wedding" is still the favoured option for many people, others are looking for ways to unite in marriage that do not involve the church. There are other marriage ceremonies, which although they may not be recognized by the state, suit many couples, particularly as they can decide for themselves the words and format of the ritual rather than following a fixed set of procedures. Weddings over the broomstick have taken place in many parts of the world, in which the couple step over a besom to indicate they are entering a new phase of a shared life. Pagans have a ceremony called "hand fasting" where the bride and groom have their hands bound together with a ribbon and there is an exchange of rings.

Although a priestess and priest officiate at pagan ceremonies, the format of the actual ceremony is always directed by the couple, allowing them to promise to love, support and remain with each other for a traditional "year and a day", or

The pagan ceremony of hand fasting involves tying the couple's hands together with a ribbon to signify their commitment to each other.

for a lifetime or forever. They usually have a pair of wedding rings blessed by the priestess and priest, and exchange these as a sign of long-term commitment. There is often a ceremonial sharing of bread and wine, and often the bride and groom break the wine glass to show that no one else can break their union. Many pagans like to conduct these marriage rites out of doors, in a sacred circle, ringed by lighted candles, flowers and ribbons. Their guests are instructed as to what may happen, as they may be from many faiths, perhaps being asked to light a candle of their own, to offer gifts or to speak personal blessings and wishes for the future of the couple. There is a wedding feast with a special cake, usually followed by a party.

NAMING CEREMONIES

Many parents today in more modern, secular societies, are not comfortable with having their baby baptized or christened into the Christian faith and are looking for other options. In former times one of the tasks of the village midwife was to bless a baby at its birth, before the priest of the orthodox religion named it. Today, pagan priestesses trained in these arts are much in demand. Within the blossoming pagan religions, new ceremonies are being constructed which can be offered to adherents, so that their children can be named and blessed in the power of the old gods and goddesses.

Affirm the life you are living now and keep mementos and reminders of the days that are passing. The stages of childhood in particular should be marked and recorded with reverence and joy.

COMING-OF-AGE RITUALS

In the Jewish religion, a boy's coming of age is marked with the "bar mitzvah" ceremony, symbolizing the end of childhood and an initiation into adulthood at puberty. For the most part, however, coming of age is not officially recognized within modern society and many people are once again looking to the pagan tradition for meaningful rites that honour the young person's passage. By officially recognizing their status in society, a young person is given a more clearly defined role and a sense of belonging that is often lacking among modern teenagers whose "difficult" behaviour can be connected with a struggle for identity.

Rituals are being set up so that young people can be seen to have passed into adulthood, and they are given the symbols of the responsibilities they are taking on. These rituals are different in character from those of earlier traditions, which might have involved a hunting ritual for boys, or a time apart for girls, but in content they can still be part teaching session and part celebration.

In a magical community, at the chosen age in years, or moment in life, a ritual is organized where the young person is presented with their own magical tools, their Tarot pack or symbol of the clan or community. They will be told of their responsibilities, which may increase if they are initiated into the Mysteries of their family, and they are shown the kind of assistance and support that is available to them within the community.

In most magical and witchcraft groups young people do not receive full initiation until they are adults. Some groups take 18 as the age of adulthood, others wait until the age of 21.

Traditions of marriage

The wedding ring: having no beginning or end, the ring symbolizes the unbroken circle of lives and the couple's commitment to each other for eternity.

The bouquet of flowers: this is a vestige of the sacrifice, which in days gone by would have been an animal or bird, offered on the altar and then becoming part of the wedding feast. Flowers symbolize beauty and perfection, with particular blooms having different meanings. Brides cast their bouquet over their shoulder to pass on the expectation to be the next to be wed.

The stag and hen night: the Stag is reminiscent of the Horned God and a symbol of male sexual potency and authority, while the Hen, with her power to lay eggs and create new life, symbolizes the fruitful mother aspect of the goddess. The traditional stag and hen parties, or bridal shower, may have evolved from the competitive games that were once held. Often, the bride had to be "stolen" from her family and taken into the groom's community, and the groom would swoop into the bride's territory on a horse and carry her off to a new life, chased by her family and his friends.

RITES OF PASSAGE: ENDINGS

While most of us welcome beginnings and the start of something new, we tend to find endings more difficult. This is partly because of the way we are taught to see life, as something that progresses from start to finish. In magical thinking, however, an ending is not something final but is merely another stage in the infinite cycle of birth, growth, decay and rebirth. It is yet another transition from one stage to another as we journey through the wheel of life. It is important to acknowledge endings as this helps us to move on to the next stage of the soul's journey.

In magical thinking, an ending is not seen as final, but as another stage in an infinite cycle which is reflected in the cycles of nature.

DIVORCE RITUALS

In the past, people struggled to make a marriage or partnership last, trying to hide their differences or finding ways of respecting them and continuing to live together for a variety of practical reasons. Today, people are more ready to separate if they have grown apart and there is less social stigma to being divorced, but as yet, mainstream society does not have any official rituals, other than legal ones, that acknowledge this transition.

For this reason, rituals of division have been created by modern pagans, which try to signify an ending that is peaceful and not acrimonious. In a ceremony, the couple acknowledge that they cannot reconcile their differences, have fallen out of love, and desire to part. Then the wedding rings are taken off, and possibly thrown into running water, or given to a goldsmith who can melt them down,

undoing the magic of joining. A ribbon that has been tied around the couple is cut and they are set free, perhaps by burning a paper on which their original bonds or promises were written. A cake may be cut in half in the presence of those assembled, or some other symbolic representation of the parting performed, to help at this difficult time.

FUNERALS

In orthodox places of worship, a funeral is usually a rather sombre and gloomy affair. While the death of a friend, family member or colleague is very sad for those that are left behind, pagan funerals try to focus on celebrating the dead person's life. Many pagans choose a woodland burial in a biodegradable coffin and to have a living tree planted over their grave, rather than a cold headstone, as a memorial. Others are cremated so that

their ashes may be ritually scattered at some sacred or beloved spot by their friends. Some funeral centres will allow for a magical circle to be cast about the coffin and floral tributes can be offered in the shapes of stars, moons or circles. Ritual prayers or poetry may be read at the service. Symbolic acts of casting off mortal life for an eternal spiritual one can be shared by family and friends, and anecdotes of the deceased's life, including photographs of them at different life stages, are often included.

OTHER ENDINGS

As we go through life, we will encounter many endings. Some of these, like death and divorce, are fairly major, but "smaller" endings, like leaving home, changing a job, or moving to a new area, all signify the ending of one phase of life and the start of something new. These endings are often acknowledged by the people we are leaving behind with cards

Severing the ties

When relationships are no longer able to sustain themselves, a ritual severing of the ties that bound the couple together helps to set them free and to heal any bitterness or uncertainty. In earlier times, the partners' names were written on a log which was then split; each partner would burn the half log bearing the partner's name on their own fire to release any lingering bonds.

As in any kind of ending ritual, splitting a log with the couple's names written on it was a way of letting go and moving on from a painful situation, and marking its passage.

For those who are left behind, a remembrance shrine can bring comfort, and a feeling of continued closeness to someone who has died.

and gifts, but we can also acknowledge them for ourselves. We can light a candle on our shrine or altar and say goodbye to the old life, acknowledging and giving thanks for all it has given us, before we embark on our new journey.

REBIRTH

Many occultists believe that after death the immortal soul is drawn towards a great light. People who have had a near-death experience often describe passing through a dark tunnel towards a place of brightness, and perhaps encountering a divine or heavenly being or spirit guide who leads them to a glorious garden. But when it is not their time to die, they return to complete their life on earth, usually as changed people. Occultists

believe that when we die, after a period of rest the soul once again prepares for rebirth into the temporal plane.

Those who have evolved through many thousands of lives and, according to the Buddhist belief, have been able to step off the wheel of incarnations, may still choose to return to earth, to teach others, or to act as a beacon, guiding lost

souls towards their heavenly or divine heritage. Some people seem to return quickly to a new life; it depends on the purpose of each particular incarnation, and time as we understand it in the physical world has no meaning in the realm of spirit. Others return after long intervals of earthly time.

IMMORTAL LIFE

In magical thinking, a burial or scattering of ashes is essentially returning the person's physical remains to the Great Mother, which is part of all life. Through the food we eat and the air we breathe, our lives are created with the substance of earth, which is also part of the cosmos. Along with the earth, moon and stars, the sun and planets, we are part of this vast creation, ever changing but immortal.

Remembrance shrine

When someone has died, the ones who are left to grieve may find comfort in marking a particular place in the house where they can go to remember and celebrate a life that has moved on. A remembrance shrine can be made using

photographs, a lit candle, some burning incense, some fresh flowers or a keepsake that reminds you of that person. Make the shrine an affirmation of the person's life rather than a continual mourning for a loss.

SPELLWEAVING

Magic doesn't just happen all by itself: spells are woven, crafted, worked and cast in order to bring about a desired result. This means making spells is an active process that requires effort, energy and commitment on the part of the spellweaver.

Essentially, a spell is a magic recipe containing many different ingredients and needs careful thought and planning. Before you start, you need to be clear why you want to cast a particular spell and to make sure your intent is in line with your highest purpose. You also need to assemble all your ingredients – and this may take several hours or even days as you search for exactly what the spell requires. And even once the spell is cast, you will need to back up your magic on the physical plane by taking whatever action is necessary to set things in motion.

This chapter contains 27 spells to bring magic into all areas of your life. The spells begin with meeting angels and guides, and then you can start to work magic for healing and protection, self-empowerment, luck and prosperity, love and romance, friends and relationships and more. It will show you how to work with a variety of magical ingredients including talismans, charms, spell bags and an assortment of stones, plants, herbs, trees and oils. You will also learn to record your efforts by creating your own spell book or Book of Shadows.

THE SPELLWEAVER'S ART

The art of weaving, or casting, spells is what attracts many people to magic. Spells are magical formulae that are designed to change or adapt reality to the magic-worker's will. They are serious matters, so be sure that your motives are pure and that your object is both achievable and desirable. You should never use magic to interfere with the free will of another, and whatever you give out in magic is returned threefold, so always make sure you are working for the highest good of all concerned. Spells are usually cast once the magic circle has been created and the otherworldly beings have been summoned. Always have your spells planned out in advance and make sure you have all the equipment gathered together before you step into your magic circle.

Spells are usually worked in a circle that is large enough to hold you and your equipment.

SIX STEPS TO SUCCESS

Natural magic requires six basic components for success, so before you embark on a spell, check that each one is in place. The first requirement is desire and need. This may sound obvious, but if you don't truly desire what you are working for then your energy won't really be behind it and your thought-forms won't take shape in the astral plane.

The second requirement is emotional involvement. This fuels your desire and need, and further strengthens the links between the astral and the physical planes: once your thought-forms are strong enough on the astral level, they cannot help but manifest themselves on the physical.

Thirdly, you need to have enough knowledge and to have set realistic targets. Knowledge is power. It includes knowing which tools to use and when and how to use them. For instance, in a spell to attract love, some herbs will be more suitable than others, and certain times will be more favourable than others. Having realistic expectations means knowing which magical goals are naturally within your reach, and which are not. No spell can make you superhuman and achieve the impossible.

How many spells?

If you are new to working spells it is likely that the first one you perform will use up a lot of psychic energy, so try not to wear yourself out. In the beginning it is probably best to confine yourself to one or two spells in a session, although as you become more practised you may do three or four.

A magic circle can be made out of individual items as well as an unbroken cord. If you are doing this kind of circle, use numbers and symbolism to add power to your spell.

The fourth component is belief. This can be difficult in the beginning, but having enough confidence and belief in the outcome of your spells is crucial. Lack of belief and negative thoughts about it will undermine what you are doing. The popular tag on the end of spells, "so mote it be"("so may it be"), is an affirmation of belief and has been used for centuries to assert a spell's reality in the here and now.

In the spirit of the old occult saying that declares "power shared is power lost", the fifth requirement is the ability to keep silent. This helps to protect the energy you have put into your spells from outside influences, some of which may be negative. Lastly, you need to be willing to take whatever practical steps are necessary to back up your magic in the everyday world. For instance, it is no good doing a spell for prosperity and then sitting around waiting for money to shower down on you from above. You will have to create and work your spell by taking appropriate action, being confident that your magic will guide you in the right direction.

KEEPING A SPELL BOOK

Get into the habit of recording your spells and other magic work in a personal magical diary, or spell book, usually known as a Book of Shadows.

Originating in the late Middle Ages, when literacy became more widespread, the practice of keeping a log has become a standard tool in modern magic. It is traditional to write up the diary by hand and to record in detail your spells and magic work, including the words that you used and any equipment, as well as the outcome. Many people also like to

The Book of Shadows

The traditional name for a witch or magician's spell book is a 'Book of Shadows'. Its title may allude to the shadows cast by the flickering candlelight that the practitioner worked by as they wrote up their magical diary, in the days before electricity. On another level, it may also refer to the fact that the book, like the magic itself, should be kept hidden and out of sight in the 'shadows'. According to legend, these books were once written in secret alphabets in case they fell into the wrong hands. The first time such a book was ever made public was when Gerald Gardner, founder of the Wicca movement, published his own early in the 20th century.

Making your own collection of precious and symbolic items will help you to be more creative with your spells. Invest time in your equipment to imprint them with emotional energy.

include transcriptions of dreams and astral travel, insights gained during meditation and other discoveries on their personal journey in their spell book. Over time, it will prove an invaluable record of your findings, failures and successes. Today, there are an infinite variety of beautiful notebooks available in the shops, made with handmade paper, coloured paper, tissue leaves and so on. Look for something that appeals to you, or spend some time making your own record book, and enjoy transforming it into a magical treasure trove.

BE CREATIVE

Once you have grasped the fundamentals of how magic works and the different attributes of the various magical tools and helpers – be they herbs, oils, gemstones, colours or deities – you can begin to create your own spells. The possibilities here are endless; it is a question of experimenting and trying out different combinations until you find something that is effective. In many ways your own formulae will be more potent, as you will have invested time, thought and emotional energy to give them an energetic imprint that is uniquely yours.

Golden rules for spellweaving

- Work from the heart and do what you do with gentleness and responsibility.
- Seek no revenge and send no ill will – for whatever you send will return to you.
- Do not manipulate the free will of another, or attempt to control events to suit yourself.
- Keep yourself, your working space and

equipment clean and free of psychic dirt.
- To insure against negative influence always include the words 'for the highest good of all' in a spell.
- At the end of every spell affirm your belief in its power by saying "And so mote it be!".

Undoing a spell

If you wish to undo a spell, write it down on a piece of paper. Light a white candle and some frankincense then burn the written spell in the candle flame and say:
This spell is undone. So mote it be.

SPIRIT AND ANGEL SPELLS

There are many different ways of connecting with angels and celestial beings, but weaving spells is an excellent method. You can use these spells whenever you are seeking guidance, clarity or inspiration from on high, during times of vulnerability or for blessings. Always remember to thank the Beings of Light; whether you sense their presence or not, they will be there.

The six-pointed star used in the Spell for Connection is a powerful mystical symbol.

A SPELL FOR CONNECTION

Sitting within the six-pointed star will help to develop your connection with celestial beings. Bless your equipment before you begin.

You will need
rhythmic spiritual drumming music
lotus oil
natural sea salt
6 violet candles
6 amethysts
gold candle

1 With spiritual drumming playing in the background, face east and anoint your head, hands and feet with lotus oil.

2 Draw a six-pointed star, made of two overlapping equal-sized triangles, in salt around you. The star should be big enough for you to sit in the centre.

3 Sit or stand in the centre of the star and place a violet candle on each of the six points, beginning at the south. Light the candles in turn, saying the following. As you light the first, say:
O Angel Gabriel, lift my spirit to Levanah, to draw down her magic into my heart.

Light the candle to your right and say:
O Angel Raphael, lift my spirit to touch Kokab that I may draw down his wisdom and truth.

Turn to the next candle, light it and say:
O Angel Zamael, lift my spirit to touch Madim that I may draw down courage and strength.

Light the next candle, and say:
O Angel Cassiel, lift my spirit to touch Shabbathai that I may draw down understanding and patience.

Light the next candle, and say:
O Angel Sachiel, lift my spirit to touch Tzedek that I may draw down righteousness.

Turn to the last candle, light it and say:
O Angel Anael, lift my spirit to touch Nogah that I may draw down love and beauty.

4 Then place an amethyst next to each candle, in the same order as above. Put the gold candle in front of you, inside the star, light it and say:
Mighty Michael, Angel of the Sun, lift my spirit to touch Shemesh that I may be drawn closer and closer to the light of the Divine. This I ask of you, that I may grow ever closer to the truth. Adonai, Lord of Light, Adonai, Adonai.

5 Now close your eyes and sit with your hands in your lap, palms up. Stay here for up to 20 minutes and feel the essence of spiritual light filling your body, mind and soul.

6 To close your spell, pick up the amethysts and blow out the candles, starting with the last one you lit and ending with the first. Close your cord circle, saying:
May divine will be done.

The colour violet, and the amethyst, are both connected to the crown chakra, the chakra of spirituality.

The angel blessing can be spoken on its own, if you feel it is needed, without candles and incense.

An angel altar should be left for 24 hours, and then dismantled.

ANGEL BLESSING

This spell can be performed as a way to bless and consecrate yourself.

You will need
2.7 m (9 ft) white cord
white candle
frankincense
charcoal burner

1 Open your cord circle and place the candle, frankincense and burner in the centre. Turn to the south and set light to the candle and the charcoal. Sprinkle some frankincense on to the hot charcoal saying:
Lord of Light, this offering I make.

2 Next, say the Angelic Invocation. While you say the first line, touch your head, as you say the second line touch your stomach, as you say the third line touch your left shoulder, and say the remainder of the invocation as you touch your right shoulder:
Uriel above me
Michael beneath me
Raphael to my left
Gabriel to my right
By the power of these Great Angels
Surround me with light.

3 Visualize an angel in each of the four directions. Bow your head and say "thank you" to each one. Ask them for what you feel you need; humility, an open heart, strength etc.

4 When you have finished thank each angel again and let him depart. Blow out the candle and close your circle.

AN ANGEL ALTAR

You can use this altar for someone you know is in need of angelic protection or healing, but never perform spells for another without their permission.

Cast a circle of salt on your altar, then place a white candle, some frankincense and a photograph of the subject within it. Light the candle and the frankincense and say the Angelic Invocation while touching the head and relevant parts of the person's body in the photograph and saying their name rather than your own. Leave the altar as it is for 24 hours, then remove the circle of salt, gathering it up so that it can be sprinkled on the earth outside, or over a pot of earth. For serious situations, leave for 48 hours, repeating the invocation after 24 hours.

A spell seeking guidance

Spells can be used as oracles when you need an answer to an important question. This simple version uses a "magical book", which could be any book containing spiritual teachings. It is best done during a waning moon.

You will need
blue candle
your thickest magical book
sheet of paper
black ink

1 Light the candle and place it beside the magical book. Concentrating on your question, write it down on a new sheet of paper in black ink. Fold the paper into a narrow bookmark shape. Say:
In this book I seek; in this book I peek.
Reveal a clue, now heed me.

2 Slide the paper into the book at random, then read the words next to the paper. This should help answer your question if it was clear. Pinch out the candle.

Spells for Psychic Help

Psychic powers can be developed by learning to trust our instinctive, intuitive responses rather than rationalizing and analysing everything that we do. Traditionally, women are said to be more in touch with this aspect of themselves than men, but this is not a hard and fast rule. Regardless of our gender it means cultivating a relationship with the "feminine" or "yin" aspect of the life force, and one way of doing this is by drawing on the powers of the moon when casting spells and working magic.

Round white stones are used to represent the full moon, or increase your connection with her.

Drawing Down the Moon

Draw on the powers of the moon to refresh and rejuvenate you for the month ahead and help you get in touch with your sensitivity and powers of intuition. The best time for this spell is 2 days before the full moon.

You will need
13 circular stones of any size
salt
aromatherapy burner
jasmine essential oil
9 white or cream candles

1 Beginning in the south, make a circle of 12 of your chosen stones in a clockwise direction. Place the 13th in the centre.

2 Sprinkle the stones with salt. Light the aromatherapy burner and put in 3 drops of jasmine oil.

3 Place 8 candles around the circle and one by the centre stone. Then light the candles as you say these words:
Magna Dei, Light of the Night, I light these candles to guide your moonrays here. I ask you to come and bless this circle.

4 Stand facing south, with your arms outstretched above your head and your feet quite wide apart. Reach towards the sky and say this lunar invocation:
Hail to thee, Sophia, holy spirit of the wise moon. I call upon you to enter and fill me with your light. Protect me and guide me on the moonway. Teach me your wisdom and truth as I seek your clarity and guidance.

5 Draw down the powers of the moon. Allow yourself to be refreshed and refilled with the feminine virtues of wisdom, beauty and grace. Let the moon bless your feelings and perceptions until you feel energized and content. Lower your arms.

6 Finish by saying "thank you". Blow out your candles and close the circle.

The spell is particularly of benefit to a woman, as the moon cycles reflect her own.

PSYCHIC DREAMS

You can encourage psychic dreams with an aquamarine crystal. Store your dream crystal in a little pouch made of shiny pale blue or silver material, decorated with moon charms and sequins. Before you use the aquamarine you need to clear your dreamtime by first using jet in your pouch under your pillow, until any nightmares you may have been suffering from are gone. Then dedicate or bless your aquamarine, place it in the pouch, and put the pouch under your pillow for perceptive dreams.

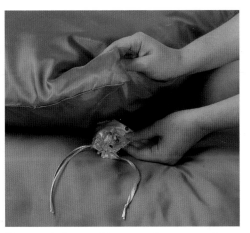

You can dedicate or bless your dream crystal every month, at the full moon, for extra potency.

OPENING THE INNER GATES

The gate of inner vision is situated at the 6th, or brow, chakra, also known as the "third eye", which is located just above the eyebrows. Seeing with this "inner" eye is associated with clairvoyance. Best time: Monday, waxing moon.

You will need
2.7 m (9 ft) white cord
flower
red candle
small bowl of water
stone
sandalwood incense
picture of an open door or gate, or the Moon Tarot card

1 Open your cord circle and place the flower in the east, the candle in the south, the bowl of water in the west and the stone in the north. Light the incense in the centre of the circle.

2 Sit in the centre of the circle with the picture or Tarot card on your lap. Close your eyes, centre yourself and focus on the intention; be sure that your wish to work with inner vision is for the highest good of all.

3 Stand up and make an opening gesture to each of the four quarters in turn, saying the appropriate sentence as you pick up each object. Light the candle as you speak the following words about candle fire:
Open my mind like a growing flower, may my vision now empower.
Open my mind to the candle fire, may my vision now inspire.
Open my mind to the water's flow, that on vision journeys I may go.
Open my mind to this stone so cold, that visions I shall safely hold.

4 Pick up the picture or card and hold it out in front of your heart. Circle or turn around four times, saying:
Open gates that I may roam,
Safely bring my knowledge home.

5 Sit down and close your eyes again. Relax and sit in meditation for a while, letting any pictures or images come and go freely.

6 When you are ready, open your eyes and put out the incense. Close the circle widdershins and dispose of your equipment appropriately.

Psychic protection

As you become more sensitive to spiritual energies, you need to make sure that you are protected. Feeling excessively tired and drained is often a sign that you are picking up too much psychic dirt. Best time: Saturday, waxing moon. Carry this spell with you for the next few days.

You will need
12 tealights
indigo blue candle
myrrh incense
carnelian stone
vervain Bach flower essence
15 cm (6in) square of indigo cloth
red thread

1 Arrange the tealights in a circle, then open it deosil, lighting the first tealight in the east. Sit in the centre of the circle, facing west, and light the indigo candle and the incense.

2 Close your eyes and visualize yourself in a golden globe of pale blue light with orange flames around the surface.

3 Take the carnelian stone and bring it to rest on your hara, the body's life energy centre about 5cm (2in) below the navel. Hold the stone here and repeat this invocation three times:
Bright angels of the astral plane, please come and bless this stone and fill it with your power, love and protection.
After the third repetition, say:
Thank you (to the angels). And so mote it be!

4 Add two drops of vervain essence to the stone and wrap it up in the cloth. Tie the parcel with the thread. Extinguish the candle and incense then close the circle widdershins, pinching out each tealight, starting in the east. Dispose of the candles with respect and do not reuse.

The carnelian is connected to the hara, the personal power centre or Shaman's Cave.

Carnelian

This deep red or orange stone has the ability to protect you from negativity. It links to your own inner power and strength during times of psychic stress.

SPELLS FOR HEALING

There has always been a strong link between magic and medicine, and any distinction between the two is often very blurred. In many cultures, spells and incantations have been used for a variety of healing purposes. Traditionally, knowledge of healing spells was the province of the village wise woman, the shaman or the medicine-man. However, it is accepted that recovery from illness has much to do with state of mind, and with a little knowledge of the art and craft of magic, it is possible for you to practise healing magic for yourself or those who are close to you.

Binding the spell with gold thread (the colour of the sun), before burying it under your chosen tree, helps to invoke the sun's healing powers.

A SPELL FOR HEALING

This is a spell to bring healing. Ask permission if you are doing it for another. Before you perform this spell, find a suitable tree – ash, birch, juniper and cedar trees are all good. You may prefer to cast your circle outside next to the tree, and work within nature. The best day for working this spell is a Sunday.

You will need
2.7 m (9 ft) white cord
gold candle
gold pen
15 cm (6 in) square of natural paper
knife
lime
gold thread
15 cm (6 in) square of orange cloth

1 Open the circle and honour the four directions. Light the candle and say these words:
Angel Och, healing spirit of the sun,
I light this flame to honour your presence
And ask you to hear this prayer.

2 Write the name of the person to be healed on the paper, visualizing health and wellbeing surrounding them.

3 Cut the lime in two lengthways. Fold the paper three times and place it between the two halves. Bind it together with gold thread and say:
Powers of lime
Health is mine/thine
Cleanse the body, cleanse the mind
Spirit pure, fill my (or say another person's name) being
With health, with health, with health.

4 Place the bound lime in the orange cloth and bind it with gold thread. Close the circle in the usual way.

5 Now take the spell and bury it near the base of the tree. Ask the spirit of the tree to help you (or another person) to return to good health. Thank the tree, and depart.

The colours of gold and orange, used repeatedly in this spell, are colours of the sun, which is renowned for its healing powers.

A SPELL TO HEAL THE EARTH

Modern magic workers like to use their skills to help heal the damage that we are causing to our planet. Choose a place where the Earth's resources are being used or abused, such as a polluted river or a quarry. This is a spell of atonement.

You will need
moss agate crystal
white rose

1 Holding the moss agate crystal in your right hand and the rose in your left, repeat the following prayer of atonement. As you say the last line, lay down your moss agate.
Spirits of this place, I come in peace but with a heavy heart. I wish to say how sorry I am for what my brothers and sisters are doing to you in their ignorance. I come to make an offering to show you that I am sorry for taking from you without respect. I ask your forgiveness. I ask you to help humanity to see how precious all life is.
I make this offering to you.

2 Transfer the rose to your right hand. Hold it to your heart, say the following:
Creator, guide us all in the ways of peace, love, wisdom and truth. I call you here to (say the name of the place) to bring the Divine to this area, to bless it with your healing love. May (say the name of the place) now be sacred again.

3 Lay down the white rose on the earth. Visualize the whole area filling with white light, embracing it with illumination. End the spell with the Native American saying:
"Mitake Oyasin" (we are all related).

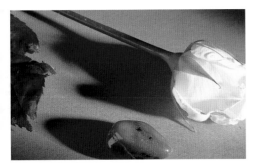

The white rose stands for purity and innocence, and is an appropriate gift for the Earth.

Frankincense is the incense associated with the sun. It is not difficult to see why when you see the rich ambers, yellows and golden colours of the loose resin.

A spell for good health

Each planet has its own magic symbol, which can be used to harness its powers. The sigil of the sun is used in this spell for health; it can also be used for success and prosperity. Sunday is the best day to perform this spell.

You will need
2.7 m (9 ft) white cord
gold candle
frankincense and burner
gold pen
15 cm (6 in) square of natural paper
a lock of your hair

1 Open the circle, taking with you all the ingredients for the spell. Light the candle, and begin to burn the frankincense, and say these words:
Angel Och, healing spirit of the sun,
I light this flame to honour your presence
And ask you to hear this prayer.

2 Take the piece of paper, and write the name of the person whom the spell is for, visualizing health and wellbeing surrounding them as you do so.

3 On the other side of the paper draw the sigil of the sun, and write the words "Angel Och". Hold the piece of paper to your heart, with the name facing inwards, and visualize golden-orange light filling your heart, and then the whole of your body. Repeat:
I am healthy and well.

4 Take the lock of hair and lay it on the spell, on the side of the sigil of the sun. Fold the piece of paper six times so that it forms a small packet. Keep it in a very safe place, or preferably, carry it with you, close to your heart.

The sigil of the sun is often used for healing.

SPELLS TO EMPOWER

The path of magic is the road towards self-empowerment. Instead of being a victim of circumstance, magic encourages us to use our free will to make creative choices for ourselves, in line with our soul's highest purpose. A universal law is that "like attracts like", so whatever we give out returns to us. Lack of self-confidence and negative self-beliefs stand in the way of us getting what we want for ourselves, but we can use spellweaving to help remove these obstacles and increase our personal power and magnetism.

Before you undertake the Aura of Confidence spell, you should perform the Golden Light Breathing Exercise, to energize yourself.

A SPELL TO REMOVE AN OBSTACLE

If you feel that you are stuck and unable to move on for some reason, and can identify the cause, try this spell to remove the obstruction in your life. For this you will need to create a gift to Mother Earth, it should be something you have made yourself, like a cake or painting, or it can be a loving action such as clearing a stream, picking up litter, or planting a tree. This spell needs to be performed outside.

You will need
*a gift for Mother Earth
a fossil or a blessed stone
natural sea salt*

1 Take your gift and fossil to the place you have chosen to perform your spell. Beginning with the east, with the salt draw a deosil circle around yourself, large enough to sit in, repeating the opening circle invocation.

2 Place yourself comfortably on the ground, facing north. Say the following invocation three times with as much feeling as possible.
*Mother Earth, I bring you a gift of (state what) because I have come to you today to ask you to help me. I wish to remove (state your obstacle).
I ask you with all my heart if you will talk with the Angel Cassiel on my behalf, and that together you help me to lift the condition. Please help me to understand why it is there, so that I may move forward, safe in the knowledge that I am part of a loving universe. Teach me, Mother Earth, to be wise and to trust in the beauty of all life. Show me the way to remove this obstacle so that I may grow in understanding and wisdom. (Take your fossil).
I ask that this fossil, when it is buried in your being, may take away my burden and help me to endure, because it is within you and you are with me.*

3 Add "thank you" at the end of the third time. Bury your fossil. Send the energies home by saying "So mote it be", while visualizing the completion of your task.

4 Leave the earth your gift, or tell her your pledge has been done, or will be done on a certain day. It is important to give, or you may not receive.

5 Starting with the west, break your circle of salt widdershins and brush it away into the surrounding area, until you are back at west again. Walk away, leaving your troubles behind you. Do not look back.

If you have a weakness for chocolate cake, make this your gift to Mother Earth.

Aura of Confidence

Tap into the sun's powers to radiate self-confidence. If you are not confident, then it is unlikely that your magic will be very successful. Make sure you practise Golden Light Breathing (see chapter 1) before you work this spell to energize you. The best time for this spell is Sunday during a waxing moon.

You will need
2.7 m (9 ft) white cord
gold candle
gold pen
15 cm (6 in) square of natural paper
larch Bach flower essence
envelope
gold ribbon
goblet of golden drink
round, golden biscuit
tin box

1 Open a circle in the east. Sit in the centre, facing south, light the candle and say:
O Michael, Angel of the Sun, I call upon your presence and ask you to shine your golden light upon my life. Strengthen my aura with your positive rays.

2 Close your eyes and visualize yourself surrounded by an egg-shaped space. This is your aura. Breathing gently, watch as the Angel of the Sun beams

Think carefully before you write down the things you would like to achieve.

his golden light rays towards you. With each inbreath, feel the light warming and energizing your whole being.

3 As you breathe out, see the egg-shaped space filling up with golden light and becoming bigger and brighter as your aura expands outwards. Repeat to yourself six times these words: *I can.*

4 Open your eyes and write down six things that you would like to achieve in the next six months. Choose things that seem out of reach at the moment, but not so far away that you feel they

As you drink the golden drink, and eat the biscuit, visualize the sun's warming powers.

are impossible. Drip six drops of larch essence on the paper, fold it up and put it into the envelope. Tie the gold ribbon around the envelope.

5 Eat the biscuit and drink the drink; both represent the power of the sun. Snuff the candle, thank the angel Michael and close the circle.

6 Put the spell into the tin box. Bury the box under a hazel tree and leave it for six months, undisturbed. When this time has passed, you may unearth the spell to check your progress.

Amulet for strengthening willpower

Making magic is about focusing your will to achieve a result. The more focused and determined you are, the better the likely outcome. Keep this amulet in your pocket and carry it with you; whenever you feel weak-willed, holding on to it will remind you of your resolve. The best time to perform this spell is on a Tuesday, during a waxing moon.

You will need
wand
red candle
haematite stone
centaury Bach flower essence
12.5 cm (5 in) square of red cloth
gold thread

1 Cast a magic circle with your wand and visualize it as a ring of fire. Put your spell ingredients in the centre and light the candle.

2 Begin in the east; hold the stone in your left hand and pass it over the candle flame, saying the first line of the following words. Then turn to the south, west and north in turn saying the second, third and fourth lines respectively and passing the stone over the candle each time.
I call the Sylphs, the helpers of Air.
I call the Salamanders, the helpers of Fire.
I call the Undines, the helpers of Water.
I call the Gnomes, the helpers of Earth.

3 Then continue with the rest of the incantation:

O elemental beings, please bless this stone so that it may remind me that I have the mental power to achieve my goal (or say whatever particular goal you are trying to achieve), sticking to what I feel is right for me. For I know that I am as firm and as steadfast as a rock.

4 Place the stone on the red cloth, together with a few drops of centaury essence. Bind the stone in the cloth with the golden thread.

5 Say "thank you" to your elemental helpers and let them depart. Blow out the candle and use your wand to close the circle.

GOOD FORTUNE SPELLS

In everyday language, a lucky life is said to be a "charmed life", and good luck charms and talismans have always played an important role in natural magic. They have been worn or carried as protection against the "evil eye" since ancient times. They have also been given to those embarking on any of life's "journeys" – whether a literal journey or a metaphorical one like a wedding, the start of a new job or the birth of a child.

A SPELL FOR GOOD LUCK

Work with the magic of the oak tree when making a good luck spell. You will need a spell bag or pouch, which you should make yourself, and a suitable oak tree. The best time for this spell is on a Thursday, during a full moon.

You will need
small amethyst
turquoise stone
oak leaves
cinquefoil essential oil
sprig of rosemary
spell bag

Turquoise brings blessings, and amethyst offers protection, so these two stones make an ideal combination for a good luck spell.

1 Greet the spirit of your tree and tell it your intentions. Place the amethyst at its base as an offering. Walking deosil round the tree, repeat the following four times:
O Sachiel, Angel of Jupiter, I ask you to hear my call.
Light my path, guide my actions, words and thoughts and those of all I am yet to meet, that by the power of your might, all will be fortunate to my sight.
Good fortune growing, growing.

2 Anoint the turquoise stone and the oak leaves with the cinquefoil oil, while visualizing yourself surrounded by the arms of the mighty oak tree.

3 Place the turquoise, the oak leaves and the sprig of rosemary in your spell bag. Hold the spell bag up to the oak tree and say the following words:
Heart of Oak, you are my heart and with honour I shall carry you by my side.
Thank you.

4 Carry this spell with you for good fortune, and store it carefully when not in use. You could also do this spell as a special gift for a friend, and then give them the spell. But ask first.

If you make the spell bag yourself it will have far greater potency than if you buy it. It can be used again and again, and don't forget, the effort, time and energy you invest will be returned threefold.

A SPELL TO IMPROVE BUSINESS

Repeat this spell regularly to keep your business affairs flowing smoothly. Giving a gift to the energies that are helping you with your business pleases them and encourages them to work positively on your behalf. Rice and wheat are symbols of new life, and they encourage fertile opportunities. Do this spell every month for a while. It is best performed on the first day of a new moon.

You will need
3, 7 or 9 fresh basil leaves
bowl of spring water
spoon
citrine stone
dried ears of wheat
rice grains
mint leaves

Potency is added to magic if you use special tools for the task. This beautiful silver spoon is used for stirring the water in the spell to improve business.

1 Bless your equipment and ingredients. Soak the basil leaves in the bowl of water for one hour, stirring occasionally in a deosil (clockwise) direction.

2 Beginning to the right of the entrance at your place of work, walk deosil round the building or work area, sprinkling the aromatic water as you go and repeating the following invocation until you are finished:
Business expand, business grow
secure and successful –
my dealings flow.

3 Bless the citrine stone, wheat, rice and mint leaves again, then place the stone where you keep your money or transactions. Offer the corn and the rice to the energies that are helping you with your business affairs by sprinkling them in discreet places around your office or workplace.

4 Carry the mint leaves with you in your money pocket or purse. Replace them with fresh ones each time you re-work the spell.

Spell for safe travel

For this spell you need to find a stone that is different in some way from other stones in your area. Ask its permission to be used in a spell for safe passage. Use it for yourself or another. The best time to do this spell is a Wednesday.

You will need
2.7 m (9 ft) white cord
yellow candle, blessed
lavender essential oil or incense
aromatherapy burner (if using oil)
an unusual stone from your area
yellow and violet or blue paints
artist's paintbrush

1 Open your cord circle in the east and honour the four directions (see The Four Great Powers in chapter 1). Place the candle and oil burner (if using) in the centre and light them, adding a few drops of lavender oil to the burner. Alternatively, light the incense.

2 Sit in the centre of the circle facing east and paint your stone bright yellow. When it is dry, paint a triangle in violet or blue, with a line near its base as shown. This is the alchemical symbol for Air.

3 Hold the stone up to the east and repeat the following invocation eight times, making sure that you say "thank you" to the angel Raphael after the eighth time.
O Raphael, Angel of the East, fill this stone with
your blessing and protection. I pray to you for a
safe journey for me (or say someone else's name).
Guard me (or say someone else's name) and guide
me (or another name) on the path this journey
takes, until I (or another name) can return.

4 Close your spell and circle in the usual way. Carry your stone with you on your travels, returning it to Mother Earth when the journey is ended and you are safely home.

This is the alchemical symbol for Air that you need to paint on the stone for the travel spell.

SPELLS FOR THE HOME

Our homes and possessions are like an extension of ourselves. In magical terms they are connected to us along fine energy pathways and we can use magic to make things happen in our physical surroundings. Traditionally, many home spells are concerned with blessing and protection, although we can also work spells to help us find things that are lost and to buy and sell property successfully.

Sweep your house with a birch broom to cleanse the physical and spiritual environment.

A HOUSE BLESSING SPELL

If you have recently moved into a new home or there have been upheavals in your domestic life, perform this blessing to consecrate the space. The best time is on a Sunday morning during a waxing moon. You should be alone.

You will need
natural sea salt
small bowl
rose geranium essential oil
white candle
aromatherapy burner
a few grains of organic rice
15 cm (6 in) square of golden fabric

1 Bless and consecrate yourself using the Angelic Invocation. Place the salt in the bowl. Starting in the top right-hand corner of your home and working deosil through the building, sprinkle a pinch of salt in the four corners of every room, door and window. As you sprinkle, say:
I cleanse and purify this room of all unnecessary or negative vibrations.

2 Take the rose geranium oil and light the white candle. Again working clockwise around the building, place the candle in the centre of each room. Anoint all doors and windows with a little of the oil as you say:

I call upon the Angels of Light and Love to bless this home and all who enter here.
May love, happiness and harmony prevail.

3 Place the candle in the centre of your main living room. Light the aromatherapy burner and add six drops of rose geranium oil to it. Sit quietly, visualizing your home filled with the qualities that you desire.

4 Let the candle burn down almost completely, then anoint it with rose geranium oil and sprinkle with rice as thanks to the helpful energies. Snuff the candle, wrap it in the gold fabric and place the spell beneath your front door mat or as close to your door as possible, saying:
This I place so that all who enter here will be blessed.

5 Leave the parcel undisturbed until the next time you perform a cleansing or blessing ceremony, when it can be replaced by a new parcel.

Grains of rice are a precious gift from the Earth and are often used in magical spells and rituals as a symbol of giving thanks.

Horseshoes, hung with the open ends upwards on front doors, provide protection and strength.

A spell for finding

This spell uses your powers of visualization in which you imagine a lost object being drawn back to you. It is best performed on a Wednesday, the day of the week associated with Mercury, the god of thieves. You will need to find a hazel tree to cut yourself a wand. Ask permission of the spirit of the tree first and leave a lock of your hair as a gift. Perform this spell during a waxing moon, on a Wednesday.

You will need
20 cm (8 in) wand of hazel
honeysuckle essential oil, diluted in carrier oil
yellow cloth

1 Find a quiet place where you won't be disturbed and draw a deosil circle around yourself with the hazel wand, saying these words:
By the powers of heaven and earth I cast this sacred circle in the name of love, light, wisdom and truth.

2 Perform the Golden Light Breathing exercise (see Preparation Rituals in chapter 5), then anoint your temples, forehead and hands with honeysuckle oil. Sit or stand in the north, facing south, close your eyes and visualize yourself on a high mountain peak made of magnetic crystals. You can see for miles in any direction.

3 Now see yourself opening your hands, palms are facing upwards. Say this invocation:
Swift and sure, my (name the object) return to me.

4 Imagine that your property is being drawn back to you, by the strength of the magnetic mountain. Draw it back with as much willpower and concentrated thought as you can. Note any pictures that come into your mind and from which direction your property returns to you in the visualization.

5 To add to the spell's effectiveness, write what you have lost on a piece of paper and pin it up where you will see it.

6 Say "thank you" to the energies that have helped you. Close your spell then move your wand widdershins from the end to the beginning of the original circle, saying:
This spell is done.

7 Wrap the wand in the cloth and store it in a safe space with the rest of your magical equipment. If the lost object is in someone else's possession, he or she should feel compelled to return it. If nothing happens, try the spell again a week later, or accept that it is irretrievable.

The hazel wand in a spell for finding gives magical protection during the ceremony.

Burning frankincense in a spell for selling will cleanse your home and purify it of old vibrations.

A SPELL FOR SELLING

When you need to sell your house, or any other object, work a spell to attract the right buyer. Burning frankincense will cleanse your home and purify it of old vibrations, making it ready for the next keeper. The best time for this spell is on a Wednesday during a waxing moon.

You will need
an altar
a vase of yellow flowers
frankincense and burner
item for sale, or a picture or symbol of it
yellow ribbon

1 Hold the item being sold, its picture, or a symbol of it in your right hand. Stand in front of your altar and turn to face west, the direction for letting go. Turn slowly, from west to east, moving deosil, as you say:

I let go of this (name the object), so that something new can come in its place.

2 Place the vase of flowers on the altar and burn the frankincense. Tell the spirit of the item you are selling that it is time to part company and that a new keeper is coming to take over.

3 Tie up the item or its symbol with yellow ribbon and put it on your altar in the east. Call on the east wind, saying:
Hail to thee East Wind. This (name the object) sells, this (name the object) sells. Please guide the next keeper here speedily so that I am free for something new.

4 Say thank you to the East Wind, saying:
For the highest good of all concerned, so mote it be!

Flowers to help a sale

To enhance the magic of a spell for selling, change the vase of flowers on the altar each day of the week for one week. Repeat the spell if the item hasn't sold, and repeat weekly until it goes.
Saturday: evergreens, cypress
Sunday: orange flowers
Monday: white flowers, river plants
Tuesday: red flowers
Wednesday: yellow flowers
Thursday: violet or purple flowers
Friday: pink flowers, roses

SPELLS FOR FRIENDSHIP

Attracting love and friendship are among the most popular reasons for spells, but remember that when you make magic you cannot use your powers to influence the free will of another. You may ask for someone to share your love with, but do not name them: whoever answers will be right for your needs. If you are having trouble manifesting results in this area, you may need to look at what is blocking you – this may be negative self-beliefs or else others may be gossiping behind your back.

Warm pink and gold are both colours associated with love and healing.

A LOVE SPELL

Try this spell for your perfect love match. Before you start, take a long bath or shower, then spray your whole body with rose water. Work this spell on a Friday, during a waxing moon.

You will need
bottle of rose water
2.7 m (9 ft) white cord
4 green candles
charcoal and heatproof burner
pink candle
rose petals
rose essential oil
cinnamon stick
gold pen
glass bowl of spring water

1 Open your cord circle and step inside with your equipment. Light a green candle in each direction. Invoke the four winds in turn, repeating the following words four times, each time substituting the next direction:
Hail to thee East/South/West/North Wind. I call for love and make this offering of light to you.

2 Place some charcoal in the heatproof burner in the centre of the circle and light it. Light the pink candle next to it. Do the Golden Light Breathing exercise until you feel full of energy.

3 You are calling for new beginnings, so face east. Put seven rose petals to one side, then rub a little rose oil into the rest. Crush the cinnamon stick and place it on the burning charcoal with the scented rose petals.

4 Focus your heart upon feeling love. Write the word "love" in gold ink on the seven reserved petals. Float them gently in the bowl of water.

5 Sit in the circle and breathe in the scent of rose and cinnamon. Take time to centre yourself and build up charged energy. Open your hands, open your heart and repeat your request seven times, with genuine feeling:
O Anael, Angel of Venus, I call upon you to fill me with love, that I may feel a joyous heart. I ask that I may share this love with another who will come to me of his/her free will and together we shall know the beauty of a loving union.
I ask this for the highest good of all.

6 At the end of the seventh request say "thank you". Blow out the candles, and close the cord circle widdershins. Pour the water and petals respectfully on the earth.

Cinnamon brings success, and is also an aphrodisiac. Breathe in its warm, sensual smell as you work.

A Spell to Stop Gossip

Gossip produces negative thought-forms that can become attached to our energy field and create problems for us. You will need to find a suitable holly tree to bury your spell under – you might want to perform your spell next to it, too. Do this on a Tuesday, during a waning moon.

You will need
2.7 m (9 ft) white cord
red candle
red pen
very small square of natural paper
snapdragon (antirrhinum) flower
thorn
red ribbon

1 Open your cord circle. Light the red candle, face south and sit down.

2 Using the red pen, write the name of the person or organization that is gossiping about you on the paper square. If you do not know the source of the gossip-mongering write "whoever is".

3 Carefully take one of the larger flower heads from the snapdragon and gently open it up. Roll the piece of paper into a tiny scroll and place it inside the flower, repeating the following words five times:
Speak only goodness, think only kind. Look to your own faults and not to mine.

4 Keep the scroll of paper in place by sealing the flower head with the thorn, and as you do this say:
Flower seal, flower heal
lips that speak not from the heart.

5 Take your spell to a holly tree. Tell the spirit of the tree your intention to bury it there and ask it to protect your good name.

6 Bury the snapdragon flower head under the holly tree. Say thank you by tying a small red ribbon to a branch.

7 As you walk away, know that you are leaving the malicious gossip behind you. Do not look back.

The colour red is associated with bringing change in difficult circumstances, and with courage, while snapdragons are used to redirect negative energies into a more creative outlet.

A spell to make friends

Perform this spell in a horseshoe shape within your magical cord circle. The colour green and the apple are both sacred to Venus, and sweet peas are the traditional flower of friendship. Work this spell on a Friday, with a waxing moon.

You will need
2.7 m (9 ft) white cord
7 green candles
aromatherapy burner
sweet pea essential oil, diluted in sesame oil
5 seeds from a sweet organic apple
gold pen
natural paper
heatproof container

1 Open the cord circle in the east. Place the green candles in a horseshoe shape, with the open end facing north and you facing south in front of it.

2 Place the aromatherapy burner in the centre of the horseshoe shape and add seven drops of sweet pea oil. Lay the apple seeds in the centre too. Light the first candle to your left and say:
Nogah, Nogah, light of love,
I honour and illuminate your beauty and call upon you to help me today.

3 Using the lit candle, light the next one. Light all the candles this way, then light the burner.

4 Using the gold pen, draw the sigil of Venus on the paper. Beneath this write your wish:
By the powers of the four directions, above me and below me, within me and without,
I call for favour with Anael, Angel of Venus,
I call for friends of the same heart, that joy and celebration shall prevail.

5 Burn your spell in the flame of the last candle to be lit, dropping it into the heatproof container. Visualize the smoke carrying your wish to the sky. Blow out the candles widdershins and close your circle in the usual way. As you extinguish the last candle say: *And so mote it be!*

6 Take the apple seeds to a prepared site or pot and dedicate them as follows:
Nogah, these apple seeds I plant to honour you and please you. And as they grow, so is my life blessed with joy of friendships new.

The seal of Venus.

SPELLS FOR PARTNERSHIPS

Many marriage customs have their root in magical thinking. In some cultures, for instance, grains of rice (symbols of fertility) are thrown as confetti, while a horseshoe is traditionally associated with luck, and the wedding ring is a symbol of the eternal bond of lives. Spells for a long and happy partnership are some of the most popular of all. These not only include spells for luck and fertility but also for removing conflict and reminding a partner of your love.

Red is the colour of Mars. Call on the energies of this planet when working with conflict situations.

A SPELL TO REMOVE CONFLICT

This spell will help remove conflict in a relationship. It will work best if both people in the relationship do it together. If only one of you wishes to do it, write down what you wish to let go of, and work to heal your own difficulties. The best time for this spell is Tuesday during a waning moon.

You will need
5.5 m (18 ft) white cord
a small round table or stool
5 red candles
charcoal and burner
coriander seeds
red pen
2 pieces of natural paper
heatproof container

1 Open your cord circle. Place the round table or stool in the centre and on it position the red candles, also in a circle, and light them, remembering which candle is the last to be lit.

2 Light the charcoal in the burner. When it is hot, face west and sprinkle on the coriander seeds, saying the following dedication:
O Zamael, Angel of Mars, we call upon you to help us today/tonight and dedicate this offering to you.

3 Breathe in the aroma of the burning seeds. Both of you should then use the red pen to write down the emotion to be let go – jealousy, anger, etc.

4 Swap papers and, without looking at what the other has written, add your negative feelings on the other side of their paper. Then walk widdershins around the table five times, visualizing the way you express your emotion.

5 When you have circled the table for the fifth time, each of you should burn your own piece of paper in the flame of the last candle that was lit, dropping the paper into the heatproof container.

Burn coriander seeds to invoke Zamael, angel of Mars. Coriander is sacred to this angel.

A joint wish

Write your names together on natural paper, stating a positive wish you both want. Place it between the two halves of an organic apple, seal the join with green candle wax and bury the apple near to your home in a prepared spot. If the apple pips (seeds) grow, tend them carefully because they represent new growth in your relationship that needs looking after.

A SPELL FOR JOINING

For a romance that is blossoming, work with the energies of spring to create this love token, which is inspired by the Maypole, an ancient fertility symbol. During the spring May Day festival (Beltane), people traditionally danced around the pole, interweaving coloured ribbons as they did so, symbolizing the joining of the male and female. Give the love token to your partner to represent the weaving together of your lives. Work this spell on a Sunday at full moon.

You will need
wand
straight wooden stick
two green ribbons
two yellow ribbons
thread or wool (yarn)
beads, pendants or stones for decoration

1 Find a comfortable place to work, then cast a circle around you. Assemble your materials in the centre. Sit facing south.

Green is the colour of new growth and fertility, while yellow symbolizes health and happiness.

2 Invoke the winds of the four directions in turn, repeating the following words and each time substituting the next direction:
Hail to the South/West/North/East Wind. I call upon your assistance in the making of this charm for (say the person's name). Please lend it your power and give it your blessings and protection for the highest good of all concerned.

3 Secure the lengths of ribbons around the top of the stick using the thread or wool. Hold the stick firmly in place and lay out the ribbons in the four directions, green in the north and south, yellow in the west and east.

4 Weave the ribbons around the stick, crossing alternate adjacent pairs in a continuous pattern, until you reach the base. Wind the north and south ribbons deosil and the east and west ones widdershins around the wood, weaving the north ribbon over the east one, and the south ribbon over the west one.

5 Secure the ends with thread or more ribbon. Tie beads, pendants or stones on to them as decoration, or leave the ribbon ends free if you prefer.

6 When you have finished, thank the Four Winds for helping you, and close the circle in the usual way.

Love's protection

In many cultures giving a cloak or scarf to a loved one signifies the offer of protection, and that the giver will always be there for the other. You can make a love charm to symbolize the cloak by using a smaller piece of fabric decorated with symbols of your love. Think carefully about the colours, patterns and fabric you wish to use. The best time to make and present this love charm is in the autumn, during a waxing moon.

You will need
square of fabric
soft pencil
needle and thread
small pieces of fabric
beads and charms
paintbrush and fabric paints or needle and embroidery thread (floss)

1 Use your hand to create a magic circle around your workspace. See it as a ring of fire and know that it protects you as you make your spell.

2 Draw out the pattern of your design on the cloth in pencil. Sew on the pieces of fabric you have chosen. You can also tie on beads and other charms if you feel they are needed, or have a particular significance.

3 Using either fabric paints or embroidery thread, fill in the pattern. Close your circle when your spell is complete.

4 Give the charm to your partner as a token of your love; remind them that you will always be there when they need you.

Spells for Separation and Endings

When relationships are no longer able to sustain themselves, many couples decide that it is best to part. This is usually the last step in a painful process that involves a lot of soul-searching and talking together. Magic can help you to achieve an ending that is peaceful and not acrimonious, that recognizes your differences without seeing one another as wrong. Ending spells may also be performed after the death of a partner to help you let go so that you are free to move on.

As you work on the talking stick, concentrate on the issues you want to resolve.

Effective Communication

Separation is a difficult and complex process, particularly if children are involved. Clear communication can help each partner let go of unspoken resentments and painful feelings, so that each can move forwards as peacefully as possible. Using a "talking stick" is a Native American technique designed to facilitate open and honest dialogue to help people move on and progress a difficult situation. The charm can be used for any problem and is particularly good for moving forward in a relationship, even if it is towards an ending rather than a reconciliation.

Making a Talking Stick

Traditionally, a talking stick was made from wood, but it can be made of any material – this one is made from paper. Decide how you are going to symbolize the relationship problem you are having, as you will inscribe this on your stick. The best time to work this charm is during a waning moon, on a Tuesday.

You will need
pencil
sheet of natural paper
coloured paints or pencils
paintbrush
coloured ribbon or string

1 Use your hand to cast a magic circle around your work area. Visualize it as a ring of bright fire.

2 Draw your inscription on paper. Spend time designing and choosing the words or symbols, remembering that they stand for the problem that you and your partner are going to discuss.

3 Using coloured paints or pencils, add colour to the design; think about talking and listening to your partner concerning this particular issue as you work, and about letting go of the problem so that you can both live without its shadow hanging over your relationship.

4 Roll the paper up into a scroll and tie it in place with the ribbon or string. The symbols, along with your intentions are now bound up into the roll of the charm.

5 Close your circle. You are now ready to use your charm. Begin by presenting it to the person you love and suggest how it may be used.

When you and your partner have finished using the talking stick it should be burned.

Before you begin using the talking stick, make sure you both agree on the rules.

How to Use the Talking Stick

One person holds the stick and talks while the other person, without interrupting, listens intently and respectfully in silence. When the speaker is finished he or she places the stick on the ground for the other person to pick up. When you both feel you have finished, throw the talking stick on to a fire, or burn it in a heatproof container. Watch the flames devour it, symbolizing the ending and letting go of an issue. This talking ceremony will need to be repeated many times during a separation process, which is a series of endings, letting go a little more each time.

A spell for helping to cut the ties

This spell can help you to say goodbye at the end of a relationship, and let go of your partner. It can be performed at the end of any relationship to ease the transition from one life stage to another. The best time to perform this spell is on a Saturday during a waning moon.

You will need
purple altar cloth
aromatherapy burner
cypress essential oil
30cm (12in) black ribbon
white candle
black candle
photograph of yourself
photograph of your partner
clean pair of scissors

1 Clean and prepare your altar space and put the cloth on top. Place the oil burner in the middle of the altar towards the back. Light the burner and add three drops of cypress oil.

2 Tie one end of the black ribbon around the white candle and the other around the black candle. Position the candles on the altar so that the ribbon forms a "tightrope".

3 Place the two photographs side by side in the middle of the altar, beneath the ribbon; the photograph of you should be on the side of the white candle, your partner's photo should be on the side of the black one.

4 Light the white candle and say:
White candle, please hear my plea and represent me.
Help me to part from (say your partner's name) in a spirit of love and friendship.

5 Light the black candle and say:
Black candle, please hear my plea and represent (say your partner's name).
Help (say your partner's name) to part from me in a spirit of love and friendship.

6 Hold the scissors over the taut ribbon and prepare to cut the ribbon as you say these words, actually cutting it as you finish the second line:
Scissors shiny, scissors sharp
Make me and (say your partner's name) move apart
Neither harmed nor alarmed
May we now go our separate ways,
Scissors clean, scissors new
Make a clean break.

7 Put the white candle on top of your photograph, and the black one on top of your partner's picture. Let the candles burn for three minutes as you visualize you and your partner happily walking away from each other.

8 Move the photographs a little further apart and repeat the visualization. Repeat once more. Close the spell by saying "thank you" to the spirits and blow out the oil burner. Repeat the spell for up to seven days.

A spell for emotional healing

Try this spell to help you through the grieving process at the end of a relationship. The best time for this is a Sunday, during a waning moon.

You will need
16 tealight candles
pink candle
rose essential oil and aromatherapy burner
pansy

1 Arrange the tealights in a circle and open it in the west by lighting the first tealight, followed by the rest of the tealights.

2 Sit in the centre of the circle, facing south, and light the pink candle and the oil burner. Add a couple of drops of rose oil to the burner. Close your eyes and breathe in the soft fragrance of the rose essential oil. As you do so, imagine yourself surrounded by a pink light. This soft pink light permeates your whole being and fills the sacred circle where you sit.

3 Bring the pansy to your heart chakra. Hold it there and, speaking softly, tell it your troubles and how you are feeling. When you are finished, slowly get up and close the magic circle in the usual way, giving thanks to the spirits for listening. Take the pansy outside and bury it in an appropriate spot.

Imagine yourself surrounded by pink.

SACRED SPACE

The idea that we can connect with higher powers through the many different spaces we inhabit is an ancient one. The Romans, for instance, believed that each home has its resident *genius loci* – the individual deity of the place – and each household had a special altar, where at certain times the family would gather to give thanks for their security. The same idea occurs in traditional Chinese and Indian thought, and similar spiritual belief systems have existed all over the world throughout the ages. Today, a growing awareness of the importance of sacred space is rekindling this ancient need to sanctify our environment – whether at home, at work or in nature – and many magical and mystical practices are being put into action.

This chapter begins with hints and tips for how we can encourage good vibrations in our homes using herbs and stones as well as creating altars for

household gods. It includes a hedgewitch salt cleansing ritual and a shamanic rattle ceremony to be used for clearing negative energies. Information is given on how to create different atmospheres, how to make a place feel special and how to change the function of a room by banishing the old spirits and welcoming the new ones. A special technique is given to clear negative energies in the workplace, as well as ideas on creating personal altars and placing altars around the home. Finally, a section on outdoor magic describes ways of honouring nature and receiving nourishment from it.

GOOD VIBRATIONS

A home where we feel secure is one of the most basic human needs, but what exactly gives us that feeling of security is something most of us would find hard to define. It has nothing to do with material wealth and luxury – some of the most palatial buildings can feel cold and uncomfortable. In magical thinking, this is because all locations have a spirit of place, or "genius loci" as the Romans called it. When this spirit is properly acknowledged and cared for, it can have a positive effect on the place and all those who occupy it. We can use many techniques based on natural magic to help generate positive vibrations in our everyday environments.

DOORWAYS

In magical terms, the doorway is very important. It is not only the means by which we enter and leave a particular space, but it also symbolizes the transition between entering and leaving different psychic realities. A doorway, therefore, is an ideal setting to affirm the atmosphere you wish to create inside your home or a particular room. Bead curtains add a sense of mystery and magic, while fairy lights strung around the doorway create a sense of light and warmth, and invite the fairies into your space. Flowers and herbs encourage connections with the natural world and convey a sense of ease and relaxation, while garlands of foliage, such as rosemary, ivy or laurel, on a door symbolize protection. Many people like to hang images or charms over the door to attract specific qualities: angels invite blessings, protective deities offer strength and coins invite prosperous

A bead curtain hung in a doorway adds a sense of mystery and magic to the place of transition.

Furnishings in the home

Today we choose our carpets because we like their colour or pattern, but the traditional designs from the Far East, Turkey and North Africa were woven to attract good fortune and domestic tranquillity. Similarly we hang pictures on our walls because we like to look at them, but originally the murals of ancient civilizations served a spiritual purpose in placating and invoking local deities. All these devices were originally intended to drive away bad vibrations and attract good or harmonious ones in their place.

In the Japanese sacred tradition, candlelight and flowers represent the innocence of the heart.

exchanges. You can also place spells for protection or good luck under the front doormat, so that you step on them each time you go in or out of the home.

HOUSEHOLD GODS

Many cultures have a tradition of honouring the household gods or ancestral deities. In ancient Greece, for instance, Hermes and Hestia were the twin protectors of the home. A statue of Hermes, the god of transition and exchange, stood by the front door, while one of the goddess Hestia presided over the hearth, representing stability and permanence. When a new baby was born, it was the tradition for Hestia's blessing to be sought by ritually carrying the child around the hearth. In the Chinese tradition, the spirits of the ancestors are venerated at the family altar or shrine, so that they will confer their blessings on the family.

ALTARS

The idea of having an altar at home may take a little getting used to, but in many parts of the East it is common practice. In the Japanese Shinto tradition, for instance, the *kamidana* is a small altar enshrining protective deities, where offerings of food, water and flowers are regularly placed. The tokonoma, an alcove in the north wall where scrolls are hung and flower arrangements or beautiful artefacts are displayed, also serves as a spiritual focus.

A domestic altar embodies the sanctity of home and family, and its presence helps to create a positive environment. It is a constant reminder of the search for spiritual fulfilment, anchored in the context of daily life. It can be a focus for prayer, a shrine to honour those you love, a place where you choose to meditate, or somewhere to spend a few minutes in quiet contemplation. An altar does not have to conform to any particular size, shape or colour but is your own unique creation.

DARK CRYSTALS AND STONES

Any dark crystal can be programmed to draw in negative vibrations from its local environment. Placing dark stones in a problem area can help to cleanse it before it is filled with symbols and objects of warmth and light. Flint, a dark stone commonly found throughout most of the world, is a powerful protector against negative psychic energies.

SHARP OBJECTS

To give protection against negative influences, you can place needles, pins, thorns, prickles or any other sharp objects in a jar, then fill it with a mixture of protective herbs. The jar should then be sealed and left in the area that seems to be causing problems. It can also be placed under the bed for protection at night. Another traditional means of protection against psychic opposition is to put rusty iron nails around a property, facing away from the walls.

A HORSESHOE

Iron is the metal of Mars – the Roman god of power, strength and courage. An iron horseshoe can be displayed with its "horns" facing to the left, in the shape of a crescent moon, to reflect the properties of Mars, and also of the moon goddess.

Protective herbs and spices

Many herbs and spices can be used to help banish negative spirits or energies and protect the home. These are some of the most common:

Angelica: an all-round protective plant.
Asafoetida: removes all negativity, but smells acrid, so is used only in severe cases.
Cactus: all spiny plants and tree branches offer protection. Prickly plants or stems in the home or workplace will deflect negativity from the surrounding area.
Fumitory: to expel negative thought-forms.
Garlic: a powerful psychic protector. Its strong smell and taste deters unwanted energies. Cloves of peeled garlic can be strung over door frames, or placed in strategic positions and replaced once a week with fresh cloves. In folklore garlic was used to keep vampires at bay.
Rowan: all parts of the rowan tree have magical protective properties. String the leaves and berries into a garland and place them around whatever you wish to gain protection for but keep the garland out of reach of small children or babies.
Salt: central to many magical practices, salt is one of the sacred items for all magical practitioners. It is a crystal and its cleansing powers mean that it is held in great respect.
Yarrow: a powerful psychic protector.

In the English folklore tradition it is believed that a jar of needles, pins and thorns, together with protective herbs, gives protection against negative influences or psychic opposition.

SPACE CLEARING

Any kind of good, positive atmosphere is welcome and wholesome, but we sometimes need to cure a negative, unwholesome one. Negative energies in the environment will have an adverse effect on the people who live or work there: common symptoms include feeling tired or drained of energy, poor concentration, loss of interest in present circumstances and being stuck in a rut. Space clearing is a way of clearing negative energies – it is like a psychic spring-cleaning. We can also perform space clearing ceremonies on ourselves to free ourselves from negative thought-forms and psychic energies.

Shaking the rattle as you say the words imbues them with the power of the rattlesnake.

SPACE CLEARING IN FOLKLORE

Many ancient space clearing ceremonies have persisted as part of the folklore tradition. "Beating the bounds" is an old custom whose original purpose was the spiritual protection of the community. The village boundary line was beaten with birch wands to ensure the safekeeping of the village by establishing a magical barrier around it that no evil spirit could cross. Similarly birch broomsticks were not only used domestically for sweeping the floor, but magically for clearing out unwanted psychic energies and for creating a magic circle. In the days of earth floors, a circle could literally be swept into the floor, this ring forming a visible barrier to the inner realm and a protection against any outside influences that might disrupt the work within. Sometimes today witches still sweep the area they use for magic.

Space clearing can also be about clearing negative energies from the body. For instance, the Northern European folk tradition of "wassailing" (the giving of a New Year salutation for health and wellbeing with a cup of spiced ale) was thought to clear away any evil spirits residing within a person's body. The term "wassail" comes from the Anglo-Saxon *waes hael* meaning "be whole" or "be well".

A HEDGEWITCH SPACE CLEARING

This ritual can be performed once a week to keep your home or workplace clear and clean. Sweep up any old salt and take it outside your property boundary before repeating the ritual.

Begin at the doorway and move deosil (clockwise) around the room. Take a pinch of natural sea or rock salt and sprinkle it in the first corner, saying:

Clean and clear this corner (or window, fireplace etc) be, from all that is not good for me.

Repeat these words as you sprinkle more salt in all four corners, then around the doorframes and fireplace before moving on to the next room you wish to cleanse.

Performing the fourfold breath will calm and centre you before a space clearing ritual.

Changing ourselves

Because "like attracts like", there is no point in space clearing the environment if we do not also change our own state of mind, banishing negative thoughts so that unwelcome vibrations are no longer received. Most psychic negativity is produced by our own mental and emotional states. Rituals that produce changes inside ourselves – changes of consciousness – need to be approached with care and sensitivity and work best when they are short and simple.

Rattles, such as this North Amerian Indian one, are made from seed pods.

SPACE CLEARING YOURSELF

To perform this self cleansing you will need a selection of white candles, including one large one, together with tealights and a rattle. Rattles conjure the ominous sounds of the rattlesnake as it warns of its presence by shaking its tail. When used in ceremony, a rattle can either summon the energy of the snake to protect, or can warn intrusive energies that they should step back and withdraw.

1 Distribute the candles about the floor of the room and light them, using as many or as few as you feel is appropriate but reserving the large one.

2 Sit on a cushion in the centre of the room. Light the large white candle and place it directly in front of you.

3 Spend some time performing the fourfold breath: breathe in for a count of four, hold for four, breathe out for four, and hold for four before taking the next breath. Then pick up your rattle in your right hand and repeat the following words, shaking the rattle at the end of each line except when you say "It is true":
Pay attention (shake rattle)
Snake is here (shake rattle)
It is true
Snake is coming (shake rattle)
So beware adversary – snake is ready to strike (shake rattle loudly).

4 Then repeat the following chant:

Life is love; love is life; let there be an end to strife.
Let the good replace all bad; let love release all spirits sad.
Let my will reveal the power, starting at this present hour,
To enhance the energy, so that I possess the key,
To allow all ills to go, and to let the goodness flow
Into this place where I now kneel, let love begin all things to heal.

5 Repeat the chant several times. Visualize all negativity departing from you at great speed as you chase it away and reclaim what is rightfully yours.

Making a space clearing rattle

If you don't have a ceremonial rattle, you can make one. You will need an aluminium drinks can, some paper, a handful of rice, glue, scissors and some sage for burning.

1 Wash and dry the empty can, making sure the ring pull has been completely removed.

2 Place the can on the paper and draw round the circular base to form a circle the same size. Cut out the circle. Pour the rice into the can through the ring-pull hole and place the paper

circle over the top of the can to cover the hole. Glue in place.

3 Cut out another piece of paper big enough to wrap around the sides of the can. Glue it around the can, decorate it if you wish.

4 When the rattle is complete, dedicate it to Sosho (the snake) by passing it through the smoke of burning sage. Call for the powers of the rattlesnake to enter your rattle and to help you in your magic.

As with all magical equipment, if you make it yourself it has greater power.

CHANGING ATMOSPHERES

N atural magic can be used to change and create atmospheres for a variety of different purposes. For instance, sometimes you may want to change the function of a room in your home, in which case you will not only need to think about how to decorate and rearrange the room, but you will also need to think about its energetic personality. If the change in use is particularly radical, like the change from a work space to a bedroom, you will need to banish the old spirits of place before the new ones can be welcomed in.

If a former bedroom, which has acquired a relaxed atmosphere over the years, is changed into a sitting room, psychically sensitive people may feel drowsy when they spend time in the room. If the planning department of a company moves out of an office and the accounts department moves in, employers may notice the accounting staff spending time in discussion. The atmospheres in these spaces are not particularly negative – they are misplaced echoes of former thought-forms, each with a residual power of subliminal persuasion, that need to be overwritten by a more appropriate one.

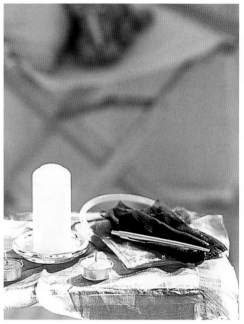

This atmosphere is being changed from the masculine atmosphere of an office – symbolized by a pen – to the gentler atmosphere of a girl's bedroom – symbolized by the little pink bag.

TO CHANGE AN ATMOSPHERE

Transmuting one positive atmosphere into another can be done with a ritual in which you begin by focusing on the old atmosphere, then swing your focus to the new, whatever it may be. This could also be described as stamping a new psychic impression upon a place. Here, the aim is to change what was a home office into a bedroom for a young girl.

You will need
4 small tumbled rose quartz crystals
altar
white candle
2–3 candles in a colour that reflects the new usage of the space
a token of the original use of the space (in this case a pen)
black cloth large enough to cover or contain the token
rose geranium essential oil and burner
a token of the new atmosphere (in this case a pink bag)

1 Set up an altar in the middle of the room using colours that suit the new atmosphere you wish to create. Put the white candle in the centre of the altar with the three coloured candles arranged in a triangle around it.

As you clap your hands, visualize the sounds driving away the old atmosphere of work, business and stressful activity.

Using colour to change atmospheres

Use this list to help you choose the most appropriate colours to represent the new function of the room and enhance the atmosphere you are seeking to create.

Red: best used in active areas, such as a living room or dining room, or to add a touch of energy to a more neutral backdrop

Orange: use in creative areas and for a supportive ambience

Yellow: best used in work places, its happy, sunny colour also works well in the kitchen

Green: use in areas of relaxation and harmony, such as a living room or bedroom

Blue: ideal for areas of peace and relaxation, such as a living room, bedroom or bathroom

Violet: as a combination of blue and pink it is ideal for areas where both liveliness and rest are required, such as a dining room

Pink: for inspiration and happiness, this could be used in a bedroom, living room or office

Purple: good for areas requiring stillness, depth and meaning, such as a bedroom, or any restful, contemplative "inner" space

Silver: symbolizes magic and dreams; can bring a touch of feminine (yin) energy into a more masculine (yang) space

Gold: symbolizes happiness and abundance; can bring masculine (yang) energy into an overly feminine (yin) space

Brown: for an atmosphere that requires stability and reliable energy; ideal when changing a mentally orientated space to a more practical one

An element of red will bring energy and dynamism to a room.

2 Put everything you are going to use in the ritual on the altar for a few moments, then take the rose quartz crystals and put one in each corner of the room.

3 Take the object you have chosen to represent the old atmosphere, and place it in the western quarter of the room. Take the object that is representing the new atmosphere of the room and place it in the eastern quarter. Light all the candles.

4 Start the ritual at the east side of the altar, facing west. Take a few deep, calming breaths and say the following:
Go! Depart! Begone ye hence!
Avaunt I say, this is my will!
Be ended, finished, changed, transposed,
Leave no disturbing echoes still!

5 Clap your hands loudly, then take the cloth over to the object in the west and cover it. Return to the altar, but this time stand at the west side facing east, in the opposite direction to the earlier part of the ritual. Say the following:
Now welcome be, now welcome stay,
Now welcome is for evermore!
Be started, newborn, fresh, unfurled,
And bring thy presence to the fore!

6 Go to the object in the east that represents the new atmosphere and bring it reverentially to the altar to place it there. Sit beside the altar and leave the item there for several minutes while you meditate on it. As you do so, absorb the new atmosphere that is emerging in the room and reflect it back at the object.

7 When you feel this is complete and the atmosphere has been altered, close the ritual by extinguishing the candles. Dismantle the altar and remove the object that represented the old atmosphere from the room. Leave the object that represents the new atmosphere in a prominent position on a windowsill or shelf.

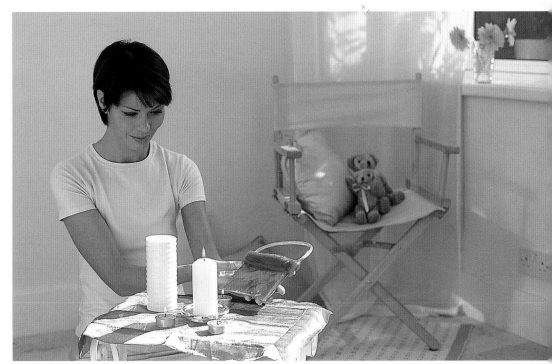

After removing the old object, bring in the new one, and place it in a central position in the room as a focal point for the new energies.

CREATING A SPECIAL FEEL

When we expect visitors and spend time preparing for their stay, our aim is to make our home feel especially welcoming. If we are holding a dinner party, we take great care both to prepare good food and to provide a pleasant atmosphere. It is important to us to provide for our guests' physical comfort, and we are also concerned about doing the equivalent on a psychic level. There are also times when a special atmosphere is called for – when entertaining friends, celebrating the season or marking some other important event, such as a wedding or naming ceremony.

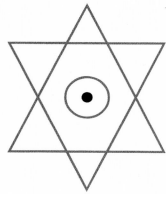

The solar hexagram is a six-rayed star with a representation of the sun in the centre.

There are two key words that relate to making a place feel special, both materially and magically, and these are "pride" and "respect". Without one, we will not feel the other. When both these elements are brought into play, our place – whatever and wherever it may be – will begin to fill with that special atmosphere of sparkle and excitement.

FOR A SPECIAL FEEL

Every now and again, we want to make a place feel especially welcoming. This ceremony uses frankincense, rose water and orange candles to create a "golden" atmosphere. Frankincense is one of the most precious incense ingredients, while rose water is delicately purifying and leaves a lingering subtle fragrance.

Orange candles symbolize the life-giving, creative power of the sun. As you perform it, you should notice your space begin to change and fill with that special atmosphere of sparkle and excitement.

You will need
altar and orange altar cloth
2 orange or gold candles
frankincense and charcoal burner
  or essential oil and burner
wand
additional orange candles for dark areas
rose water in small bowl

1 Position the altar so that you will face east when standing before it. Arrange the cloth and the two candles in holders upon it, together with the incense or essential oil burner and the wand.

2 Place the additional candles around the room in the shadowy areas that light does not normally illuminate, and where the candle glow will enhance the richness of the room's appearance. The aim is to achieve a depth of perspective in the room, so arrange the candles in a non-linear way, and avoid having them at a similar distance from the altar.

3 Light the candles, then stand in front of the altar and bow your head. Take several deep and calming breaths.

4 Use the wand to "draw" a solar hexagram in the air in front of you, above the altar. The hexagram, a six-pointed star (identical to the "Star of

The many candles that are randomly arranged in this ritual will brighten every corner.

As you perform this spell, focus your mind and concentrate on what you are doing, and visualize a sphere of happiness being created.

Elemental imbalances

Sometimes the atmosphere of a place is spoilt by an elemental imbalance, that is to say, where there is either too much or not enough of one of the four elements. These elemental imbalances can be corrected by introducing any of these quick fixes:

Air: music, wind chimes, images of air creatures such as birds, lavender fragrance;
Fire: candlelight, gold or orange materials, fire creatures such as the phoenix, lion or dragonfly, frankincense or copal fragrance;
Water: an indoor fountain, water garden, fish-tank or bowl of water, images of water creatures or plants, jasmine fragrance;
Earth: plants, herbs, crystals, images of earth-dwellers such as prairie dogs or badgers, cypress fragrance;
Elemental lightbulbs: Another way to change the atmosphere is by replacing a plain lightbulb with one you have painted with particular designs, using glass paint. To introduce more Air use a patterned lightbulb painted with violet circles on a yellow background; to add more fire to a room use a lightbulb painted with red flames on a green background; to add Water use a lightbulb painted with blue bands on an orange background; and to introduce Earth use a lightbulb painted with citrine and russet-brown diamonds.

Painted lightbulbs add instant elemental influences to a room.

David"), is associated with the zodiac, the planets and the sun.

5 At the centre of the hexagram, "draw" the symbol of the sun: a small circle with a dot in the middle. As you do this, visualize the outline appearing as a line of brilliant golden light. Then, in a commanding voice, say:
Let none undo the spell I cast,
For it is well and three times good;
This place is special now at last,
Be it now full understood!

6 Now pick up the bowl of rose water and, as you walk clockwise around the edge of the room, dip your fingers in the water and then brush your hand over the walls and floor areas. As you do so, say, "Blessed be this boundary". Where there are areas of the room that might be damaged by the rose water, pass your hand over the walls a little distance away. It is helpful to visualize the blessing water creating a sphere of happiness and peace, as you mark out the boundary of the room.

7 To close the ritual, extinguish all the candles, starting with the furthest away from the altar and ending with the nearest. Then give thanks and go outside to discard any remaining rose water into the earth.

MAGIC IN THE WORKPLACE

Unless you have a private office or work from home, it may be difficult to imagine using magic in the workplace. However, there are a number of ways of using magical tools and equipment to protect against negative energies at work. It is a good idea to do this, as we are exposed to many vibrations that can adversely affect us. Common problems include allergies, poor concentration, high stress levels and feeling tired all the time. Such problems have been linked to excessive exposure to artificial light, electromagnetic radiation (the energy waves emitted by electronic equipment such as computers, mobile phones and photocopiers), and "sick-building syndrome". The latter is a term used to describe a cluster of health problems associated with inhabiting certain kinds of buildings.

As offices are usually crowded and busy places, space clearing at work often needs to be a private, mental exercise.

THE POWER OF THE MIND

It is a good idea to perform regular space clearing rituals at work to transform negative energies. Although it can be awkward to conduct any kind of overt ceremony or ritual, there are ways around this. At its purest and most powerful level, magic needs no special equipment or physical actions, not even speech: the entire ritual, including all scents, colours and tools, can be imagined through creative visualization. An occult master can use his or her mind and willpower to achieve astonishing results using this technique, but fortunately even a shadow of this ability is good enough for your needs.

PREPARATION

Try to choose a time when you are unlikely to be disturbed. Even though your outward actions will not raise any eyebrows among your colleagues, you will be better able to concentrate if you are alone. Beforehand, you will need to obtain a small notepad suitable to make into a scrapbook. You will also need to collect a number of appropriate images to represent your working environment. These could be taken from magazines and catalogues. Your tools for this ritual will be nothing more complicated than scissors, glue and paper.

Cut out the pictures you have collected and use them to assemble a collage, or compound image, of your workplace, by arranging and sticking them together. Remember that it does not need to be a realistic impression of the place, nor does it need to be artistic or to scale, or to have perfect perspective. You are simply aiming for a symbolic general impression of your working environment, not an accurate representation.

Create a scrapbook of images that represent your working environment, and use this as a focus for your thoughts.

Crystals

As natural parts of the earth's structure, the energies of crystals are radiated at natural frequencies. You can use these to help balance the emissions of modern appliances by placing them around equipment such as computers and printers or televisions. To remain effective, the crystals will need to be cleansed once a month.

SYMPATHETIC MAGIC

Everyone is familiar with the voodoo practice of sticking pins into a doll that represents someone you don't like. This is based on the principle of sympathetic magic: the idea is that the doll and the target become inextricably linked, so that whatever happens to one will transfer itself to the other by association. Though this practice is a form of destructive magic and is not recommended, the principle of sympathetic magic can be used in a positive way – in this instance, to clear negative energies at work.

So just as the doll is only a rough image of a real person, your workplace collage need only be an approximation of the actual place. You can make a single collage or as many versions as you like, until you find an image that you resonate well with. Once you are satisfied, sit quietly with the image and visualize it being filled with golden light. See the light filling up the picture until everything is surrounded by a golden glow – pay particular attention to areas of heavy or particularly negative energy,

such as photocopiers, computers and other machines. Say these words quietly to yourself:

Darkness be gone! May this space be filled with golden light. And so mote it be!

Repeat the visualization regularly for maximum effect; each time you practise it your powers of visualization will become more powerful and effective.

GUARDING AGAINST NEGATIVITY

There are other steps you can take to repel negativity and to promote good vibrations at work. Keeping the area clean and free from clutter is one of the most basic – negativity attaches to dirt. If you are having trouble with another worker, a cactus plant positioned between you will offer protection.

If when you are at work you feel a sudden vulnerability, use your mind to project an image of a guardian figure standing next to you. This could be your guardian angel or guide, a totem animal or someone you know with whom you feel safe and happy. Remember the guardian will never take the offensive against the person or situation that is causing you to feel vulnerable, but will offer a mantle of protection around you, strengthening your auric field so that negative energies cannot get to you.

PROTECTION STRATEGIES

There are also other ways to keep your workplace psychically protected:

◇ Display plants and flowers that have protective qualities, such as fern and geranium. Put them in waiting rooms

If you need protection from a difficult colleague, position some cacti on your desk between you.

and reception areas to reduce invasive effects from the energy of visitors.

◇ Place smoky quartz crystals in the four corners of the room to help absorb stray energies. Make sure you clean them once a month.

◇ Position clear quartz crystals near computers and electronic equipment to help to absorb and transform electro-magnetic radiation.

◇ Include plenty of green plants in the building to provide oxygen, and let their vibrations help to connect you with the natural world.

Altars at work

In many parts of the East, you are just as likely to find an altar or shrine in a shop or office as at home. You can make an unobtrusive "altar" at work by creating a small display of personal objects on your desk or workstation. These could include a photograph, a natural object, such as a stone or crystal, a piece of fruit, and some fresh flowers or a plant.

If you need protection, make a display of suitable plants and keep it on your desk.

Smoky quartz crystals, placed in the corners of a room, will absorb stray energies.

PERSONAL ALTARS

Creating a personal altar is a way of inviting magic into your home. The sacred space it occupies is available to you all the time; it is a meeting point where the divine reaches down to touch the everyday world and where you can concentrate your intentions and desires for spiritual growth. There is a two-way flow between the individual and the world of spirit, and the altar is its channel. It can be both a setting for a journey into a spiritual dimension and a place to gain deeper understanding of your own character and place in the universe.

A personal altar is probably best used for prayer or meditation rather than spell-making, ritual or ceremony, when special altars are usually set up for that particular purpose. As it is used, it becomes energized and its influence widens, flowing out through and around you, to bless your home and everyone in it. A personal altar can be a physical expression of your deepest attachments and longings: by giving them form you bring them into your daily life and empower yourself to achieve what you desire. There is no set way of creating your own personal altar – the form it takes is up to you. What is important is that it has meaning for you.

Stones represent the Earth element. Their presence on an altar can help stabilize stress-filled places.

NATURAL OBJECTS

In natural magic, a personal altar would usually contain symbolic representations of the natural world. Placing natural objects on an altar helps to reinforce its connection with earth energies and underlines our commitment to preserving the natural world. It is also a reminder of our own connection with the web of life. When looking for objects for your altar, you may prefer to take only things that have fallen ("found" objects), rather than by cutting flowers or trees, for instance. Remember to always give thanks for what you have taken by leaving an offering or by a simple action, such as clearing away litter.

SACRED IMAGES

Deities from any religion may have a personal symbolism for you that you would like to represent on your altar. For instance, a statue of the Buddha in meditation could help you to focus on your own meditation, while the Goddess could be represented by a fertility figure or a statue or painting of one of her many aspects. By invoking the Goddess and seeking her ancient wisdom you will find an aspect of her in yourself. Bringing her into the heart of your home in this way upholds a tradition that has been practised throughout history. Similarly, if you call on a guardian angel for spiritual support, you can place a picture or figurine of an angel on your altar to focus your prayer.

ABSTRACT SYMBOLS

Symbols predate writing as a means of conveying ideas. Ancient symbols were carved, painted, stitched and worked in metal for magical purposes, to ward off evil or to invoke gods. A symbol gains its significance from the emotional and spiritual weight that it carries. Some of the most compelling symbols are the simplest, such as the circle that

Feathers represent birds, who are honoured as a link between earth and heaven.

Natural symbolism

The natural world is full of symbolism, whether in trees and plants, rocks and shells, or feathers, flowers and pieces of wood.

Feathers: represent the Air element and also symbolize the connection between the earth and the heavens.

Stones: bring grounding, Earth energy to the altar. A stone also brings some of the character of the place where it came from.

Fossils: even more than stones, a fossil is a striking reminder of the antiquity of the earth and carries the resonance of millions of years of history.

Seashells: a reminder of the ocean and the element of Water. Seashells are associated with the unconscious and feminine energy. They also have traditional links with regeneration, baptism and prosperity.

Fruits, nuts and grains: are a reminder of the abundance of nature and the changing seasons of the year.

Flowers, herbs and trees: plants are great healers, with particular species being linked with different properties. For instance, ash is associated with purification and cleansing, roses with love and beauty, and basil is said to protect from pain.

Driftwood: a piece of driftwood, carried by the oceans, conveys the blessings of the Goddess.

---

represents the wheel of life, death and rebirth. The spiral too stands for the cycle of existence, but its outward motion also symbolizes growth and energy. The pentacle, or five-pointed star, is an ancient symbol of harmony and mystic power. Placing ancient graphic symbols such as these on your altar will bring their energy and associations into your life. By painting or carving them yourself, you will enhance your connection with them further.

PRACTICAL CONSIDERATIONS

A personal altar is essentially a work of intuition and imagination. Any flat surface can become an altar when it is hallowed by intent. The surface could be a shelf, a windowsill, the top of a chest or even the top of a refrigerator. Some people like to know that their personal altar is completely private to them. If you feel this way, you could arrange a beautiful shrine inside a cupboard or box. A small wooden box makes a lovely

Elemental altars

Another way of creating a personal altar is through a symbolic representation of the elements. For instance, if you are working on creative issues, then you would focus especially on the Fire element, for relationship issues on Water, on Earth for stability and material prosperity, while Air represents freedom, change and new ideas.

Fire: symbolized by the colours orange or red and by yellow or gold flowers

Air: symbolized by incense, scented candles, a fan or feathers and silver-coloured cloth or ornaments

Water: symbolized by the colours blue and green, and by water, wine or any liquid

Earth: symbolized by stone or terracotta objects and earthy colours such as russet, brown and deep orange

---

altar because you can arrange all your sacred things on the flat lid and it is also portable. Having a portable altar is a good idea if you are often travelling away from home and wish to carry the essence of home with you.

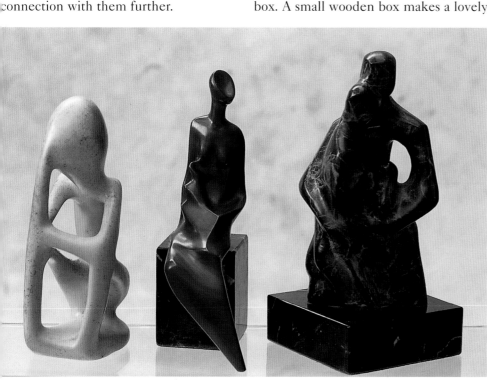

Statues of female or male figures can be used to represent the archetype you wish to honour.

A portable altar will remind you of home.

ALTARS IN THE HOME

Most people have one room that feels special, where the sense of positive energy is most complete. It could be the living room, the kitchen, or a welcoming entrance hall. Traditionally the hearth is regarded as the centre of the home and it is really a prototype altar. Deciding where to position your altar will influence its style as well as how you use it. For instance, your altar can be for you alone, or to share with others. A family altar can work for cohesiveness, like the traditional ancestral altars of the East, while a couple could share in the creation of an altar to promote a deeper commitment to one another. In each case certain locations in the home are more suitable than others.

POSITIONING THE ALTAR

All the different activities that we pursue create distinct types of energy in each room. This is why it can be very difficult to go to sleep in a room that has been full of lively conversation, for instance, or to concentrate on a piece of analytical work in the kitchen. Similarly, every altar will be influenced by the energy of its surroundings. You can use this power to create a life-enhancing altar in any room by drawing on the intrinsic energy of the space, and there is no reason why you shouldn't have several small altars around the house, wherever you feel they are appropriate.

To help you position your altar, you could look into Feng Shui, the ancient

This simple bedside altar to Gaia, the goddess of dreams, includes lilies to invoke calm.

Chinese art of placement. There are many good reference books available on the subject, but essentially the different rooms in a building as well as the different corners in a room correspond to

A bedroom altar could include the scent of lavender to help promote peaceful sleep.

An office altar dedicated to Thoth, the scribe and guardian of knowledge to the Egyptian gods, encourages inspiration.

A child's altar

Children have a wonderful ability to invest all kinds of objects with magic. A handful of toffee wrappers can become jewel-coloured windows, and fragments of translucent sea-worn glass are as valuable as any precious gemstone. Young children naturally make collections of their favourite things. Creating a special place for them – or an altar – will encourage the child to build a magical relationship with their spirit, which grows and develops as they journey through life.

particular areas of life. For instance, south-west-facing rooms are linked with love and relationships, while those that are north-facing suit business affairs. Alternatively, you could use a pendulum to dowse for the most suitable spot (see Divination), or follow your gut feeling and be guided simply by your intuition.

THE BEDROOM

Most of us want our bedroom to be a sanctuary where we can be wholly ourselves. It is where we take our secrets and prayers, joy and grief. A bedroom altar acts as a focus for these, and for daily rituals to help you greet the day and prepare for night.

For peaceful rest, place sleep crystals on your altar: amethysts, a piece of jade or obsidian. Burning a little lavender incense or essential oil will also help you sleep. Honour the earth deity and goddess of dreams, Gaia, with barley grains or laurel, or include an image of Nephthys, who sheltered the sleeping pharaohs beneath her protective wings.

At bedtime, set a bowl of water scented with jasmine oil near your bed and place your sleep stones or crystals in it. To help your wishes come true, write what you wish to come to you in your sleep on willow leaves.

THE STUDY OR OFFICE

An altar in the workplace will generate positive energy to help you concentrate. Wisdom and inspiration are personified by Thoth, the scribe of the Egyptian gods, who wrote down the wisdom of the universe. Yellow candles assist communication and learning. Helpful crystals include emerald to give insight, azurite for clarity, and haematite to aid reasoning and memory. There are also many fragrances that are useful for mental work. Eucalyptus, peppermint and camphor can clear muddled thinking and are an antidote to daydreaming, while rosemary and basil have head-clearing properties, aid concentration and sharpen the intellect.

THE HALLWAY

An altar or shrine in the doorway or near the entrance to the house is traditional in many parts of the world. The Roman god Janus is a traditional protective deity, while a guardian totem animal such as a dog, lion or tiger is also appropriate. Sacred objects at the entrance to your home help to sanctify the whole of it and you and your visitors will carry blessings with you as you leave.

To create the welcoming smell of home, warm and spicy fragrances such as cinnamon, cassia, star anise and clove work well in the winter season, while summer blooms such as stocks, lilac, sweet pea or cabbage rose can permeate the whole house with their fragrance and particular characteristic.

THE KITCHEN

At the hub of the house, the kitchen is a potent place. The magical process of preparing and cooking food transforms the energy of the earth into a form that we are able to take in. An altar for hospitality could be dedicated to Hestia, the goddess of the hearth, or to Demeter, goddess of abundance and unconditional love. Leave offerings of rice, grains, fruit or honey for the nature spirits and light the altar candles each time you prepare a meal. A shrine behind the sink would engage your attention as you work there. You could hang herbs and flowers, chilli and garlic around the window like a garland, or decorate it with evergreens.

THE LIVING ROOM

To promote harmony between your family and friends, set up an altar to the four elements in the living room. This could combine salt for Earth, a red candle for Fire, sea shells for Water and feathers for Air. You could also put photographs of loved ones on the altar.

Create a prayer bowl, placing a clear quartz cluster in a bowl filled with spring water, with floating green candles for harmony. Invite members of the family to write down their prayers and tuck them under the bowl.

A kitchen altar could include offerings of food in honour of Demeter, the grain goddess.

A prayer bowl in the living room can be a family focus for wishes and requests.

OUTDOOR ALTARS

Magic is about relating to the natural world and finding our place in it. Visiting nature is a good way to find peace, tranquillity and inspiration and most people have a particular place that they visit when they need time alone, to meditate or just to relax. Such a place could be anywhere – part of a garden, a spot near a favourite tree, a rock on a hillside, or a cool, leafy forest – it doesn't really matter as long as it is special to you. Like the traditional holy sites, these places have a natural power, but they also take on the energy of those who visit them: they become magical or sacred space.

NATURAL ALTARS

You can set up an altar in your sacred outdoor space. This may be a temporary or more permanent feature depending on the location. A flat rock or a tree stump can work well, or a sacred circle can be made with stones, twigs or cones, although nothing should be done that disturbs the natural harmony of the place. An outdoor altar can be adorned with anything that has a special significance for you, such as crystals, feathers, flowers or sticks. It can show appreciation for the moment and it has the advantage that others might see it and add their energy. Remember to leave an offering on your altar when you visit.

TREE ALTARS

Trees make very beautiful natural altars, pleasing to the eye and very calming when attention is focused upon them. Being firmly rooted, a tree has a deep

A flat rock makes a good outdoor altar, especially when it is in a spectacular setting.

Ritual sites in nature

Increasingly, those involved in magic today are looking to ritual sites in nature and ancient stone monuments to contact the energies of their ancestors, those who practised the "Old Religion". These sites, which often date from the Neolithic era, are often viewed as places of female mysteries and the land itself is thought of as the Goddess incarnate. Believed to be gateways into the otherworld, a "dreamtime" that enables magic workers to connect with a sacred place within themselves, these places are the locations for healing, divination and the conducting of life rites, such as hand fastings (pagan weddings).

Salt is part of the crystal kingdom and is the blessed representation of the earth. Use salt to purify, consecrate and protect.

connection with Mother Earth, and that energy can be tapped into when you talk to it, leave offerings and pray or meditate there. You can tie things in the branches for decoration, or place tiny items in the trunk. A flat rock placed at the base of the trunk can serve as an altar stone. Be aware of which trees attract you, because they all have their own attributes and symbolism. For example, oak is the keeper of wisdom and possesses great strength; willow represents love and regeneration, being very ready to grow a new tree from a cut branch; the tall and graceful beech symbolizes aspirations to higher ideals; yew, associated with ancient burial sites, represents transformation and inner wisdom.

ROCK ALTARS

Rocks are the bones of the Mother, supporting her and therefore us. Because they take millions of years to form, they hold ancient Earth wisdom and knowledge, power and strength. They can help you to connect with these primordial energies and you can call upon this strength when you pray or meditate at a rock altar. Feel the strength of its timeless wisdom helping, supporting and connecting you.

THE GARDEN SANCTUARY

Whatever the size of your garden, you can create an outdoor sanctuary to connect with the magical powers of nature. If space permits, this can be achieved through planting trees or shrubs to form an enclosed area. This can contain seating, such as a wooden bench or chair, as well as a shrine or grotto. A water feature is also recommended; this could be a fish pool, or some kind of running water in a stream or fountain. It does not need to be very big, but the energy of water is refreshing and cleansing for the subtle bodies. A statue of the Goddess and/or a nature deity such as Pan can be part of your garden altar. If your garden area is small, consider creating a miniature garden with Japanese bonsai trees, or arrangements of pebbles, or making a nature table to reflect the changing seasons of the year.

Trees have enormous symbolic and magical powers, and are also vital for the sustenance of life on our planet. Offer them respect and reverence in your magical work.

Making a cairn

The beauty of making something to use as an altar is that your energy is blended with the materials in a focused way. A cairn looks like a haphazard pile of stones but, to make it stable, care must be taken in selecting stones that fit together well. Take time to gather the stones.

1 Begin by selecting a few large, flat, roughly circular rocks to act as the base of the cairn. Start to build up a tapering dome by laying smaller flat rocks in an overlapping pattern.

2 As you work, keep the intent of honouring creation, and that will help focus your energy. Work slowly and methodically so that the stones are evenly balanced.

3 When the cairn is complete, decorate it with objects found close by.

Making a cairn takes time and care, and so gives the end result greater significance.

MAGIC IN DAILY LIFE

Caught up in busy schedules and coping with the demands of everyday life, it is easy to forget to take care of your own needs and to become disassociated from the core of who you are. But at the centre of everything that is going on in your life, ultimately there is only one person – you. If you don't take care of yourself then everything else in your life will suffer. Practising natural magic puts you firmly at the centre of life's wheel and encourages you to look for practical ways to nourish yourself in body, mind and soul and to reconnect with the magic of daily life.

The focus of this chapter is finding ways to use magic for everyday concerns. It begins by recognizing that care of your inner self forms the basis from which the rest of your life will grow and blossom, before turning to specific areas of life such as your goals and ambitions, the quality of your relationships and your health and wellbeing. It also offers suggestions for

how to increase wealth and prosperity by focusing on abundance, and how to deal with change with the minimum of stress. It concludes with a special section on lunar gardening, which shows you how to work with the cycles of the moon for strong and healthy plants. By bringing magic to bear on all aspects of your life, you will be enriched on many levels.

THE INNER YOU

It is what you are within, rather than what you do, that is important so far as the life of your soul is concerned. The meaning and purpose of your life, and your connection with the greater whole, are to be found deep within you. There are many ways of nourishing your connection with your inner self, but before you begin you should take care of your physical, mental and emotional needs. Natural magic is based on balance and harmony between all aspects of creation, and you need to reflect this before you can succeed.

BODY CARE

Physically, you are influenced by your lifestyle and what you choose to eat and drink. You may like to consider changing things in your daily life that do not serve you – or are actually harmful to you – such as too many late nights, poor eating habits, or addictive patterns such as alcohol or drug consumption. On a physical level, it is helpful to be disciplined about transcending your "bad" habits, as a weak or sick physical body will significantly affect your emotional, mental and spiritual health.

Taking the Bach flower crab apple essence can help you to detox, while walnut and chestnut bud can help reduce addictive cravings.

MENTAL AND EMOTIONAL WELLBEING

Albert Einstein once said; "A clever mind is one that is trained to forget the trivial." On a mental level, being unable to switch off our thoughts is associated with many common stress-related problems such as tension headaches, anxiety and insomnia. White chestnut flower essence can be helpful, and it is

Regular meditation is a very good method of staying in touch with your inner self.

also advisable to consider physical exercise, or to begin practising a spiritual discipline such as yoga or tai chi, all of which will help reduce stress levels.

On an emotional level, you need to consider "relationship" – how you relate to others and from what emotional

Take time out, find a private space, and don't let yourself be distracted by other people. Cultivating self-awareness will give you the confidence to take a break when you need one.

A woman's moontime

The female menstrual cycle mirrors the cycle of the moon in duration, and both the hormonal changes in the body and the phases of the moon have a profound efffect on the emotions. The time of ovulation, when a woman is at her most fertile, is likely to occur during a full moon. During their menstruation, women are sensitive and highly perceptive; it is particularly important at this time of the month for women to look after themselves. Book a date with yourself and use your "moontime" to let go of the past and to allow the flow to cleanse and take away any problems or difficulties in preparation for the new cycle ahead.

perspective you see things. When you look closely at your emotional responses to life, you may realize that they are out-dated, linked to wounds from the past that have yet to heal. There are several Bach flower remedies that can help with emotional healing, including using honeysuckle for someone who dwells on the past, holly for jealousy, anger and destructive feelings and impatiens for irritability and excessive reactions. Understanding and sorting out your feelings will help to alleviate heated arguments, high stress levels and heavy atmospheres.

LIVING LIFE CREATIVELY

The spirit of creation flows through every one of us. We may describe it as divine inspiration, chi, life force or quintessence, but it is the energy that we put into everything that we do – whether this is carving a sculpture, writing a letter, making a meal, or simply interacting with others. In this sense, creativity is not restricted to "artistic" pursuits, and everything you do can be approached with the spirit of creativity, giving spiritual value to all aspects of your daily life. Being mindful of this is one of the best ways of staying in contact with your inner self as you go about your daily affairs.

Mindfulness is another name for meditation, and meditation is one of the best ways of connecting with your creativity and inner self. Its benefits have been well documented: it allows you to relate to who you truly are without falling into the common traps of everyday life. It also helps you to think clearly and sharpens your intuitive, spontaneous responses. Spending regular time in meditation each day is a good discipline to foster; it is like washing your inner senses and will give you the eyes to see the magic that is all around us, ever-present all of the time.

AN ALTAR FOR INSPIRATION

The creative process is about inspiration, hard work, discipline, exercising judgement and discernment and the courage to make mistakes and learn from them. Making an altar to inspiration will encourage you to go beyond your limits, so that your open mind will attract fresh ideas like a magnet, faster than they can be expressed. It is in this state of intuitive awareness – a form of meditation – that creativity flows and life itself becomes a magical experience.

There are really no rules for making an inspirational altar. You might like to make it very vibrant, dressing it with a variety of colours so that its flamboyance

Playing music is just one of the ways to express the creativity you hold within you.

will give you the confidence to express yourself in your daily life. Or you may choose a theme or colour scheme and work with that. The objects you choose to put on the altar can reflect the creative opportunities you want to explore, such as brushes and paints for artistic endeavour, or pens and paper if you are searching for the courage to express yourself. Use this special place to try out your dreams, and bring your own creations to beautify your altar.

HARMONIZING WITH NATURE'S CYCLES

To a greater or lesser extent, most of us are disconnected from the natural rhythms of nature, the journey of the sun and moon through day and night, the months and the seasons of the year. Effectively this cuts us off from our own nature, our innate, inner wisdom that is central to who we are. Spending time in nature and observing the seasons through ritual and celebration, as well as changing our diet and lifestyle to adapt to nature's patterns, can help us to reconnect with nature's cycles and our central core.

Imbolc: the light of inspiration

At the beginning of February, the festival of the return of light, or Imbolc, honours the Celtic triple goddess Brigid, a fire deity, and celebrates her union with the god of light. It is a time of inspiration and creativity, when rituals are performed to bless new love, fertility and the planning of new projects. Imbolc is predominantly a female festival and Brigid blesses women's self-expression and creativity. By tradition, if a white cloth is left outside overnight at Imbolc, the goddess will bless it with inspiration.

GOAL-SETTING

Wherever our real ambitions lie, striving for achievement is necessary if our lives are to be fruitful and valuable. If we aim for nothing, we may end up achieving just that. And if we don't set our own priorities, someone else will. So setting out the things we want to achieve over the next week, month, year or five years, is a valuable exercise in establishing what our goals are. We can then use magic to help us in our journey towards them.

If your goal is physical fitness, picture yourself running along a beach or climbing a hill.

ESTABLISHING GOALS

Achieving something that we want to do is a great boost to confidence and self-esteem, helping us to raise our sights to even higher goals. Aspirations need not be set in stone: they need re-evaluating as we learn from experiences and as our outlook and priorities change. Re-evaluating current goals is therefore the first step. Very often we find ourselves pursuing ambitions that no longer satisfy us and, in some cases, maybe never did.

For instance, our work may leave too little time for relationships, family life or creativity, or perhaps we realize we are doing the wrong job altogether – a career path chosen perhaps to satisfy our parents – in which case it might be time to change track and consider retraining for something that we would really like to do. To help establish your goals you can divide your life up into different categories and look at each one in turn:

Asking yourself what you want from life and then thinking about the practical steps you can take to achieve it is part of goal-setting.

Setting goals

- Visualize your long-term goals and set short-term targets – weekly or monthly – to help you get there.
- Set specific daily goals to keep you motivated.
- Goals should stretch you, but not defeat you before you begin. If you make them too easy, they won't motivate you. Make each goal a challenging and positive one.
- Limit the number of your stated goals and make sure they don't clash or contradict each other.
- Write a list of your goals and read it at the start of every day.
- Re-examine your list from time to time; if your goals have changed or seem unrealistic, you can change them.
- Give yourself small rewards for each of your achievements.

A wishing box

One way of working towards your goals is to create a wishing or dream box. Write down your wishes and then keep them in a special wooden box on your altar. Surround the box with oak leaves to sanctify and protect your dreams. The sacred oak will aid your rituals with its strength and bring the promise of success. If you are unable to find oak leaves, you can sprinkle a few drops of the Bach flower oak essence on the wishes.

Keep some frankincense in your wishing box. This most ancient incense has been burnt on the altars of many cultures to summon the aid of the divine. Its uplifting scent banishes negative thoughts and promotes success. Burn a little each day as you visualize the goal you are working towards manifesting.

relationships, work, home, health, creativity, leisure and money. Some of these categories may overlap and you may notice that some areas are more important to you than others. Take as much time as you need, until you have found goals that have meaning for you and are going to help you create the life you want for yourself.

THE POWER OF NOW

Magic only recognizes the here-and-now: the past has gone, the future is not yet, and the point of power is in the present moment. So when working with goal-setting, always use the present tense for your targets. For instance, instead of saying "I want", begin with "I now have /am". Similarly, visualize the result you desire as if it is already happening. For instance, if your goal is to get a new job, you can visualize yourself opening the letter of appointment telling you it is yours. Or if your goal is a return to health and fitness, visualize yourself striding up a hill or running across a beach. Hold on to your vision for as long as you can, so that it sinks into your unconscious mind, forming a new pattern into which you can grow. Even when you seem to be making no progress, your spirit will still move in the direction you have chosen.

RITUAL FOR WORLDLY SUCCESS

For material achievements such as making money and success at work, include Earth element as well as Fire on your altar. Earth is the element of stability and prosperity, and supports us in taking responsibility for our own destiny. Fire is the element related to ambition and creative projects and helps burn away any resistance there might be to achieving our goals.

1 To represent the Earth, use the colours of the land, such as olive green and russet, and place two green candles, and one darker one, on the altar, together with some salt or a stone.

2 Place a bowl of the Fire incense, frankincense, on the altar; it is best to use pieces of frankincense resin.

3 Now write your goals (remembering to use the present tense) on a piece of paper. Fold the piece of paper up and put it into the bowl of resin.

4 Close your eyes and visualize the realization of your ambitions, seeing the successful outcome rather than the process of getting there. When you have fixed the images in your mind, take the piece of paper and burn it in the candle flame, dropping it into a fireproof bowl.

5 To finish, pinch out the candles and take a few moments to gather your thoughts. Remember that you need to remain open to whatever happens and that you always seek the highest good of all concerned.

Burning the paper symbolizes letting go and trusting the universe to bring you a result.

When working for worldly success, Earth colours such as greens or russets and symbolic representations of Earth, such as salt or a stone, will help your magic along.

Magic as Medicine

Originally, medicine and magic were not two separate disciplines but one. Medicine has largely moved away from magic, but there are many ways of using magic therapeutically, whether with herbs and plant medicines, with the assistance of cosmic powers and divine beings, or by using the vibrations of colour, sound or crystals. You can use magic as medicine to treat yourself or another (with their permission of course), to restore harmony in body, mind and soul. It is about listening to your body and working in harmony with its innate self-healing powers to restore wholeness.

A quartz crystal will help you to transmit your healing power as you voice your prayer.

A Healing Ceremony

Healing ceremonies play an important part in magic and medicine. Traditionally they are conducted by the shaman or medicine man, who uses a combination of ritual, spells and charms to drive out the bad spirits causing the illness from the sufferer. This ceremony enlists the healing energy of Water.

Set up an altar for healing in the west and stand facing towards the west to make your offerings or to say prayers. Make the altar a vision of pure watery beauty, fresh with the colour blue and decorated with flowers such as jasmine, lilies, lotus, iris or poppies, or with water-smoothed pebbles or seashells. These beautiful natural items will speak of the vibrancy of the world outside that waits to be enjoyed.

Choose sandalwood incense, which is associated with purification and healing, or camphor or eucalyptus for their cool, cleansing scents.

A healing ceremony will be most effective during the time of a waning moon – particularly in the four days following full moon. This is the time when things can be cast away or released,

The goddess of compassion

Chinese worshippers flock to the shrines of Kuanyin to seek her favour because they believe she can cure almost every sickness and alleviate every distress. Her name means 'One who sees and hears the cries of the whole world' and her image stands on many family altars in the East. She is usually shown carrying a vial containing the dew of compassion, and she cures the seriously ill by sprinkling a few drops on their heads.

On your healing altar, place a bowl of water, a quartz crystal, the colour blue, and some beautiful white flowers, such as lilies, to echo the vibrancy of the outside world.

including grief and anger. To perform a healing ceremony on behalf of someone who is ill, light two blue candles on the altar and present a bowl of clear spring water as an offering.

Ask for the healing help of Archangel Gabriel or Ceridwen, the white goddess of the Celts, or try appealing to the compassion of Kuanyin, the Buddhist goddess of mercy. Using a silver pen, write down the name of the person and their ailment on white paper or a petal from the lily, and then float it in the water. Visualize the ailment being lifted out of the sufferer and give thanks for their recovery. Place a clear quartz crystal in the water, and hold a second crystal in your hands while voicing your prayer, so that the healing power is transmitted.

Magical Herbalism

Every culture has had its own tradition of plant medicine, sometimes widely known and sometimes kept as secret wisdom by certain members of the society. Today many people in the western world are turning to more natural, plant-based medicines, but to understand this vast subject fully and use plant material safely takes many years of study and commitment. It is not recommended that you try to treat serious conditions yourself, but there are some traditional herbal remedies that you can use to treat everyday complaints. Generally, the herbs are best made into a tea or decoction and then drunk. If you are unsure about the safety of any herb, seek professional advice before using it.

Moon medicine

The phases of the moon are associated with important healing energies. The new moon is for health, vitality and regeneration; the full moon for fertility and empowerment; and the waning phase is the time when unwanted symptoms and ailments may be banished. The following moon medicine combines the power of crystals with the appropriate moon phase, depending on what is being treated.

To make the moon medicine you will need to make sure the moon is in the correct phase of her cycle and perform it either outside on a calm night, or inside by the light of the moon. Choose an appropriate stone that has been cleansed. Traditionally, all white, clear or watery bright stones are associated with the waxing and full moon ('bright moontime'); examples include moonstone, pearl, aquamarine and clear quartz. Black, dark or cloudy stones are used at the time of the waning moon ('dark moontime'); examples include jet, smoky quartz, obsidian and black tourmaline.

You will need
9 white tealights
matches
glass bowl
appropriate moon stone
spring water

1 Place the glass bowl on the floor in front of you, then position the nine tealights in a circle around it. Light the tealights, starting with the one in the south, saying while you do so:
Hail to thee Levanah, Queen of Heaven.

The nine tealights correspond with the moon's magical number of nine.

I call for your blessings and ask that your moonrays fill this essence with healing.

2 Put your moon stone in the bowl and pour in the spring water until the stone is completely covered. Leave it in place for at least three hours. Do not leave the tealights burning unattended and replace any that burn out.

3 After three hours, blow out the tealights, remove the stone, pour the infusion into a glass and sip slowly while visualizing yourself being touched by the moon's gentle rays.

Traditional ways with herbs and spices

The use of herbs and spices for healing, spiritual cleansing and magic has a long history. Many remedies are tried and tested, and almost every plant is useful in some way.

Feverfew leaves: eaten in honey sandwiches these are a traditional cure for migraine. This daisy-flowered herb with its peppery scent is fairly common, growing wild in some places.
Lemon balm: this is said to make the heart merry and the soul joyful. Bees love this plant

and bee-keepers traditionally rub their hives with it to keep their bees contented and settled.
Garlic: this offers protection from negative influences, including everyday infections such as the common cold, as well as bad spirits like vampires and ghosts.
Dandelions: these have a detoxifying and cleansing action. At one time, dandelions were a rustic oracle for telling the time: the flowers were said to open at five in the morning and close at eight in the evening.

Camomile: this brings down a fever, soothes the stomach, and is cooling and calming; it is also a tonic for blonde hair.
Ginger: this is warming and energizing; it is said to be a prescription for a happy love life in your later years.
Rosemary: said to be an aid to memory and concentration; it is also used as a conditioning tonic for dark hair.
Cloves: this warming spice is a traditional remedy for toothache in its oil form.

CHAKRA BALANCING

When our chakra system is balanced we enjoy good health. However, the chakras can be thrown out of balance by many things, including poor diet, lack of sleep and exercise, stress and modern medicines. Negative environmental influences such as electrical energy fields, geopathic stress and pollution also upset the chakra system. There are many ways to balance the chakras. For instance, you could work with colour therapy and gemstones, placing the appropriate coloured stone on each of the chakra points. Or you could use the healing properties of sound by intoning the mantra (healing sound) relevant to each energy centre, beginning from the base and ascending to the crown, and going down again. The box below on chakra properties tells you what colours and sounds to use for each chakra.

To diagnose which chakras are out of balance, you can use a pendulum to dowse them; you can also use dowsing after the treatment in order to check that the imbalance has been corrected.

The healing power of colour

Choose colours according to your healing need or preference.

Colour	Healing uses
Red	low energy, sexual problems, blood disorders, lack of self-confidence
Orange	depression, mental disorders, asthma, rheumatism
Yellow	detoxifying, hormonal problems
Green	antiseptic, balancing, tonic; soothes headaches
Blue	insomnia, nervous disorders, throat problems, general healing
Indigo	painkiller, sinus problems, migraine, eczema, inflammations
Violet/purple	psychological disorders; fosters self-love and self-respect
Magenta	emotional hurts and upsets, accepting life's problems
Black	for when you need to hide (such as when grieving)
White	tonic, replaces all colours
Gold	depression and low energy; digestive disturbances
Silver	hormonal and emotional balance, calms the nerves

Bottles of dual-coloured liquid can be used to diagnose colour imbalances. The bottles you are drawn to will tell you what colours you need more or less of in your life.

Chakra properties

Each chakra governs distinct organs and functions, and corresponds to a colour and sound.

1st chakra, colour; red, mantra; "lam":
Governs the gonads or ovaries, skeleton, large intestine and lower body; physical survival, energy distribution, practicality

2nd chakra, colour; orange, mantra; "vam":
Governs the bladder, circulation, sexuality; feelings, emotions, creativity and pleasure

3rd chakra, colour; yellow, mantra; "ram":
Governs the adrenal glands, spleen, pancreas, stomach; identity, self-confidence, personal power

4th chakra, colour; green, mantra; "yam":
Governs the thymus gland, immune system, lungs; relationships, personal development, self-acceptance, compassion

5th chakra, colour; blue, mantra; "ham":
Governs the thyroid, lymphatic, immune and neurological systems; self-expression, communication, trust

6th chakra, colour; indigo, mantra; "om":
Governs the pituitary gland, central nervous system; understanding, perception, intuition, spiritual "knowing", psychic abilities

7th chakra, colour; violet, mantra; silence:
Governs the pineal gland; openness, connection to higher energies, self-realization

Crystal healing

Gemstones and crystals are attributed with specific healing powers. You can use them to transform poor health (whether physical, mental or emotional) into wellbeing by placing them on the chakras. You can also programme stones to deal with specific complaints, and then place it on the relevant part of the body to draw out the sickness. It is important to use only cleansed stones in healing and to clean them again afterwards.

Amber: relieves depression

Amethyst: protects the immune system; calms fear; aids sleep

Aventurine: soothes the emotions

Bloodstone: blood detoxifier; strengthens physical body

Carnelian: increases physical energy

Chrysocolla: assists in the relief of grief, worry and pain

Clear quartz: a powerful talisman for healing, known in many cultures as the "all-healer". guards against loss of vitality and strength; draws out pain, raises self-esteem, balances emotions, increases insight

Garnet: relieves depression, boosts sexuality and fertility

Haematite: helpful for blood disorders, anaemia; eases the effects of jet lag

Jet: dispels irrational fears; protects from illness and infection

Malachite: releases trauma, relieves depression, protects against negativity

Rose quartz: comforts and heals the emotions; strengthens the heart

Tourmaline: good for psychic protection; relieves stress

Crystals whose colour corresponds to a chakra will enhance its natural qualities, whatever the situation. For a simple chakra balancing, place a stone on the relevant chakra for a few minutes.

COLOUR HEALING

There are many different ways of harnessing the vibration of colour for health and wellbeing. You can wear it, use it in your surroundings, make colour infusions, eat coloured food or even bathe in coloured light.

A colour infusion draws on the energizing, health-giving powers of the sun. To make one, use coloured stones, fabric or any other colourfast item and soak the "colour" in a bowl of mineral water. Leave the bowl in sunlight for several hours, then pour the water into a glass and drink the infusion. Always make sure the coloured item you are using is clean before you soak it.

Coloured foods can also be used for healing. Red, orange and yellow foods are hot and stimulating. Yellow foods can help with weight loss and red foods restore energy. Green balances and detoxifies and is a tonic for the system. Blue, indigo and purple are soothing; blue curbs activity so is useful when you are trying to gain weight.

Another way of healing with colour involves shining coloured light on to the body to relieve physical, mental and emotional problems. You can try it yourself on everyday ailments. Place a coloured gel over a spotlight, making sure it is not touching the hot bulb. Turn off any other lights, and bathe in the coloured light, taking in the healing vibrations of your chosen colour. The main colour choice is often followed by its complementary opposite. For instance, if you are being treated with green, this may be followed by magenta to ensure a healthy balance in the body.

FLOWER ESSENCES

The subtle vibrations of flowers and trees are contained in flower essences. These are very useful for treating negative mental and emotional states and helping to rebalance the body's subtle energy system.

These properties of flowers were first discovered in the early twentieth century by Dr Edward Bach, who found himself drawn to certain flowers when suffering from particular emotions. The essences are made from flowers that are gathered when the dew is on them, floated in water and placed in the sun to allow the water to absorb the subtle vibrations. There are 38 Bach remedies, each one representing a negative emotion, plus rescue remedy, a mixture of five essences that is used for treating shock.

HARMONIOUS RELATIONSHIPS

The people in our lives can be one of the greatest sources of happiness, yet they can also present us with some of our biggest challenges. Every relationship will have its ups and downs and you should consider the effect your moods and emotions have on those around you as well as vice versa. Relationships require a level of self-discipline and a commitment to work things through if they are to be nourishing and supporting. There are many ways of using your magic skills to foster an atmosphere of love and understanding and to honour your closest relationships.

To help communication between members of your family, use blue stones on the altar.

A FAMILY ALTAR

Making a family altar is a good way of celebrating and deepening the bonds between you. It is best positioned somewhere that is at the heart of family life, such as in the living room or kitchen.

An old piece of furniture that has been handed down to you through the generations could be the perfect site for an altar dedicated to your family. It will carry the blessings of those it served in the past. You could place the altar in the west where the Water element governs relationships. If you wish to observe Feng Shui principles, the area of your home or room that corresponds to the family is positioned in the west, and to love and relationships, in the south-west.

You might invite all the members of the family to help you make the altar, each bringing an object that symbolizes an aspect of themselves. Photographs of your loved ones will act as a focus for your prayers and thoughts about your

Place pictures and gifts from children on the altar, to honour their contribution to the family.

Zodiac candle colours

Each sign of the zodiac can be symbolized by a coloured candle as follows:

Aries: dark red
Taurus: green
Gemini: yellow
Cancer: silver
Leo: gold or orange
Virgo: yellow
Libra: sky-blue or rose
Scorpio: burgundy or red
Sagittarius: purple or black
Capricorn: black
Aquarius: rainbow
Pisces: sea-green or indigo

family. To honour your relationship with your partner, choose a happy and harmonious picture of the two of you together. Other items could include gifts to you from your children, especially presents or drawings made by them, which bring with them fond memories and the resonance of the love that motivated the gift. But remember to include objects that represent family members as they are now – acknowledging your children as complex teenagers, not just as enchanting toddlers, for example – so that the altar grows with the family and remains relevant. If pets are part of your family, you can also include reminders of them on the altar.

RELATIONSHIP DIFFICULTIES

When you or other family members are going through a difficult time, try to stay open and talk about what is happening. Because of their link with the throat chakra, all blue crystals aid communication. You can put the stones on the altar, or else use them as a charm and carry them with you. Blue lace agate helps you express feelings, turquoise fosters partnership, light blue angel stone heals anger and lapis lazuli aids in the release of emotional wounds. Rose quartz is the stone of love.

If someone close to you is having problems in their relationship with others, perhaps with friends or at work, surround a picture of them with rose

The symbolism of flowers

In folklore, flowers are believed to speak the language of the heart. Using flowers and herbs is another way of working with whatever qualities are being expressed or are needed in a relationship.

Apple blossom: love, friendship
Clover: fidelity
Coltsfoot: peace and tranquillity
Cyclamen: love and truth
Gardenia: peace and healing

Hyacinth: love and protection
Jasmine: friendship
Lavender: peace and happiness
Lily of the valley: peace, harmony and love
Narcissus: harmony
Passion flower: peace and friendship
Rose: love
Sweet pea: friendship and courage
Vervain: inner strength and peace
Violet: contentment

quartz crystals for harmony. While you do this, think about the person close to you and imagine them at ease with themselves and others.

GIVING BLESSINGS

When someone leaves home or begins a new life journey, write a protective blessing and tuck the folded paper into the frame of their picture on your altar. When loved ones are away, you can light candles that represent their sun sign to send them your love and support. You can also burn candles to bolster confidence and self-esteem or to celebrate significant dates such as birthdays and anniversaries.

HONOURING THE ANCESTORS

In cultures with an established tradition of family altars, the ancestors are the most honoured family members.

Photographs and mementos of your forebears keep those you loved as a positive influence in your life, and provide a sense of continuity for your children, helping them to see themselves as links in a chain of existence.

In Spanish-speaking countries – particularly Mexico – the Day of the Dead is when the dead are entertained as respected members of the family. One of the most important religious occasions of the year, families have picnics in the cemeteries and build altars covered with flowers and food to welcome their dead relatives home for the night, burning candles and copal incense to help them find their way. Veneration of the ancestors is also an important tradition in the East. To prevent their spirits from becoming restless or vengeful, rituals are conducted that ensure proper respect and provide the family with a means of consulting the wise elders; the family includes past and future generations, as well as the present.

Copal

One of the most important and valuable incense burning substances used by the Mayans, Incas and Aztecs of Central and South America was copal, the gift of the jaguars. According to the Mayan's holy book, copal resin was extracted from the Tree of Life and given to humanity as a gift. There are three types of copal resin: black, golden and white.

If someone in the family needs special love and care, surround their picture with rose quartz.

COPING WITH CHANGE

Our lives follow cycles that are continually changing, evolving and shifting from moment to moment, and nothing in the physical realm remains the same forever. In modern society, we have come to fear or abhor most endings, seeing them as associated with failure or as the loss of something we value or want to keep. However, natural magic teaches us that change is good, and when we are able to let go of things that do not really serve us, or of an experience that has run its course, our lives can open up in very positive ways.

ENDINGS

To attract a new beginning, we must first close the door on that which is ending. This could be a work contract, a relationship, a house move or perhaps grown-up children leaving home; whatever the situation it is important to create an ending that honours the change, while remaining positive about it. The simplest way to honour an ending is to voice the fact, and give thanks for what you have experienced as you

A ritual purification of your new home, using sun-charged water and rosemary, will cleanse the psychic space to make it yours.

indicate your intention to let it go and move on to a new beginning. The ceremony can be as simple or as elaborate as you wish. For instance, you could light a candle on your altar and say a prayer, or give some other offering as a thanksgiving for what is ending. Water is the element associated with letting go, so you could also include this on your altar.

MOVING HOUSE

If you are moving house, cleaning and clearing out is something that you will do naturally in the process of moving on. After the physical clearing and cleansing has been finished, an ideal way to acknowledge the act spiritually is to sweep the house symbolically with a bundle of birch twigs or a birch broom, imagining each area being purified as you do so. In ancient times, brushwood from the birch tree was used to sweep out the spirits of the old year, preparing the way for the beginning of the new one. Let the house know of your intentions in performing this act and thank it for having been your home. You can also use the birch broom to sweep the new house you are moving into, as a

A traditional witch's broom made from birch twigs can be used symbolically to sweep away the old to make way for the new.

first step to claiming it as your new home. Here, it will have the effect of sweeping away the atmosphere created by the previous occupants, making space for your own spiritual energy.

To prepare your new home for the beginning of your life there, you can bless it by walking around all the rooms and sprinkling them as you go with drops of water that you have charged with the energy of the sun. Use a sprig of rosemary to sprinkle the water, as it is a protective herb that favours new beginning. This will add vitality and vigour to your new environment.

A TALISMAN FOR CHANGE

Endings and beginnings may be accompanied by feelings of insecurity, fear, and sadness, and you can use this talisman to help you come to terms with your feelings. Make it during a waxing moon if you are more concerned with beginnings, during a waning moon for endings and letting go.

You will need
2 silver or white candles
silver pen
23cm (9in) square of natural paper
moonstone

1 Light the candles, saying these words as you do so:
Hail to you Levanah, I light these candles in your honour and ask for your help with the endings/beginnings (whichever you are working on) in my life at this time.

2 Draw the symbol for Alpha (beginnings) or Omega (endings) in the middle of the paper, depending on whether you are working with endings or beginnings. If you want to work with both, then draw both symbols.

3 Fold the four corners of the paper into the centre to make a diamond shape, then fold in the same way twice more.

4 Pinch out the candles, place the moonstone on your talisman and leave it in moonlight for several hours. Afterwards, put it in a safe place or carry it with you.

Symbols of new beginnings

Add a wish to a bowl of pumpkin seeds.

A white lily holds a rolled-up wish paper.

There are many ways in which you can call for a new beginning, once you have recognized and acknowledged an ending in your life.

● A pair of lodestones placed together in a central area of a room will call for the attraction of a lover.

● If you see shooting stars and comets together in the sky, wishing upon them calls the Sky Father's protection and blessing for any wishes you make.

● The cowrie shell is sacred to the Goddess and empowers wishes for love, friendship and family. Decorate a small pouch with cowrie shells and drop your written wish inside.

● A bowl of seeds (such as sesame, sunflower or pumpkin) with a wish tucked into them, placed on an altar or on the kitchen windowsill, will encourage the growth of whatever you have called for.

● A birch broom propped up beside a doorway will encourage the old to depart and the new to arrive, and will also provide protection for your home.

● When you are seeking new work or prosperity opportunities, turn silver coins in your pocket on the first night of a new moon to invite growth in your finances.

● Write a wish on a piece of paper, fold or roll it and place the paper within the cone of a white lily flower; this bloom is sacred to Ostara, the goddess of birth and new life.

● Written symbols, such as Beth from the Druidic tree alphabet, or the Greek letter Alpha, will encourage new beginnings. Write them in places of significance, such as over a written wish, or trace them in the air in a space where new beginnings are being called for. You could also include them on a talisman.

A talisman to the moon can help you cope with change.

ABUNDANCE AND PROSPERITY

Prosperity is not only a matter of material possessions, physical or otherwise – feelings of satisfaction with our lot often bear little relation to what we actually possess. Abundance is about tuning in to the blessings of life, shifting emphasis away from personal limitation and all that we lack, and opening ourselves to new and prosperous possibilities. It has long been acknowledged that if you have a clear idea of what you want you are far more likely to achieve it. Magic recognizes that thought is a form of energy, and positive thinking contributes energetically to the fulfilment of your desire: ideas are the first step to abundance.

An altar of abundance, dedicated to Lakshmi, should reflect Earth colours and scents.

PERSONAL BELIEF SYSTEMS

When you want to focus on creating abundance a good place to start is to examine your belief systems. For instance, many people believe that material wealth is at odds with spirituality, and that being poor is somehow virtuous. Another widely held view is that you have to work hard in order to have wealth, or that only money that is "hard won" is deserved. Similarly, many wealthy people are unable to enjoy their riches as deep down they harbour a sense of guilt, alternatively some people are actually afraid to have more money for fear that they won't be liked or won't fit in any more with their social group, or even that they will become a target for people's jealousy.

Most of us have many barriers that stop us from receiving the abundance that we deserve – whether on the material plane (money), on the emotional (love) or on the spiritual (godliness). The first step in bringing more abundance into your life is to feel that you are worth it and deserve it: a person living in abundance has much more to offer than someone who is living in lack or "poverty consciousness".

One way of increasing your feeling of self-worth is to practise "affirmations", sayings that you use to help redirect your thoughts from negative to positive. The words you use for attracting abundance can be whatever you feel fits the situation, but here are two suggested affirmations;

I (say your name) am now open to receive (say what it is you are wishing for),
or *I (say your name) give thanks for the ever-increasing blessings in my life, now, today and always.*

One of the best ways to find abundance is to have gratitude for everything you have, as well as anything else you may receive.

An Altar to Abundance

Dedicating an altar to abundance is a powerful symbol of your intent to welcome more of life's goodness and to give thanks for the gifts you have already received. As Earth is the element associated with the material plane, use warm earth colours such as russet, deep yellow, rich browns and olive greens. Add spicy scents to your altar to attract prosperity, scents such as patchouli, star anise, clove and cinnamon are ideal – or make up some prosperity incense mix.

Make an offering of some silver coins, and as you do so, think of all the things that already enrich your life and represent them on the altar to create a positive reminder of what you have already been given and to express your gratitude. If you focus your attention on what you have, and keep giving thanks for it, you will find greater abundance being drawn into your life, based on the "like attracts like" principle.

Hindu Gods of Abundance

If you are seeking to manifest greater wealth, call on the Hindu goddess Lakshmi and/or the god Ganesha.

In the Hindu tradition, Lakshmi is the personification of abundance, wealth and harmony. She is portrayed as a beautiful woman seated on a sacred lotus throne; with two of her four hands she offers blessings of love and joy, while gold coins

---

Chai Shen, the god of wealth

For generations, Chinese families have set up an altar outside their homes on the eve of the Lunar New Year, in the hope of receiving the blessings of Chai Shen, the god of wealth, for the coming year. Each year, the god arrives from a different direction and this must be carefully calculated to make sure the altar is correctly positioned, otherwise it would welcome the god of evil instead.

All the family members say prayers and make offerings that symbolize abundance and good fortune, including sweets, fruit and wine. Everyone writes their wishes for the year on red paper, which is burned with offerings of incense. The previous year's portrait of Chai Shen is burned, and firecrackers are set off. After the ceremony, the god's portrait is carried inside to watch over the household for the year to come.

---

fall from the other two into the ocean of life. She is a symbol of everything that is fortunate and it is the nature of good fortune that it is distributed randomly. Deepavali, the third day of Diwali (the Festival of Lights), is dedicated to her worship; lamps are lit inside every home to welcome her and fireworks are exploded in her honour.

Ganesha, the elephant-headed god and lord of obstacles, helps to clear the path of anything that stands in the way of us receiving Lakshmi's blessings, so his presence can also help to bring abundance into your home.

A Prosperity Box

To help you focus on what you want to bring into your life, choose a suitable container to be your "prosperity box". Using black ink, make a list of what you

wish for. Be specific with what you are asking for – for instance, if you would like more money, state how much you need. Then write another list using energy-enhancing orange ink: this list should contain all the things you are prepared to do to help you achieve your desires. Remember: you have to take practical steps to help magic happen.

Fold the pieces of paper and place both lists in the box, together with a handful of prosperity incense, a few silver coins and a small piece of jade. Keep the box on your altar. When you receive a gift, place it on the altar for a while and give thanks to sustain the flow of abundant energy.

Prosperity incense

1 part cassia bark or cinnamon
1 part grated nutmeg
1 part finely grated orange rind
1 part star anise
few drops orange essential oil
2 parts frankincense grains

Pound the first four ingredients using a pestle and mortar, sprinkle on the oil and mix in the frankincense resin. Burn small amounts of the mixture on a charcoal block placed in a heatproof bowl.

A mixture of frankincense and rich spices can help in your prosperity magic.

Prosperity boxes can be filled with wishes for others, and offerings to a wish-granting power.

LUNAR GARDENING

Because the moon has such a strong influence over crop yields, for hundreds of years farmers, agriculturists and gardeners have all observed the moon's phases when planting, tending and harvesting crops. The phases of the moon, and also the zodiac sign that it is passing through, seem to affect the way plants grow, so timing gardening activities according to the moon helps make them more effective. The principles of lunar gardening take a while to adjust to, but after a while, you will find that your flowers bloom brighter, crops grow more succulent and flavoursome, and trees have stronger roots. In fact your whole garden will benefit from this ancient way of gardening and be filled with healthy plants that are a joy to behold.

Watery or fleshy plants, like courgettes and cucumbers, should be planted during a full moon.

GARDENING BY THE MOON

If, to begin with, you find it a little too complicated to check the zodiac signs for your gardening tasks, you can simply follow the moon's phases of waxing and waning. The moon is increasing in influence between the new and full phases (brightmoon) and decreasing in influence during the waning and dark phases (darkmoon).

NEW MOON

Seeds of plants that flower above the ground should be sown at the new moon. This is also the time for farmers to sow cereals such as barley and sweetcorn (maize), and for leafy and fruiting crops such as asparagus, broccoli and Brussels sprouts, squash and tomatoes to be planted. This is also the time for fertilizing and feeding anything that you wish to flourish.

FULL MOON

Because full moon has the strongest influence over the Water element this is the best time to plant watery or fleshy crops like marrows (zucchini) and cucumbers. This is also a good time for harvesting the leaves, stems, or seeds of herbs for drying, especially when the moon is transiting a Fire sign. It is important to pick your herbs on a dry day, so that they dry quickly, without rotting. The best time to harvest is just before midday. String the stems together

and hang them upside down in an airy, cool but dry atmosphere, until ready for use. The full moon is also an excellent time for baking bread. The influence of the full moon proves the yeast better and encourages the dough to rise.

Traditionally, mushrooms are picked at full moon, the best time being just after dawn, when the dew is still on the grass. Take them home and have them for breakfast. Remember that some fungi are poisonous, so be very careful that you

pick only edible mushrooms and do not eat anything you are unsure about.

WANING MOON

The waning moon is the time in the moon's cycle for root vegetables, peas and beans, and garlic. Anything undertaken during this time will benefit

Tend leafy plants and feed the garden well during the new moon. This is also the best time for sowing many types of seeds.

underground development or retard growth. This is therefore an excellent time to mow the lawn, as its new growth will be slowed, or to plough and turn the soil. Gather and harvest crops during the waning moon, especially in late summer, the traditional harvest time. This is an excellent time to prune trees, roses and shrubs, and to water the garden. Making jams and pickles should also be done during a waning moon, for best results.

Crops that are suited to planting during the waning moon are endive (chicory), carrots, garlic, onions, potatoes, radishes, beetroot (beets) and strawberries. All flowering bulbs, biennials and perennials should be planted during this time, especially when the moon is in a Water sign. Saplings also benefit from being planted during the waning moon, when it is in Cancer, Scorpio, Pisces or Virgo.

DARKMOON

The fourth quarter, or darkmoon, is the best time for garden maintenance: for weeding, cultivation and the removal of pests. Start a compost heap during the darkmoon time, or harvest and dry herbs and everlasting flowers, especially if the moon is in a Fire sign. A watermoon is the best time to water fields and gardens.

Carrots and other root vegetables develop best during the time of a waning moon.

Elemental gardening table

When gardening according to the moon's sign of the zodiac, your timing needs to be a little more accurate than is the case with the moon's phases. The moon takes only about a couple of days to pass through each sign, so to coordinate both factors will take careful planning. For details on the moon's phases and when it is passing through a particular star sign, you will need to refer to a lunar almanac or an ephemeris. Then check the chart below to discover which zodiacal sign is most appropriate for each activity.

AIR
Gemini (barren and dry): weeding, clearing, pest control
Libra (moist): plant fruit trees, fleshy vegetables, root vegetables
Aquarius (barren and dry): garden maintenance, weeding and pest control

FIRE
Aries (barren and dry): weeding, clearing, garden maintenance
Leo (barren and dry): bonfires, ground clearance, weeding
Sagittarius (barren and dry): plant onions, garden maintenance

WATER
Cancer (very fruitful and moist): best sign for planting, sowing and cultivating
Scorpio (very fruitful and moist): very good sign for planting, sowing and general cultivation, especially vine fruits; start a compost heap
Pisces (very fruitful and moist): excellent for planting, especially root crops

EARTH
Taurus (fertile and moist): plant root crops and leafy vegetables
Virgo (barren and moist): cultivation, weeding and pest control
Capricorn (productive and dry): good for root vegetables

LUNAR PLANTS

Particular plants and trees come under the influence of the moon. These have been used in ceremonies and rituals to the moon goddess, and were also depicted in traditional art and sculpture. Flowers of the moon include all aquatic plants like waterlilies, seaweed and lotus, as well as jasmine and poppy. All flowers that are white or that blossom at night, such as jasmine or night-scented stock, are also moon flowers.

Trees of the moon include sandalwood and camphor, both of which were used in the ancient world in ceremonies to attract the attentions of the moon goddess, as well as the willow, aspen, eucalyptus, pear, plum and lemon. The willow is also known as the moon's wishing tree, and calling for favour by tying white, silver or light blue ribbons to her branches on lunar festival days can help to empower a wish.

Foretelling the weather

Because the moon influences weather patterns, it is possible to predict changes in the weather according to where the moon is in her cycle, or her appearance.

- a new moon always brings a change in the weather, and if the horns of the moon are sharp it indicates the onset of windy weather
- a crescent moon cupped and on its back means rain
- if you can see a star close to the moon, expect to have "wild weather"
- a bright full moon heralds good weather and a mottled full moon will bring rain
- storms and other dramatic weather patterns are more likely just after a full moon

ARTS OF DIVINATION

The word divination shares the same Latin root as divine, meaning sacred, godly or pertaining to the heavenly realm. Divination is a sacred art; it is the means by which we can discover the unknown (or what is hidden) by means of intuition, inspiration or magic. In ancient times, it was very much a part of both religious and secular life. In Old Testament times, for instance, the priest would cast stones or lots when important decisions had to be made, while in the Ancient and Classical world, oracles were regularly consulted to assess the best time for an undertaking or to predict the outcome of a course of action. In all cases it was believed that God or the gods were speaking through the divining tool.

Divination embraces a number of arts that use symbols or patterns to help you focus your clairvoyance or psychic vision on matters that may be occurring at a distance, back and forth in time, or simply at a deep level within yourself.

There are a variety of different methods by which the doors to your own psychic abilities are opened in a way that permits intuition to work. This chapter includes some of the most widely popular systems of divination in use, including numerology, astrology, the Tarot, the I Ching and runes. Dowsing, a relatively straightforward art, is also included, along with scrying, which is perhaps one of the trickiest to master.

DIVINATION

Above the entrance at the celebrated Delphic Oracle in ancient Greece was carved the inscription, "Know Thyself". Indeed, increasing self-awareness can be said to be the ultimate purpose of divination. Rather than being a method to predict a future that is already certain, it is a way of seeking guidance from the gods or our "higher self" about possibilities. If we accept that we are the creators of our own destiny, it follows that the more information we have at our disposal, the more we are able to make choices that are in line with our highest purpose or destiny.

The I Ching can give you greater insight into your situation and help you make wise decisions.

HIGH AND LOW MAGIC

At its most elevated level, divination is a sacred art designed to exalt the consciousness of the individual seeking guidance (the inquirer) and to increase self-acceptance. At the other end of the spectrum, divination is also associated with "fortune-telling" and prediction.

This can place the inquirer in a passive position, a victim in the hands of fate. Practitioners of natural magic are more inclined to use divination for its original sacred intent. This puts the onus of responsibility firmly in the hands of the inquirer and means that the divinatory arts are approached with the same care and respect as any other aspect of natural magic. When interpreted correctly, a reading will direct the inquirer's attention to the forces shaping his or her path in life – and present choices or suggest a course of action.

SYNCHRONICITY

The practice of divination stems from a desire to know in advance what is going to happen. Through the ages many

Divination can be done for yourself and for others. If you undertake to perform any kind of reading for someone else, be careful about how you give them difficult or challenging information.

Uses for divination

Divination can be used to:
- analyse problems
- clarify a decision-making process
- help you to understand yourself and others better
- reveal aspects of a situation that are out of conscious awareness
- stimulate intuition
- open up your mind
- assist healing
- predict future patterns or trends

Ethics – the dos and don'ts of divining

Traditionally the divinatory arts were taught by oral and practical exposition, where the student would naturally assimilate the level of responsibility needed to stand as mediator between the inquirer and the spiritual realm. Whenever you undertake to perform any reading for another person, you should treat them with respect and compassion: do not give them more information than they can handle, and do not frighten them if you see difficult or challenging aspects in their reading. The following guidelines may also be helpful:

1 Do not use divination for guidance obsessively: this can be counter productive and indicates giving away your power and responsibility.

2 Always obtain the permission of another person before doing a reading for them.

3 Do not use divination for entertainment or in inappropriate circumstances.

4 Respect your spiritual allies; seek their advice seriously and remember to give thanks.

5 Don't divine when you are low in energy or feeling upset; wait until you feel balanced and centred.

6 Remember that divination is a means of spiritual clarification, not sorcery.

7 Dedicate your art to the highest good of all.

8 Encourage the inquirer to see the reading as a pattern of possibilities based on their current situation; remind them that they have choice.

different methods have been used to foretell the future, from signs and portents in the sky to the patterns made by tea leaves or the innards of slaughtered beasts. Sticks, coins, coloured stones, pictures and dreams have all been used to predict events, often with an uncanny accuracy. No one really knows how divination works, but the theory of "synchronicity" may come close to giving us a plausible explanation.

It was the twentieth-century psychologist, Carl Jung, who used the term synchronicity to account for "meaningful coincidences". In rational thinking, mysterious or amazing coincidences are ascribed to chance, but during the course of his work Jung noticed a pattern of coincidences in seemingly unrelated events that caused him to challenge the predominant scientific view of cause and effect. He ascribed this to a deeper level of the mind, which he referred to as "the collective unconscious". Archetypes and symbols operate at this level.

According to magical thinking, nothing happens at random; everything is connected and has meaning, as events in one area of the web of life correspond to patterns in other areas. This means that in theory, almost anything can be used for divination; it is all a question of being able to read the signs or patterns. A divinatory reading can reveal a minute part of the greater pattern; during that moment, it is as though a veil is twitched aside and we glimpse the otherworld.

Palmistry has been used as a divination tool for centuries and can take years of study and practice to perfect.

PREPARATION

Before divining, it is important to create a calm environment with soft lighting. Too much background noise or bright lights can disturb your concentration. Privacy is also vitally important because quite personal and intimate subjects may be discussed while doing any kind of reading. Eye contact and a friendly smile always helps the other person to feel at ease. Before you start, the inquirer should focus on the subject or issue that they are seeking guidance with. If you are using any tools – such as Tarot cards or the Rune stones – let the inquirer handle these as they focus on their issue. Some people will take only a short time to get their issues clear in their minds, while others will take longer to focus. The inquirer should then pass the cards, stones or whatever is being used back to you so that you can begin.

NUMEROLOGY

Aside from their practical use in counting, numbers also have a symbolic value. Numerology is the art of understanding life by studying the symbolic value of numbers and the relationships between them. Since time immemorial, cultures and religions all over the world have either devised their own system of numerology or borrowed from and expanded on existing ones. All of them have been used to explain and gain a deeper understanding of ourselves in relation to the cosmos, and numerology has always played a part in magic and divination.

The numbers of our birth date help us discover and express our core personal qualities.

LIFE CYCLES

The numbers 1 to 9 form the basic building blocks of numerology. Aside from zero, all other numbers can be reduced to arrive at one of these single digits. For example, 39 reduces to 3; this is arrived at by adding 3+9=12; 12 is then reduced to 1+2=3. Numerology is based on the principle of reduction, which mirrors the process of life. For instance, our time in the womb from conception to birth is nine months, which consists of three terms, while traditionally our lives are said to be made up of three cycles of three nine-year periods. The first cycle (ages 0–27) is concerned with the birth and growth of the individual; the second cycle (ages 28–54) is about how we engage with the world; while the final cycle (ages 55–81) is about engaging with the spirit. Similarly the numbers 1 to 9 form three nests of three with their symbolic meanings fitting within this bigger framework.

NUMEROLOGY AND YOU

Numbers affect every area of our lives and almost any set of numbers can be broken down and have meanings assigned to them. Many numbers are uniquely ours, from our telephone or house number to the number on official documents such as passports, driving licences and bank accounts. Many people also have a number that they consider "lucky". In numerology, however, the most significant numbers are those that relate to your date of birth (the life path number) and to the letters of your name (personality number).

THE LIFE PATH NUMBER

Everyone has a life path number that represents their potential. It is derived from the sum of the digits of their birth date. For example, a birthday of 9 November 1968 (9/11/1968) has a life path number of 8, reached in the following way: 9 + 1+1 + 1+9+6+8 = 35, then 3 + 5 = 8. Your life path number is a guide to what you need to do in life.

THE COSMIC AND PERSONAL YEAR

Like astrology, numerology can also provide a clue for the best timing of

The personal year number helps us all to work in harmony with unfolding events.

events. Every year, the calendar changes and different possibilities are available to us. The cosmic year number is calculated by adding up the digits of the current year. For example, the year 2004 is a 6 year, showing that there will be a potential for universal peace and harmony (the vibration of 6) that year. While the number of the cosmic year symbolizes the potential that exists around you, there is also a personal year number that relates more directly to you. To calculate this, you use your birth date, substituting the current year for the year of your birth.

NUMBERS AND THEIR MEANINGS

Traditionally, the symbolic meanings of numbers are ascribed as follows:

0: The lens; the all-seeing eye that encompasses everything but cannot act; reflective; withdrawal from life to take stock before embarking on the next adventure.

1 Initiative and independence; the leader; goal-setting and ambition; Great Father; the sun.

2 Nurturing and relationship; balance; carer, mediator; Great Mother; moon.

3 Creativity; self-expression; the birth of ideas; aspiration; Cosmic Child.

4 Structure and order; stability; material structures; discipline and consolidation.

5 Breaking free from limits imposed by structures leading to growth and change; restlessness; adventurous; exploring new possibilities; self-discovery.

6 Emotional harmony and sensitivity; perfection and ideals of family life; love of heart and home.

7 Spiritual transformation; meditation, mysticism; spiritual learning and development; life and spirit combine.

8 Strategist and organizer, regulating relationship between spirit and matter; moves between spheres of heaven and earth; connects with cycles of life. Karmic number.

9 Wisdom gained through experience; the great teacher; completion and ending before a new cycle begins.

11 Speaking with inspiration; channelling the spirit; visionary; the prophet or seer.

22 Building the dream; the master builder; systematic approach combined with gentleness and sensitivity.

33 Unconditional giving; devotion to great causes; saint or martyr; the tireless helper.

Personal year numbers

Your personal year number is calculated by adding the day and month of your birth with the current year.

1 Fresh beginnings, both in your personal and professional life

2 Finding peace; revising and strengthening what you have started

3 Self-expression; personal as well as professional development

4 Discipline and consolidation; application, hard work and self-discipline

5 Exploring new possibilities; change

6 Self-esteem; love and romance

7 Soul-searching; self-awareness and personal spiritual growth

8 Go with the flow; try to connect more with inner self and others

9 Resolution; assess the past and note and enjoy your achievements

The personality number

Although many people will have the same life path number, the unique path that their life will take will be influenced by their personal attributes. A clue to these can be gained from the personality number. This number represents your identity; by recognizing and using its inherited qualities, you are better able to express yourself. In numerology, every letter of the alphabet has a numerical equivalent. The personality number is obtained by finding out the numerical value of every letter in your full name and reducing it to a single digit. For example, the name Ann Helen Myers consists of the numbers 1+5+5 + 8+5+3+5+5 + 4+7+5+9+1 = 63 which reduces to 9. Name changes and nicknames will reflect the personality number most representative of you at the time.

Numerical equivalents of the alphabet

1	2	3	4	5	6	7	8	9
A	B	C	D	E	F	G	H	I
J	K	L	M	N	O	P	Q	R
S	T	U	V	W	X	Y	Z	

The letters of our names can give us clues to our inherited patterns.

ASTROLOGY

Before the modern scientific age, it was widely believed that the movements of the celestial bodies regulated life on earth. The cycles of day and night, the waxing and waning of the moon and the movement of the planets across the starry night sky follow regular and predictable patterns. Our ancestors related these patterns to natural phenomena, including not only the weather and seasons, but also different kinds of destiny. Astrology is the study of these cosmic patterns pin pointed in the continuum of time and space and represented symbolically on an astrological "chart" or horoscope.

The universe is constantly evolving and new planets are still being discovered today.

ORIGINS OF ASTROLOGY

Astrology is one of the most ancient of all the magical arts. It seems to have evolved in Mesopotamia, where it was practised by priests who concerned themselves with the prediction of major events, from whether or not the harvest would be good to the destinies of kings and princes. Later it became the province of mathematicians, and the Greeks and Chaldeans used their knowledge of the heavens to delineate

The zodiac signs

In modern-day Western astrology, there are 12 signs of the zodiac, each related to a constellation.

Aries: The leader; "me first"; loner, pioneer, go-getter; enjoys action, adventure; quick to anger; ruled by Mars

Taurus: The builder; practical, patient, steadfast; enjoys material comfort and wellbeing; ruled by Venus

Gemini: The talker; quick-witted, restless, easily bored; enjoys travel, new ideas; constantly on the look-out for new experiences; ruled by Mercury

Cancer: The nurturer; empathic, sensitive to needs of others; imaginative; enjoys home and family; ruled by the Moon

Leo: The actor; plays centre-stage, dramatic, generous, warm, affectionate; enjoys good living, romance, and "to play"; ruled by the Sun

Virgo: The perfectionist; precise, meticulous, pays attention to detail; enjoys work in the service of others; sincere, dependable; ruled by Mercury

Libra: The adjuster; seeks to bridge or reconcile opposites, to balance; relationships important and need for peace and harmony; enjoys aesthetics and beautiful things; ruled by Venus

Scorpio: The transformer; death and rebirth, endings and beginnings; going to the depths, emotional intensity; enjoys the occult, the mysteries of life; ruled by Pluto and Mars

Sagittarius: The traveller; journeys to expand horizons; free spirit, adventurous, buoyant and exuberant; enjoys humour, having fun, new experiences; ruled by Jupiter

Capricorn: The climber; works hard to achieve ambitious and lofty goals; patient, cautious, responsible, committed; enjoys the status of success, black humour; ruled by Saturn

Aquarius: The reformer; intellectual revolutionary, seeks social justice, a "brotherhood of man"; freedom of thought, originality and emotional independence; enjoys gadgets, machines, electronic media; ruled by Uranus and Saturn

Pisces: The dreamer; impressionable, imaginative, sensitive and artistic; psychic development, meditation, spiritual transformation; refines and idealizes; enjoys the arts, but also has a tendency towards escapism; ruled by Neptune and Jupiter

certain characteristics associated with each pattern that could be applied to life on earth.

USES OF ASTROLOGY

A horoscope involves plotting the position of the celestial bodies at a given moment in time. It is possible to draw one up for almost any life situation: we can use it to help us determine the best time or place for an event, such as a wedding or business venture, or we could also examine the potential of a relationship by comparing two charts and looking at the symbolic interaction between them. However, the most useful place to start with astrology is with your own birth chart.

The birth chart can be used as a tool for self-awareness: personality types and psychological traits as well as information on the building blocks of life – such as career, health and relationships – are all covered in the birth chart. It can also be used to predict future life-trends, although be aware that these are "trends" and not absolute certainties. Drawing up a birth chart involves complex numerical calculations and unless you want to spend the time learning how to do this, it is a good investment to get your chart drawn up by a professional astrologer. Once you have your chart, it is yours for life. The next step is learning how to make sense of it.

UNDERSTANDING ASTROLOGY

Your horoscope will be drawn as a circle divided into twelve sections, each section representing a sign of the zodiac

Astrology is the study of the patterns made by the planets and how these can influence life on Earth.

(Aries, Taurus, Gemini and so on); the word zodiac itself comes from the Greek meaning "a circle of animals". Each of the celestial bodies (referred to as "planets" for convenience) will appear in a sign of the zodiac. Most probably you already know your "Sun sign" (often referred to as your "star sign") but in addition you will find that you will also have a zodiac sign for the Moon, Venus, Mars and all the other planets. The basic layer of the birth chart shows the disposition of the planets and how they are influenced by the nature or character of the signs in which they fall. The next layer is to look at the relationships or "aspects" made by these planets to one another; some of these aspects will be easy and harmonious, while others will be stressful and present challenges. On top of this, the chart is further divided into twelve "houses". These represent areas of life – such as work, relationships, creativity and health for instance – that show us where the energies of each planet are expressed.

The symbolism of the planets

The word planet is derived from the ancient Greek "wanderer". In ancient times, the planets were regarded as mysterious wanderers of the night sky and linked with the gods and goddesses of classical mythology. Each of these divinities is contained within the horoscope, and can be seen to represent different energies or aspects of the psyche. How these are expressed will vary according to which of the 12 zodiac signs the planet falls in, and whether this is a Fire, Water, Earth or Air sign.

Planet	Symbol	Function
Sun	☉	Wholeness; integration of the self; inner purpose; vitality; conscious authority; the heroic impulse to "be"
Moon	☽	Emotional response; imagination; receptivity; rhythm and mood; memories
Mercury	☿	Thought and communication; mental faculties; intelligence
Venus	♀	Love, beauty, art; relationships (friends and lovers); harmony; money and resources
Mars	♂	Action; self-assertion; desire, ambition, competition; physical energy; ego
Jupiter	♃	Expansion, freedom, opportunity; search for meaning; luck, learning, philosophy
Saturn	♄	Limitation, structure, perseverance, responsibility; life's lessons; karma
Uranus	♅	Originality and inventiveness; eccentricity; urge to reform; radicalism; change, the unexpected, intuition
Neptune	♆	Idealism and inspiration; spiritual values, transcendence; clairvoyance, the subconscious
Pluto	♇	Transformation; death, rebirth and regeneration; intensity, power

THE HOUSES

Just as there are 12 signs, there are also 12 astrological houses that closely reflect the meanings of the signs. The houses are "areas of life", compartments of experience that indicate where the energies of each planet are expressed. If the planets show us "what" then the houses indicate "where".

The first house is concerned with childhood and the development of personality. It governs physical appearance and is the way we present ourselves to the world. The second house represents possessions and values; it is the domain of accumulated wealth, income and everything to do with material comfort. It is connected with a person's capabilities and resourcefulness. The ability to communicate is contained within the third house. This house also governs neighbours, relatives and the immediate environment. Home is the domain of the fourth house; this includes our homeland, as well as the actual building in which we live. The fifth house is about pleasure and creativity, and includes love affairs, our sex life and children, as well as creations of an artistic sort. Our health and wellbeing falls into the sixth house, which also includes our work and how we fulfil our role in society. Close relationships and partnerships (both marriage and business) fall into the seventh house, while the eighth house is the house of transformation and covers endings, death and rebirth. Inheritances, wills and life's challenges and upheavals are found in this house. Travel, higher education and spiritual voyaging are ninth house matters, while the tenth is concerned with public position, our reputation and status in the world. Friends and social groups are contained in the 11th house, while the 12th house is the area of spirituality and transcendence.

Aspects

Reading a birth chart is extremely complex. Not only does the astrologer take into account the position of the planets in the signs and houses and where they fall in the circle, they will also look at the "aspects" or relationships between the planets. Like relationships, some aspects are easier to handle than others. The challenging aspects are often what motivates psychological growth. The main astrological aspects are as follows:

The conjunction (0°): planets are in close proximity to one another. The conjunction is like a marriage, with each planet strongly influencing the other; it is usually a harmonious aspect, depending on the planets and houses involved.

The opposition (180°): planets are placed on opposite sides of the circle, suggesting tension and confrontation. The opposition is a challenging aspect and means that we will struggle to integrate these opposing forces.

The trine (120°): planets are in a harmonious relationship forming one (or more) sides of a triangle, enabling easy synthesis. If all three points of the trine (or triangle) are completed, it is known as a "grand trine".

The square (90°): planets are in tension with one another, forming one (or more) sides of a square. The square produces restless striving in order to get to grips with the planetary energies involved; being at right angles to one another, the planets involved may also go off at a tangent, causing blocks.

The sextile (60°): planets are in harmony; sextiles produce motivated activity, a working relationship between the planets and the angles involved.

The first of the 12 astrological houses is concerned with childhood.

Our love affairs and our sex life are governed by the fifth house, which is also about pleasure and creativity.

Work comes under the governance of the sixth house, which also includes our role in society.

THE ASCENDANT AND DESCENDANT

The houses of your horoscope begin with the ascendant. This is the precise degree of the sign on the eastern horizon at the time and place when you were born. Also known as the rising sign, the ascendant is very influential; it is like the outer mask or persona that we present to the world and is largely how we create a first impression with others. So, for instance, someone with Leo rising but with a moon in Pisces may seem bold and brash, but their moon sign indicates sensitivity and that they are liable to be easily hurt. Opposite the rising sign is the descendant; this marks the cusp of the seventh house (the house of relationships) and describes the "other", the natural partner. The ascendant and the descendant form a polarity, so that neither can be understood without the other. The ascendant-descendant axis divides the circle into upper and lower halves, the upper part symbolizing the "world out there" and the lower part our subjective, inner experience.

THE MIDHEAVEN AND THE IC

The uppermost point of the chart is known as the "midheaven"; this point symbolizes the height of worldly success and public position, and with most house

The moon through the signs

Unlike the Sun, the moon travels through all the signs of the zodiac in a month, spending two or three days or so in each sign. Because the moon is so important in magic and ritual, it is especially useful to understand how it functions through the different signs.

Moon in ...	Key word	Magic for ...
Aries	energy	starting new projects; leadership; goal-setting
Taurus	dependability	love, money and material things
Gemini	communication	talking, writing; travel (short journeys)
Cancer	nurturing	home and family, emotional support; issues to do with motherhood
Leo	courage	creativity and fertility; daring to take risks
Virgo	self-improvement	work (on self or in the world); health; attention to detail
Libra	balance	emotional harmony, giving and receiving; artistic and spiritual work; legal matters
Scorpio	transformation	making real changes in your life; sexuality and desire
Sagittarius	exploration	travel (long journeys); pursuit of spiritual values
Capricorn	achievement	getting organized; pushing forwards with career, ambitions; status in the world
Aquarius	revolution	freedom and originality; any work that involves creative expression, problem-solving
Pisces	compassion	healing; working with dreams, psychic abilities, clairvoyance and telepathy; trusting intuitive powers

The 11th house governs our friends and our social groups.

systems is on the cusp of the 10th house. It describes our aspirations and the type of career we are likely to develop.

At the other end of this axis is the IC, or *imum coeli* (Latin for "bottom of the sky"), on the cusp of the 4th house. It describes the least exposed parts of ourselves and is a link to our personal and ancestral past. The IC and the midheaven form an axis of innermost and outermost life experiences, which further divides the circle into eastern and western hemispheres. The eastern hemisphere is concerned with the self, while the western hemisphere is linked with the impact of others.

THE TAROT

The origins of the Tarot are shrouded in mystery. Some say it dates back to ancient Egypt, while others see strong links with Hebrew mysticism. However, we do know that in fifteenth-century Italy the wealthy Visconti family commissioned an artist to paint a set of 78 unnamed and unnumbered cards that depicted religious allegories, social conditions and ideas of the time, to celebrate a family marriage. These cards formed the deck for an Italian gambling game called "Tarocchi", and by the late eighteenth century we find them being used as a divinatory tool. Since then, hundreds of different Tarot decks have been produced but the core meanings of the cards remains largely unchanged.

Pick a Tarot card each day and meditate on the image, or think about what you feel it shows.

WHAT IS THE TAROT?

Essentially the Tarot is a deck of 78 cards, which divide into two clear parts: the 22 cards of the Major Arcana and the 56 cards of the Minor Arcana. The Minor Arcana is further sub-divided into four suits, each of which is related to one of the four elements: Wands (Fire), Swords (Air), Cups (Water) and Pentacles (Earth). The Minor Arcana closely parallels a normal pack of 52 playing cards with its suits of clubs (wands), spades (swords), hearts (cups) and diamonds (pentacles). It is therefore possible to transpose the meanings of the Tarot cards on to a deck of playing cards and to use these for readings.

The word "Arcana" is related to arcane, which means mysterious or secret, and the Tarot has also been known as a "Book of Secrets". The Major Arcana deals with archetypal themes and reflects the major turning points in our lives: our commitments, triumphs and tragedies, our greatest challenges and most powerful impulses. The cards of the Minor Arcana deal with more day-to-day aspects of life, such as work, relationships, our ideas and our ambitions. Taken together, they constitute a guidebook to the incidents and issues that we have to handle in our lives, from the past, in the present and looking to the future.

DECODING THE TAROT

Most modern Tarot decks have a picture on every card, and the best way to learn the meanings is to shuffle a new pack thoroughly and take one card each day. Place it somewhere you can see it and think about what it seems to show, or meditate on the image. Write down your conclusions in a book kept for the purpose, and next day go on to another card, until you have examined all 78. You may simply focus on the name or number of the card, or try to decide what the picture shows at first, but gradually meanings will start to emerge.

Many books on interpreting the Tarot system are available and they take a wide variety of approaches – from light-hearted fun to a deep magical or psychological orientation. It is best not to rely too heavily on the meanings given in books, however, but to use your own intuitive understanding.

Understanding the cards

This numerical guide can be used as a quick reference to the Minor Arcana definitions, by cross-referencing the generic numerical meaning for any card with the general background to a particular suit. Take the Nine of Cups, for example. The suit of Cups is concerned with emotional issues, whilst a general definition for any of the number nine cards concerns fulfilment. By combining these two pieces of information, you can work out a general definition for the Nine of Cups to signify emotional contentment.

King:	Competition, realization
Queen:	Fulfilment, deep satisfaction, skill, maturity
Knight:	Focus, single-mindedness
Page:	Information
Ten:	Culmination and change
Nine:	Integration, contentment
Eight:	Organization, evaluation, experience, commitments
Seven:	Imagination, options, variety of choice
Six:	Poise, contentment, relaxation, victory
Five:	Adjustment, challenge, possible conflict
Four:	Manifestation, creation of a plan
Three:	Clarification, plans made public
Two:	Affirmation, some sort of choice, commitment
Ace:	Potential, new beginnings; the "raw" energy of the suit

THE MINOR ARCANA

The 56 cards of the Minor Arcana are divided into four suits. The suit of Wands is concerned with energy and ambition, our goals and desires; it is also connected with sexuality. The suit of Swords is concerned with the mental realm of thoughts and ideas; it is also the area where conflicts are likely to surface. Emotions are connected to the suit of Cups dealing with love relationships, artistic endeavours and contentment. Lastly, the suit of Pentacles is concerned with everyday material matters, such as money and property.

The Major Arcana

The cards of the Major Arcana represent the powerful cosmic forces at work in our lives and are always the most important cards in a reading. These cards represent archetypal forces and have traditional astrological correspondences.

Number	Card	Correspondence	Traditional meaning
0	The Fool	Uranus	Fresh beginnings; spontaneity; taking risks and stepping into the unknown; change
I	The Magician	Mercury	Manifesting results in the material world; communicating; bringing different elements of life together
II	The High Priestess	Moon	Trust your intuition; don't take things at face value but look behind the scenes; patience
III	The Empress	Venus	Fertility or pregnancy; domestic bliss; abundance and the good things of life; enjoyment of sensuality. The 'mother' principle
IV	The Emperor	Aries	Power and authority. Established structures and organizations: banks, schools, offices, companies. The 'father' principle
V	The Hierophant	Taurus	Traditional ways of doing things; seeking advice from figures in the establishment or a higher authority (a teacher or spirit guide)
VI	The Lovers	Gemini	Intensity and choices in relationships; instant chemistry and attraction between two people; the feeling that something is 'meant to be'
VII	The Chariot	Cancer	Moving forwards on the path through life towards success; staying focused on goals
VIII	Strength	Leo	Recognizing and using your inner strength; having self-confidence
IX	The Hermit	Virgo	Look before you leap; take time out to be alone; cultivating wisdom and self-awareness; the guide
X	The Wheel of Fortune	Jupiter	Luck, expansion and growth; fate taking a hand in your life and possibly redirecting the path you are on
XI	Justice	Libra	See what is out of balance and make necessary adjustments; reaping what is fair and just
XII	The Hanged Man	Neptune	Sacrifice and letting go; reversal of fortune, a time to sit back and wait until circumstances improve
XIII	Death	Scorpio	Changes and endings (not usually a physical death), followed by regeneration and rebirth
XIV	Temperance	Sagittarius	Testing the waters before diving in; compromise and cooperation, allowing feelings to flow. Treading a middle way and not jumping in where angels fear to tread
XV	The Devil	Capricorn	Trapped by fears, compulsions and addictions; being overly attached to security; can also be rediscovery of passions and sexual energy.
XVI	The Tower	Mars	Disruptive changes that are sudden and unexpected; life will never be the same again; a radical upheaval
XVII	The Star	Aquarius	Realizing dreams and visions, a wish comes true; renewal of hope and faith
XVIII	The Moon	Pisces	Dreams and illusions, everything may not be as it appears at face value; the power of the subconscious
XIX	The Sun	Sun	Extremely positive card denoting growth, life and an increase of potential in all or many areas of life; vitality, joy and happiness
XX	Judgement	Pluto	Decisions are pressing and need to be made; coming to terms with the past. Moving forwards with a more positive attitude; the lifting of karmic restrictions
XXI	The World	Saturn	The most auspicious card in the deck. You have come a long way and can now enjoy great success in all areas of life; completion of a cycle

USING THE TAROT

One of the main differences between using the Tarot compared to other divinatory tools, such as astrology or numerology, is that it is a pictorial system. The visual images give this system an impact that is real and immediate. It is even possible for some people without any knowledge about the Tarot to give accurate readings simply by looking at the images, having an instinctive response and then conveying what is seen, felt and understood.

We can use the Tarot for many purposes: to ask for advice about a best course of action, to gain insight into life's spiritual "lessons", as a tool for meditation and self-discovery, and also to develop our psychic ability and interpret what we see for others.

TAROT FOR YOURSELF

It is possible to do readings for yourself. One way of doing this is to begin each day with a simple question such as "What kind of day is in store?" Shuffle the pack, then pick a card. At the end of the day you may be able to understand how the card related to the day's events; it will also help you come to terms with a card's meaning, as experience is the best form of learning there is.

A quick three-card reading is also useful. Shuffle the pack and pick three cards, laying them out from left to right. The first represents yourself and your current situation; the second and third cards represent the situations and people you are about to encounter, respectively.

READING FOR OTHERS

When giving a Tarot reading, almost as much thought needs to be put into the preparations as into the actual reading itself. It is important to create a calm environment, preferably with soft lighting and no disturbing background noise. Privacy is also very important because quite personal and adult subjects may be discussed while doing a reading for another (the inquirer). Eye contact and a caring smile can help the inquirer to feel at ease when you are reading their cards, and remember it is not part of your remit to make scary predictions or give negative feedback. Always focus on the positive messages of the cards.

Ask the inquirer to concentrate on the subject or issue of their reading, as they shuffle the cards. Some people will take only a short time to get their issues clear, while others will take longer to focus. When the inquirer feels they have shuffled for long enough, they should pass the deck back to you. Now you are ready to lay out a spread. There are many different types of spread you can choose from, with two of the most popular being the "Celtic Cross" pattern, or one based on astrology. There are many good books on the Tarot, which will give information on different spreads for you to try.

Lay out the cards, face up, in the correct sequence. Notice any patterns or clusters of cards (for instance two or more

Before you begin to work with your Tarot cards, take some time to get to know them.

Care of your cards

Many people like to keep their Tarot cards wrapped in silk or in a special pouch or box. Do not loan out or let others handle your cards (except when giving a reading), as they will absorb your psychic impressions and become special to you.

of the same number, or a predominance of a particular suit), as this will give you a clue to the overall theme of the reading. You should also pay particular attention to any Major Arcana cards.

When you have interpreted all that you can from the cards, draw the reading to a conclusion and gather them together.

A Tarot Spell for Insight

The Tarot is a powerful divination system. Use this spell to empower a new pack of cards, or before doing a particularly important reading.

1 Take your cards and a square of silk, either red or bright blue, and a large surface with a clean flat cloth on it. Place a tall yellow or gold-coloured candle in a gold-coloured holder and light it.

2 Place the cards face down on the cloth and, with both hands, mix them up very thoroughly, saying the following:
Cards of wisdom, cards of grace, cards with magic on their face,
Open in me the holy power, to answer truly at any hour.
Open in me the skill of sight, to speak the truth by day and night.
Let the knowledge in me rise,
Let all I speak be good and wise.
Help me, Lord of the Tarot,
Help me.

Keep your Tarot cards in a safe place, and don't let anyone else use them.

3 Clap your hands over the cards three times, then select three cards and turn them over. These will show how well your spell has worked by their meanings. Snuff out the candle.

4 Collect up all the Tarot cards, wrap them in the silk square, place them in their box and put it in a safe place to retain their power.

The Celtic Cross formation is one of the best Tarot spreads to use.

Tarot meditation

One of the best ways of getting to know the Tarot is through meditation. To do this, sit quietly and comfortably with your eyes closed and take a few deep breaths to calm and centre yourself, allowing your thoughts to settle. Keeping your eyes closed, reach out and pick a card, feeling its energy in your hands. Open your eyes and allow your gaze to softly focus on the image, absorbing all its details, colours and characters.

Now close your eyes again and start to re-form the image in your mind's eye. Let it become bigger and bigger, until it becomes like a doorway. See yourself walking through it and into a living world peopled with the characters and symbols of the card. Notice your thoughts and feelings, and let yourself interact with the figures you find there. When you have finished, say goodbye and step back through the doorway. See the scene you have visited shrinking until it is once more the size of a card. Take a deep breath and open your eyes. Record your findings in your Book of Shadows.

THE I CHING

Paradoxically, the only certainty in life is change. In all change, however, there are certain patterns, and it is this predictability that the shamans of ancient China referred to when they were called upon to give advice and divinations on forthcoming events. Originally, an answer to a question was divined from the patterns on animal hides or tortoise shells; later this developed into the I Ching, or the Book of Changes. As the I Ching developed, it became more than an oracular device; the ancient sages saw that it could be used as a blueprint for understanding the way the whole universe works in all its complexity.

You may be able to obtain some old Chinese coins to use for divining, but any coins will do.

WHAT IS THE I CHING?

At its root, the I Ching is made up of eight trigrams, said to represent the eight fundamental forces of nature. At some point they were arranged into an octagonal form known as the Bagua, showing opposing pairs or forces, and were given specific names taken from nature. As its name suggests, a trigram is an arrangement of three lines, with a solid line used to represent yang energies, and a broken line to depict yin. In Chinese thought, yin and yang are the

Throw combinations

3 heads	= 9	__._ changes to __ __
2 heads, 1 tail	= 8	__ __
1 head, 2 tails	= 7	____
3 tails	= 6	__x__ changes to ____

two opposing principles that underlie all of creation, the complementary opposites that are apparent in everything. When combined with one another, the trigrams make up the 64 hexagrams of the I Ching.

CONSULTING THE ORACLE

A physical way of constructing a hexagram is needed and the most common is to throw or cast three coins. It is a good idea to dedicate your coins to the I Ching and only use them for this purpose. The "heads" side of a coin is considered yang, and is given a value of three, while the "tails" side is thought of as yin and has a value of two. When the coins are thrown, a total of six, seven, eight or nine is obtained, giving lines that are either yin (even numbers) or yang (odd numbers).

Begin by preparing yourself and letting go of everyday thoughts and concerns. Light some incense and burn a candle to help put you in the right frame of mind. When you are ready, hold your question in your mind's eye and then drop the coins on to a hard surface, making a note of the pattern to give you a number. Repeat this process a further five times until you have six totals. The hexagram is then constructed upwards, following the path of organic growth, so that the first total makes up the bottom line.

CHANGING LINES

A line totalling six (old yin) or nine (old yang) changes to its young opposite. The changing lines give deeper insights into a reading, being used to produce a second hexagram. The initial hexagram relates to present conditions, while the second hexagram relates to the future outcome of a situation, or can help to clarify the original question.

The eight forces of I Ching

Ch'ien/Heaven: the creative
Chen/Thunder: the arousing
K'un/Earth: the receptive
Sun/Wind: the gentle and penetrating
Li/Fire: the clinging
Ken/Mountain: the stillness
K'an/Water: the abysmal
Tui/Lake: the joyful

When you are consulting the I Ching, light a candle to help focus your mind.

The 64 hexagrams

1 Ch'ien:	The Creative	Masculine, dynamic, inspiring
2 K'un:	The Receptive	Feminine, yielding, receptive
3 Chun:	Difficult Beginnings	Immaturity, new growth, sprouting; perseverance
4 Meng:	Youthful Folly	Inexperience, guidance, enthusiasm, tuition
5 Hsu:	Waiting	Correctness, patience, perseverance, nourishment
6 Sung:	Conflict	Opposition, disengagement, communication
7 Shih:	The Army	Unity, harmony, acting in concert, strength, division
8 Pi:	Holding Together	Union, bonding, cooperation
9 Hsiao ch'u:	The Taming Power of the Small	Patience, yielding, strength; gentle action
10 Lu:	Conduct	Caution, courtesy, simplicity, innocence
11 T'ai:	Peace	Balance, harmony, new growth, prosperity
12 P'i:	Standstill	Lack of progress, barriers, stagnation
13 T'ung Jen:	Fellowship with Others	Cohesion, bonding, strength in numbers, co-operation
14 Ta Yu:	Possessing Plenty	Feminine, yielding, receptive, gentle, providing, bountiful
15 Ch'ien:	Modesty	Quietly progressing, steadfast, deepening, developing
16 Yu:	Enthusiasm	Energy, opportunity, support
17 Sui:	Following	Acceptance, following, joy
18 Ku:	Work on Corruption	Disruption, decay, disorder, spoiled, repairing
19 Lin:	Approach	Advance, waxing power, strength, benevolence
20 Kuan:	Contemplation	Meditation, understanding, perceiving, example
21 Shih Ho:	Biting Through	Clarity, decisiveness, obstacle, unity
22 Pi:	Grace	Adornment, beauty, simplicity
23 Po:	Splitting Apart	Strong, enduring, patient, non-action
24 Fu:	Return	Change, turning point, improvement
25 Wu Wang:	Innocence	Purity, innocence, sincerity, intuition
26 Ta Ch'u:	The Taming Power of the Great	Keeping still, tension, practice, staying firm
27 I:	Corners of the Mouth	Nourishment, discipline, meditation, fulfilment
28 Ta Kuo:	Preponderance of the Great	Pressure, regeneration, growth, cautious progress
29 K'an:	The Abysmal	Depths, despair, danger, alertness
30 Li:	The Clinging	Dependence, passion, brilliance, creativity
31 Hsien:	Influence	Harmony, mutual benefit, coming together, courtship
32 Heng:	Duration	Persistence, progress, endurance, stamina
33 Tun:	Retreat	Withdrawal, conserving strength, stillness, order
34 Ta Chuang:	The Power of the Great	Self-possession, strength, heaven, patience
35 Chin:	Progress	Advancement, dawning, rising
36 Ming I:	Darkening of the Light	Oppression, damping, sunset, inner light
37 Chia Jen:	The Family	Harmony, togetherness, loyalty, health, balance, structure
38 K'uei:	Opposition	Misunderstanding, contrary resistance, adversity
39 Chien:	Obstruction	Obstacles, barriers, blockage, stuck
40 Hsieh:	Deliverance	Relief, release, growth, progression
41 Sun:	Decrease	Discipline, simplicity, limited, drawing in, restriction
42 I:	Increase	Improvement, gain, progress
43 Kuai:	Breakthrough	Resoluteness, determination, resistance
44 Kou:	Coming to Meet	Caution, awareness, temptation, tolerance
45 Ts'ui:	Gathering Together	Peace, harmony, cooperation, prosperity, leadership
46 Sheng:	Pushing Upwards	Direction, ascending, growth
47 K'un:	Oppression	Exhaustion, stretched, adversity, endurance
48 Ching:	The Well	Spiritual nourishment, counsel, guidance, wisdom
49 Ko:	Revolution	Change, advance, devotion
50 Ting:	The Cauldron	Growth, sacrifice, nourishment
51 Chen:	The Arousing	Shock, movement, stimulation
52 Ken:	Keeping Still	Stillness, observing, quietness, clarity, readiness
53 Chien:	Development	Gradual progress, patience, steady growth
54 Kuei Mei:	The Marrying Maiden	Impulsiveness, disturbance, desire, proper conduct, discipline
55 Feng:	Abundance	Fullness, power, wise actions, plenty
56 Lu:	The Wanderer	Moving, restless, temporary, transient
57 Sun:	The Gentle	Gentle, penetrating, wind, persistence
58 Tui:	The Joyous	Inner strength, fulfilment, harmony, joy
59 Huan:	Dispersion	Division, dissolution, rigidity, stubbornness
60 Chieh:	Limitation	Restraint, moderation, guidelines
61 Chung Fu:	Inner Truth	Prejudice, understanding, acceptance
62 Hsiao Kuo:	Preponderance of the Small	Non-action, caution, patience
63 Chi Chi:	After Completion	Order, balance, awareness, culmination
64 Wei Chi:	Before Completion	Caution, regeneration, potential, clarity

THE RUNES

A system of sacred writing from northern Europe, Runes are said to have appeared to the Norse god Odin, during a shamanic initiation rite. The runes then became his gift of knowledge to humanity and as such they are empowered with ancient wisdom. The word "rune" comes from the Middle English *runa*, meaning "a whisper" or "a secret", and traditionally knowledge of the runes was granted only to a runemaster, who guarded it closely. A runemaster performed a similar role in Norse communities to the shaman, or medicine man or woman.

Runes can be written on small round pebbles, or on specially cut rounds of wood.

RUNE LAW
Runemasters underwent many initiatory experiences to discover the secrets of rune lore. They knew how to use them for divination, but also for magical and healing work. Runes can still be used as guides for meditation, as protective talismans, and in spells and charms.

THE RUNIC ALPHABET
The angular script of the runes points to the fact that they were not intended for writing but for carving. Many stone memorials bear runic inscriptions and it is likely that the earliest alphabets were inscribed on to pieces of wood, stone or bark. There are many different varieties of runic writing, but the most widely used runic alphabet is the Early Germanic or Elder Futhark. The word "futhark" refers to the first six runic letters f, u, th, a, r and k, just as our word "alphabet" refers to the first two letters of the Greek alphabet, Alpha (or a) and Beta (or b). The Elder Futhark has 24 letters and some scholars believe it was probably in existence as early as the 2nd century BC. Traditionally, it is divided into three "families", or aetts, of eight runes each, which were named for the Norse gods Freyr, Hagal and Tyr.

In the ancient runic alphabet, each inscription (also known as a glyph) possessed a signifying sound and a meaningful name. Over time, they have also become associated with particular trees, colours, herbs and gemstones.

A rune bag is essential for storing your runes, and it is also important that you keep them cleansed and that no one else uses them, as they are imbued with your unique energy.

Care of your runes

The following guidelines will help you take care of your runes:

- cleanse them regularly with spring water, salt or by smudging
- to empower your runes, leave them outside for 24 hours to let the sun and moonlight energize them
- keep them in a special bag or box, and do not lend them to anyone

A guide to the runes

There are 24 rune symbols, each of which stands for a different letter of the Early Germanic, or Elder Futhark, alphabet. Each of these inscriptions has a divinatory meaning, as well as tree, colour, herb and gemstone associations.

Sign	Name	Meaning	Divinatory meaning	Tree	Colour	Herb/plant	Gemstone
ᚠ	Feoh	Cattle	Spiritual richness	Elder	Light red	Nettle	Moss agate
ᚢ	Ur	Auroch (recently extinct cattle)	Strength in time of change	Birch	Dark green	Sphagnum moss	Carbuncle
ᚦ	Thorn	Thorn	Contemplation before action	Thorn/oak	Bright red	Houseleek	Sapphire
ᚬ	Ansur	A mouth	Messages and new opportunities	Ash	Dark blue	Fly agaric	Emerald
ᚱ	Rad	A cartwheel	The wheel of life, a journey or quest	Oak	Bright red	Mugwort	Chrysoprase
ᚲ	Ken	A torch	Enlightenment and inspiration	Pine	Light red	Cowslip	Bloodstone
ᚷ	Geofu	A gift	A spiritual gift, love and partnership	Ash/elm	Deep blue	Heartsease	Opal
ᚹ	Wynn	Happiness	Success and achievement; balance	Ash	Yellow	Flax	Diamond
ᚺ	Hagall	Hail	Strength to face a challenge	Ash/yew	Light blue	Lily-of-the-valley	Onyx
ᚾ	Nied	Need	Everything is as it should be; your needs are met	Beech	Black	Bistort	Lapis lazuli
ᛁ	Is	Ice	Standstill, preparation before moving on	Alder	Black	Henbane	Cat's eye
ᛃ	Jara	Harvest	Harvest, reward for past effort	Oak	Light blue	Rosemary	Cornelian
ᛇ	Eoh	A yew tree	Transformation; letting go, endings ready for beginnings	Yew	Dark blue	Mandrake	Topaz
ᛈ	Peorth	A dice cup	Choice, taking charge	Beech	Black	Aconite	Aquamarine
ᛉ	Elhaz	An elk	Protection within	Yew	Gold	Angelica	Amethyst
ᛋ	Sigel	The sun	Good fortune	Juniper	White/silver	Mistletoe	Ruby
ᛏ	Tyr	The god Tyr	Initiation	Oak	Bright red	Sage	Coral
ᛒ	Beorc	A birch tree	New beginnings	Birch	Dark green	Lady's mantle	Moonstone
ᛖ	Ehwaz	A horse	Progress	Oak/ash	White	Ragwort	Iceland spar
ᛗ	Mann	A human	Destiny	Holly	Deep red	Madder	Garnet
ᛚ	Lagu	Water, sea	Attunement to creation	Willow	Deep green	Leek	Pearl
ᛜ	Ing	The god Ing	The inner spark	Apple	Yellow	Self-heal	Amber
ᛞ	Daeg	Day	The light	Spruce	Light blue	Clary	Diamond
ᛟ	Othel	A possession	Focus and freedom	Hawthorn	Deep yellow	Clover	Ruby

Consulting the Runes

The runes can be used in a variety of ways. A single rune may be picked to give you guidance for the day ahead or to help clarify a problem or issue. The message of a single rune can help bring you back down to earth when you are losing touch with reality, or reassure you about a course of action you have already decided upon, confirming what you already know. You can also draw a rune to honour significant events, such as birthdays, anniversaries, a wedding, or getting a new job, or to celebrate the changing seasons and festivals throughout the year. The most common issues or questions on which people seek guidance, whether from the runes, Tarot, I Ching or any other divinatory method, tend to fall into categories such as love and relationships, work, home and family, health, and general life guidance.

When using the runes for clarification or guidance, avoid asking "closed" questions that demand a "yes/no" answer. Instead, turn the question into an "issue" statement: for instance, the question "should I change my job" becomes "the issue is my job". The runes will never tell you what to do, but what they can do is comment on a situation, giving you a new perspective.

Keeping your issue in mind, focus your thoughts on it while holding your runes. This will send a vibration of your

The three-rune spread

A line of runes is referred to as a "spread", and a three-rune spread is helpful for giving an overall picture of an issue by placing it in its context. It is like a signpost at a crossroads showing where you are, where you have been, and where you can potentially go if you learn the lessons you need to learn. Focus on the situation and pick out three runes from your bag. Lay them one by one in a row, and read them in turn as follows:

1 The past: this provides background to the situation and shows events that led up to it.
2 The present: the issue as experienced now.
3 The future: the most likely developments given 1 and 2.

thought-forms into the runes, and then you will unconsciously be attracted to pick out the rune that resonates with you. You can pick a rune directly from the bag or box, or else lay them all face down in front of you and then pick the one you are most drawn to. You may notice your body becomes warmer as you are drawn to the right rune; you will just need to trust that whichever one you pick is right for you for this moment.

Advanced Divination

As well as providing insight into everyday situations, the runes can also be used to give deeper insight to help you on your spiritual path. The following spread is based on the World Tree and is designed to act as a guide to the next stage of your spiritual journey. Similar to the Tree of Life, the World Tree is one of the very oldest and most universal symbols in the world. Known as Yggdrasil in the Norse tradition, its roots are said to connect to the underworld, home nature spirits and elementals, while its upper branches ascend to the sky and the realm of angels, advanced souls and supernatural entities.

Beginning at the base of the tree and working upwards and from left to right, lay the runes out in the correct positions,

Rather than picking the runes one by one from the bag, you might prefer to spread them all out in front of you and then pick the one you are most drawn to.

For guidance for the day ahead, simply pick one rune from the bag.

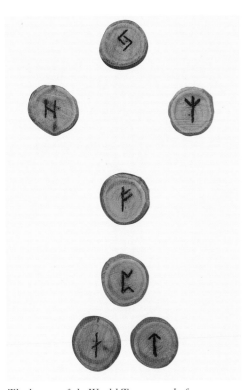

The layout of the World Tree spread of runes.

Working with a partner to read runes will help you to work out their meaning.

asking the following questions of the runes as you pick each one:

1 *What do I need to learn?*
2 *What will challenge me?*
3 *What is my guiding rune?*
4 *What power will help me?*
5 *What comes to warn me?*
6 *What do I need to let go of?*
7 *What will be the outcome of learning this lesson?*

INTERPRETING THE RUNES

The meaning of a particular rune may change depending on whether it is picked upright or upside down (reversed). This is largely a question of individual preference, and there are many books available with more detailed meanings for each of the runes, including upright and reversed meanings. However, as with any other method of divination, to become adept at interpretation you need to train your intuition. This is the connection to your higher self, the part of your being that knows everything, including your purpose in life and how it can best be achieved. Meditation is one of the best ways for training intuition.

At the beginning of each day, pick out a rune and sit with it quietly in meditation for ten minutes or so. As you go through the day, reflect on its symbol and notice any particular themes or patterns to your day; at the end of the day, you can check the rune's official meaning and see if it relates to your experience. When checking the rune's official meaning, pay attention to any particular passages or words that seem to jump out at you, as these will be the ones that have the most relevance for you at this time. When we look up a meaning, a lot of what is said doesn't seem to apply, but then suddenly we will come across something that strikes a chord and that seems to speak to us directly. This is when divination is at its most powerful.

Creating your own rune set

If you want to get to know the runes, a good way of doing this is by making your own set. The two materials from which runes are commonly made are wood and stone, although other materials such as crystals, glass beads or clay can also be used. If you are using stones, you will need to collect 24 of a similar size. Some of the best stones for rune making can be found on beaches and in streambeds; remember to leave behind an offering in thanks for what you are taking.

For stones: using a fine paintbrush and an acrylic paint in your chosen colour (preferably a neutral, earthtoned shade), paint the runic inscriptions on each stone. When the paint is dry, apply a coat of varnish over the stones to protect the paint. For wood: you will need a long branch. Ask permission from the tree before you cut it. Use a handsaw to cut the branch into 24 slices. Burn the inscriptions into the runes with a soldering iron. Rub over with beeswax to protect the wood.

Making your own runes makes them personal.

DOWSING

Everyone has the ability to dowse and it is a skill that every witch and magician should hone and perfect. Dowsing is essentially the art of asking a "yes/no" question and using the movement of a dowsing device – usually a pendulum or rod – to divine the answer. It is a simple process that connects the rational, intellectual part of ourselves with the intuitive, wise part. It is like a doorway between the mind and spirit, using the body as a threshold. The more respect we bring to our dowsing, the more reliable and effective it will be.

When holding a pendulum, keep your fingers pointed downwards, to allow it to swing freely.

HOW DOWSING WORKS

A genuine need to know is a key factor for dowsing to work well. You ask a clear and unambiguous question in your mind, to which the answer can only be "yes" or "no". The second important step is then being able to let go of the question and any emotional attachment to the answer one way or the other, and waiting with a "detached curiosity", or an open mind, for the answer to come back from your inner self.

The most familiar tools that are used in dowsing are the pendulum and L-rods, although other devices such as Y-rods and "bobbers" are also used. The movement of the dowsing tool occurs involuntarily, in the same way as a yawn or a laugh, without your needing to make it happen. But before dowsing can start, you need to establish your personal basic dowsing responses.

PENDULUM RESPONSES

Before you begin, you need to establish the pendulum motions that will mean "yes" and "no" for you, as these vary from person to person.

1 Sit in a relaxed, upright position and hold your pendulum in a central position just above the height of your knees. Start swinging it in a to-and-fro motion towards and away from you. This is the "neutral" position and indicates that you are ready to start.

2 Now move your hand over your dominant-side knee (right for right-handers, left for left-handers). State clearly to yourself the following words: *Please show me my "yes" response.*

3 Notice what the pendulum does; it may swing in a clockwise or anti-clockwise direction, or from side to side, or even diagonally. Whatever it does, this is your signal for "yes".

4 Take the pendulum back to the neutral position and move your hand to the other knee. Repeat the procedure as in step 2, this time asking for your "no" response. It should be something clearly different to "yes" and will be your signal for "no".

5 Repeat the exercise several times to become confident and familiar with your responses. After a short period of time, your chosen responses will become automatic and spontaneous and you will be able to dowse with confidence.

DOWSING AND HEALTH

There are an infinite number of possible situations in which you can use dowsing, but using it as a tool for information and

Crystal pendulums are widely available and are also very beautiful objects to work with.

Choosing a pendulum

Almost anything that swings freely can be used as a pendulum, but ideally it should be symmetrical and attached to its cord centrally so that it can swing in any direction. Natural materials such as wood, stone, metal or crystal can all work well, but find one that feels right when you pick it up and swing it, or make your own from whatever you feel is appropriate.

With practice, you can learn to detect problems in specific parts of someone's body.

guidance around your health is one of its most valuable uses and also one of the best ways to build up experience and confidence. You can experiment with lists of herbs, vitamins, massage oils, Bach flower remedies or forms of treatment with which you have become familiar, so that you can dowse along the list, picking out things to try in a particular case.

You can also dowse for someone else, but you should always get their permission first. Unless you are very experienced and able to hold them in mind as you dowse, it is a good idea to obtain something from them, such as a

You can use a pendulum for sensing the energies around a person's aura to judge their health.

lock of hair or a ring, to help "link" you to them while you investigate. If they are present, you can ask questions while swinging the pendulum over their hands, or you might feel more confident if they

supply the sample and allow you to work on their problem by yourself. Always be sure that you are dealing with an ailment you can handle, and if either of you are in any doubt, seek medical advice.

Typical dowsing responses

This is the kind of pattern of responses that you might establish:

Anti-clockwise for "no"

Towards and away for "neutral"

Clockwise for "yes"

Diagonal to the left for "no"

Diagonal to the right for "yes"

Dowsing the life-force in food

As well as its nutritional properties, our food carries the "life-force", or vital essence. This is most intensely present when the food is at its freshest and diminishes over time. Food that has high life-force tastes better and gives us more nourishment; we may find that we need to eat less of it. You can dowse over your food to assess its vitality, using a scale of 0–10, with 0 being

absence of life-force, and 10 being the optimum. As you dowse over the food, ask questions such as "is the vitality of this (say what it is) higher than 5? Higher than 8? Does it have a vitality of 10?" and so on to assess the score. You will find that freshly picked fruit and vegetables have the highest score, while packaged foods and ready-meals will be at the lower end of the scale.

DIVINING THE LAND

In magical thinking, etheric energy (known as "chi" in Chinese thought) flows through every energy system, including that of the earth. We can use dowsing to detect energy patterns in nature and to observe the different effects they have on us. We can also use dowsing to repattern chi paths and to bring healing to traumatized environmental energies.

Although you can use your pendulum for dowsing in relation to earth energies, it is often more useful to use another of the basic dowsing tools, the L-rod. So called because of its shape, the L-rod can be constructed from any material, including an ordinary wire coat hanger, cut and bent into shape. You will need a pair of rods, one for each hand. Mostly used for searching for things while the dowser moves around, they can also be used for "yes/no" questions in a sitting or standing position.

L-ROD RESPONSES

To establish your "yes" and "no" responses, stand in a comfortable upright posture, spine straight and shoulders relaxed, and hold the shortest "handle" part of the rods. The rods should be pointing straight out and away from you, parallel with each other. This is the neutral or search position.

Keeping the rods the same distance apart, move them over to the dominant

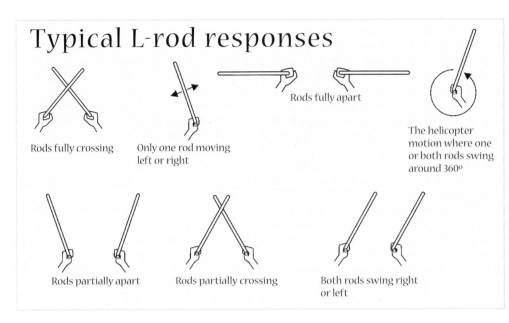

Typical L-rod responses

Rods fully crossing

Only one rod moving left or right

Rods fully apart

The helicopter motion where one or both rods swing around 360°

Rods partially apart

Rods partially crossing

Both rods swing right or left

side of your body and ask to be shown your "yes" response. Return to neutral and repeat on your non-dominant side to be shown "no".

DRAGON ENERGIES

In traditional Chinese thought, the chi paths of the earth's subtle body are known as dragons. Dragons inhabit every landscape. Typically described as having the body of a serpent, the scales of a fish, wings of a bat and claws of a bird, they symbolize the energy that is present in all animals and throughout nature. Sinuous and mercurial by nature, their energies fluctuate and change with sunrise and sunset, with the waxing and waning of the moon, with the passing of the sun through the seasons and with the deep, quiet cycles of planetary time. The West recognizes its own dragons or energy lines, referred to as ley lines, which form more or less rectilinear grids across the earth. Where ley lines cross are points of power. In addition, there are energy paths for each of the elements of Earth, Air, Fire and Water.

SEARCHING FOR DRAGONS

Centre and calm yourself and standing comfortably with your rods in their neutral position, say the following:
I wish to dowse for earth energies; is this timely and appropriate?

To establish your own responses, first hold the rods straight out and away from you, parallel with each other; this is neutral.

Saying in your mind, "please show me my response for yes", move the rods over to the dominant side of your body and note the signal.

Go back to neutral, then to the opposite side of your body, asking for the "no" response. Observe the signal. Test the responses several times.

If the response is "yes", ask:
Please show me any energy paths of significance to my health.

Walk forwards at a slow but steady pace. When you reach the first path, your rods may start to split apart as though meeting something solid like a wall. Once they are completely apart you have arrived at an energy line. Conversely, you may find that the rods cross – this is an equally valid "here it is" sign. You can continue to dowse to find out more about the dragon, such as how big or small it is (some lines are very narrow while others are several metres wide). You can also ask if the line is predominantly yin or yang, and find out how strong it is, using a scale of 0–10. The effect of being in a predominantly yin chi path slows us down, rather like a glass of wine or heavy meal. Predominantly yang chi, on the other hand, acts like coffee, stimulating and speeding us up. These effects increase with the intensity of the etheric field, and are more extreme the more strongly the etheric field is polarized to yin or yang.

HEALING TRAUMATIZED ENERGIES

Traumatic changes to the surface of the landscape, such as quarrying or excavation or new construction projects, can create stress and trauma in an otherwise healthy energy field. If the chi has been traumatized it is likely that one or more blocked, stagnant or overly stimulated chi paths runs through the space. Let your dowsing guide you to where to work.

Place your hands where your L-rods indicate and visualize yourself channelling healing energy from the divine source, asking that the etheric field receive whatever healing energy that it needs in order to regain a state of health and balance.

At the end of each session, visualize yourself filled with golden light and give thanks for the healing that has occurred.

Dowse intermittently to see if the process is complete. It may take several healing sessions over a period of days, weeks, or even months, the earth's cycles of time being much slower than those of a person.

Repatterning energies

If you find a chi path that is detrimental to your health, you can ask the spirit of place that the energy be repatterned. Remember that the energy itself is neither good nor bad, and that something that may be harmful to us, can be helpful to other species. Repatterning may take hours or days, but once you have begun the process you don't need to stay. You can return to the place every few hours and check with your dowsing to find out when it is complete. You can use a pendulum to do this exercise.

1 Hold your pendulum and begin by checking with the spirit of place if it is timely and appropriate to communicate with it. If the answer is "Yes", continue by saying:
I wish to spend time in this space and need the energy here to be supportive to my health. Are you willing to repattern the energy here to be supportive of my health?
If the spirit of place is not willing, then you might want to ask it to suggest an alternative place where you can work.

2 If the spirit is both willing and able, make a special request almost like a prayer. You may also visualize golden light filling the entire space as you make your request:
I request that the energy in this space be repatterned at this time to be supportive of human health at every level, and that it may remain so for as long as may be the divine will.

3 Once your dowsing indicates that the repatterning has occurred, give thanks to the spirit of place by leaving an offering.

L-rods are probably the most popular and widely used tools for water dowsing.

SCRYING

From the earliest times, people have seen supernatural images in shiny surfaces such as a pool of dark water, a black stone, a concave mirror or a crystal ball set against black velvet. In Tibet, seers sometimes gaze at a wetted thumbnail. The process is called "scrying", which means "perceiving", and it is an art that many magicians aim to master as a way of answering questions about the future. To be able to scry you need to be able to switch off from the distractions of everyday life and enter an altered state of consciousness. It uses the same kind of inner vision as dreams, so you may find that by improving dream recall, scrying gets easier, or conversely if you learn how to scry you will remember your dreams.

An ordinary picture frame can be turned into a scrying vessel by placing a piece of black paper behind the glass.

FINDING YOUR RELAXED STATE

To improve your success at scrying, it is necessary to be able to enter a deeply relaxed state, so performing this preparatory exercise might help.

Find a time and place where you won't be disturbed for at least half an hour. You will need an upright chair and a notebook and pen for keeping a record – you may wish to use your Book of Shadows or else create another magical diary which you keep for recording your work with dreams and/or visions.

1 Sit with your feet flat on the floor or on a thick book so that your knees are at a right angle, and find a comfortable relaxed position. Close your eyes.

2 Breathe out fully and then, counting at your own speed, breathe in for a count of four. Hold your breath for a count of four, breathe out for a count of four, then hold your breath out for another count of four.

3 Repeat this entire breathing cycle at least 10 times. If you lose count, it will be necessary to start again from the beginning. You may find this pattern difficult, in which case you can try a slower 10–5–10–5. You can count quickly or slowly or, if you can feel your pulse while sitting in a relaxed position, count that.

4 Focus all your mental attention on breathing slowly and rhythmically, and relaxing physically. Gradually, you will find that this helps you to become calm and focused.

5 Bring your attention to the scrying glass, and gently open your eyes. You are in your relaxed state and ready to begin scrying.

Scrying within a magic circle of candles will protect you from harmful or negative visions.

Steps to scrying

You can learn to develop your ability to "see" by following these steps.

1 Allow yourself to sink into a relaxed state. Open your eyes to regard the glass, crystal, sphere or other "speculum".

2 Look within the glass, ignoring any reflections or points of light on its surface. Sink within it, forming the question in your mind. In a while, you will find that the glass seems to cloud over, or become dim. Through the mist, a dark patch may appear.

3 You might find yourself sinking into this dark patch, then pictures, signs, numbers, words or other symbols may appear before you. This will probably not happen in the first experiments you perform but will come with practice.

4 Continue for a number of regular sessions and you will gradually master this ancient and very valuable skill.

LEARNING TO SCRY

Scrying is not a skill that you can learn automatically. Like riding a bicycle or swimming, there is a knack to it and it takes time, practice and concentration. A common mistake in beginners is that they try too hard, which only creates tension. Rather relax, and you will see words, images, still pictures or actions flitting through your mind's eye, rather like watching a film. The trick is not trying to hold on to what you see, but to let it go.

After a while, you will find that the film slows down and the images or non-visual concepts remain visible long enough for you to study them. Like remembering dreams, you may need to tell yourself what is happening in order to fix it in your longer-term memory, but it does get easier with practice. You may find that it helps to cast a circle around yourself and the table with the scrying vessel (known as the "speculum") on it, or that to light a candle and some sweet incense will bring on a more psychically open state of mind. Really it is a matter for patient experimentation to see what works best.

TRUST WHAT YOU SEE

In order for scrying to work, there must be no distracting reflections on the surface of the object, so the ambient light where you are working should be soft and diffuse. If a vision is to emerge, the mind and body need to be stilled and calmed by a period of quiet contemplation, with the eyes closed so that residual images fade from the retina.

Once you feel you have reached the right state of mind you are ready to begin to gaze into your scrying object. Gazing into the speculum induces a trance-like state and allows ideas to emerge from the unconscious mind, as they do in dreams. The first impression may be of a mist, which eventually darkens and resolves into colours, shapes, symbols or complete images. Like the images seen in dreams, these are likely to relate to deep-seated issues and offer information that the conscious mind does not have access to. They may seem inexplicable at first, but become relevant later.

Making your own scrying vessel

Real crystal balls are difficult and expensive to obtain, so before you decide whether to get one you can make your own scrying vessel. Use black enamel spray paint to coat the outside of a balloon-shaped wine glass. You may need several coats. Alternatively try scrying in a clear glass bowl of water. You can also make a simple mirror by painting the glass of a picture frame, or as follows, using a sheet of black paper.

1 You will need a picture frame, a piece of black paper and a pair of scissors. Take the frame apart and cut out a piece of black paper to fit. Place the paper in the frame behind the glass and put the frame back together again.

2 Once the frame is properly secured, polish the glass thoroughly with a soft cloth. Your scrying glass is now ready to use.

Crystal balls are closely associated with magical arts, especially the ability to see into the future.

Interpreting visions

Although visions in a scrying vessel can only be interpreted by the individual who sees them, like the symbols perceived in dreams they sometimes seem to represent archetypes that have universal significance. Some visions are simply a mist of colour.

White: good fortune

Yellow: obstacles to come

Orange: troubled emotions, anger

Red: danger

Blue: business success

Green: health and happiness

Grey/dark: misfortune

Rising clouds: affirmative

Sinking clouds: negative

Far-off visions: the distant past or future

Foreground visions: the present or near future

DEVELOPING THE SUPER SENSES

From ancient times, every worker of magic has made use of psychic abilities of one kind or another. Some of these are immediately available, inherited perhaps as a gift from the gods, from ancestors, or from past lives; others may be less accessible, but can be developed just like any other skill. Most magical training is aimed at working with these "super senses", but it will require commitment, dedication and hard work.

The ability to enter an altered state at will is probably the most important key to developing psychic abilities. Meditation and creative visualization

are two of the most powerful tools in this respect and this chapter begins with a variety of techniques designed to develop these skills. This is followed by information on psychic training using games and experiments to develop telepathy and intuition, as well as how to sense auras and chakras. Astral travel and dreamworlds – including information on dream control and lucid dreaming – are also included, as well as how to journey to the otherworld and inner planes. Through psychic powers it is possible to meet spirit guides, teachers and angelic beings, while exploring past lives can provide many valuable insights into your current situation here on the Earth plane.

MEDITATION

Psychic ability may be seen as the gift of the Goddess, the great Earth Mother. A heightened sensitivity to the unseen relies on a strong intuitive sense that we can develop through cultivating a strong relationship with the Goddess or "feminine" aspect of ourselves. For men and women alike, this means learning to trust our body sensations and having a "felt sense" that is accurate and reliable. To be able to do this we need to be as relaxed and free in body, mind and spirit as possible. Meditation is one of the best ways of achieving this; it helps to ground and centre us in the root of our being and opens up the doorway to the otherworld.

Burning white sage before you begin to meditate clears the head and promotes insight.

THE POWER OF MEDITATION

Many ancient religions and many cultures in both East and West have practised the art of meditation, and today we have a huge variety of techniques at our disposal – some active, some passive. What is important is to find a method that works for you and to practise it regularly; over time, you will be able to "switch off" from everyday concerns and enter an altered state more readily, while along the way you will be developing an increased sensitivity, heightened perception and intuitive awareness.

Essentially, meditation is the quality of awareness that we bring to an act. It is about raising our levels of consciousness so that we are aware of our activity and of any thoughts and emotions that we are experiencing in the moment as we do it. In which case, any act can become a meditation; if you enjoy walking for instance, you can make this activity your meditation. Instead of hurriedly rushing to be somewhere, slow down and take the time to feel your feet connect with the earth as you take each step. If you enjoy dancing or jogging, you can also make this your meditation, allowing yourself to relax ever more deeply into your body's natural rhythm and movement.

Active meditations such as these are particularly helpful when you are feeling stressed and find it difficult to sit still

Meditation is the best gateway to inner wisdom, opening you up to previously unknown dimensions.

Going in

Meditation is a way of "going in" to meet yourself. As everyday concerns begin to fade and your conscious mind quietens, the deeper more subtle senses begin to awake and inform your conscious awareness. Unless you can withdraw from the everyday world for a few minutes each day, there is no way that these inner forces can develop.

The three "S's" for meditation

Follow this checklist of the 'three S's' – Stillness, Silence and Sensitivity – to help make meditation easier.

Stillness. If you sit relaxed and completely still, this helps you to drift into the poised state of awareness where inner material can begin to flow. As soon as you start to wriggle about, or become aware that you are not comfortable, you will break the stream of concentration.

Silence. Don't be tempted to use background music to blot out noises in the environment. It is far better to find a quiet time of day and learn to create inner silence. This matters because as well as seeing images many people also hear sounds, and any music will make this much harder. The more you focus inward and allow any images or feelings to surface, the less you will be distracted.

Sensitivity. You need to listen, watch and perceive whatever images, sounds, symbols or other sensations start to occur in your mind. These will be vague and fleeting to begin with, but the more physically and mentally still you become, and the quieter the background noises are, the sharper your own awareness will be.

breath to relax a little more deeply. Many meditation practices involve working with the breath in a sitting or lying down position, as the mind and body can most easily unwind in these positions.

ACTIVE AND PASSIVE MEDITATION

Active meditations can include dance, walking, jogging or any day-to-day activity, providing it is performed with conscious awareness. With a modern sedentary lifestyle, there are many advantages of using active meditation methods. They help to burn off excess energy, which if it is not used, has a tendency to produce an imbalance in the mental body, making it much harder to quieten the mind. They also help to move energy through the body's subtle energy system. Passive meditations usually involve sitting or lying down in a comfortable position and letting go of tensions held in the mind or body through focusing on the breath.

EMBRACING DARKNESS

From a seed that sprouts in the soil to a child growing in the womb, all life begins in the dark. The darkness is a place of mystery and tremendous power; it is the realm of the Goddess and is associated with the "feminine" creative force. In modern society, we have become afraid of darkness and have created many sources of light to help us escape from it; but being able to embrace darkness is a necessary part of life. It is also essential if we are to develop as a worker of magic and to feel comfortable entering the otherworld, itself a place of mystery.

A DARKNESS MEDITATION

This guided meditation is a good way of connecting with the beneficial power of darkness; it may be a little tricky to master at first, but with practice it does get easier. It is best done in the evening.

1 Sit in a relaxed, upright position in a darkened room. The darker it is, the better, with no chinks of light coming in through the curtains or under the door. Breathe gently and, keeping your eyes open, stare into the blackness. Feeling at ease, imagine the darkness

Using the flame of a candle to help your mind to focus is a good meditation technique.

that is all around you entering your open eyes. It should give you a deep, soothing feeling.

2 At this point, you may like to close your eyes and imagine yourself disappearing into the darkness, just as a shooting star disappears in the rich dark of the night sky. Feel yourself being absorbed, so that just for this moment in time, you don't have to be or do anything. Allow yourself to fully experience the deep relaxation of letting go.

3 Come out of the meditation slowly, lighting a candle to allow your eyes to get used to the light, before you turn on electric light or allow daylight in.

4 As you go about your usual activities following the meditation, imagine that you are carrying a patch of this darkness within you; silent, deep and relaxed. If you do the darkness meditation before bed, try and carry this patch of dark silence with you into sleep.

and relax; they help to "burn off" your outer layers of energy and bring you back into contact with your inner self.

LETTING GO

Meditation teaches us to relax and let go of everyday concerns as we move into deeper levels of our being. It is from these deeper places in ourselves that we are able to experience our connection with the universe; the more deeply we can let go, the more powerful our experience of the hidden realm and cosmic oneness. Many meditation techniques are based on passive "non-doing" states. Bringing awareness to the breath is a good way of bringing attention into the here and now, using each out

THE MIND'S EYE

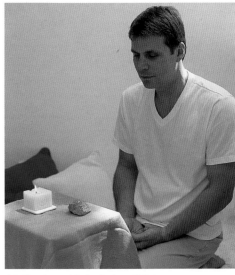

Meditating with lapis lazuli helps promote a lively silence, and aids thought processes.

Perhaps the most powerful tool of any witch or magician is their mind. It is estimated that we use only a tiny percentage of our mental powers, leaving vast reservoirs untapped. Learning to train and use the mind is one of the most basic yet far-reaching skills of any magic worker. The ability to exert control over our thoughts and to direct the focus of our attention is a necessary prerequisite for successful magic; it is also how we can develop the extraordinary powers of the mind to travel in space and time. One of the best ways of doing this is through the faculty of imagination. This is because the imagination deals in pictures, not words, and can influence the unconscious mind on a much deeper level.

THE IMAGINATION

The words imagination and magic share the same root. To imagine is to allow our thoughts to wander freely and conjure up pictures or concepts that are not actually present but seen in the mind's eye as though they are – and the more vivid our imagination, the more real these things seem. Imagination can be seen as the ability of the mind to be creative or resourceful. William Wordsworth, the eighteenth-century English poet, described it as "another name for absolute power and clearest insight".

A vivid imagination, directed by magical training, is the most effective tool we have for changing the world from within, yet for most of us it is something that has lain dormant since childhood. Creative visualization is a way of accessing and training the imagination and beginning to harness its power.

Using creative visualization

Creative visualization can be used in many areas of life, including personal relationships and health and business situations, as well as to improve memory, overcome problems and counter negative thinking. It is also one of the most powerful tools for developing psychic abilities.

A grounding visualization is helpful whenever you feel unconnected to reality, or to the natural world. Sit in front of a green candle on a wooden table to represent the earth.

CREATIVE VISUALIZATION

Essentially, creative visualization uses the power of the mind to consciously create pictures at will. For instance, if you are sick, you could use creative visualization to imagine or see yourself healthy and well; this is much more effective than simply using positive thinking, although accompanying a visualization with a positive thought or affirmation increases its power. Techniques similar to creative visualization have been used for centuries in some parts of the world to heal or prevent disease, although it can be used for any aspect of life.

For instance, creative visualization is a good technique to use for grounding and protection. When developing your mental powers it is particularly important to take care of yourself. Being grounded (or "earthed") is essential; a lack of grounding makes you unable to channel higher energies successfully. You can become overwhelmed by extra-sensory perceptions and get swept away. Similarly it is also a good idea to learn how to protect yourself so that you don't become drained or tired, or else vulnerable to negative energies.

GROUNDING VISUALIZATION

Practise the following grounding visualization before undertaking any work on the mental plane. It will help to connect you with the natural world and to focus, stabilize and renew your positive energies. To do it, you will need a green candle and a dark stone, such as black onyx or smoky quartz.

1 Light the candle and sit on the floor in front of it, or else sit on a chair with your feet on the ground. This is to connect you with the earth. Take the stone in both hands.

2 Breathing slowly and deeply, visualize the roots of a tree gradually growing down into the earth. Think of the strength of numerous small roots, locking themselves into the fertile soil, anchoring the tree firmly and working silently down towards the earth's core. See yourself connecting with the earth.

Holding a grounding stone can reduce feelings of confusion and anxiety.

3 Concentrate on your out-breaths and with each one, feel the energy flowing downward through your body into the ground. You can also see it as a stream of light, passing through you and "earthing" through the soles of your feet. Become aware of the constant, sustaining strength that lies beneath you, supporting you.

4 Now on each in-breath, feel the earth's strength flowing back into you. Picture it as a green energy flowing up through the roots of the tree into the trunk and branches that is your body. Visualize its power flowing into you until you feel calm and centred. When you feel you have come to the end of the visualization, release the stone.

Stones for grounding

Black onyx: protection against negative energy, good for emotional stability; encourages connection to material goals and their achievement

Black tourmaline: grounding and protective, absorbs negativity.

Haematite: banishes fuzziness and aids concentration, memory and self-discipline; self-healing

Jet: grounding, earth power; wards off nightmares and avoids ill-health

Obsidian: very powerful grounding crystal; dissolves anger and fear; snowflake obsidian has a softer effect, restores balance and clarity

Smoky quartz: lightly grounding and balancing, counteracts hyperactivity, fosters self-acceptance and awareness of divine protection

PSYCHIC TRAINING

Y ou may already have found that your magical interests have led to your getting "hunches" about doing, or not doing, certain things, or that hints and clues are found in dreams, or that you actually perceive future events clearly in meditations or during divination sessions. Gradually, these psychic impressions will become clearer and easier to interpret, especially if you are able to devote some time to learning which skills you already have, and which need to be rehearsed. There are many simple techniques that you can practise to train your psychic abilities, but it is important that you work at a level and pace that feels comfortable for you; too much progress too quickly could make you feel overwhelmed by your ability to pick up impressions from the otherworld.

The human mind can be trained to realize its full psychic potential.

PSYCHIC GAMES

Some of the most valuable training techniques are psychic "games" which you can experiment and have fun with. It is worth trying some experiments in extra-sensory perception (ESP), psychokinesis (PK, affecting material objects by "mind power"), and expanding psychic awareness. You and your magical companions, or perhaps a slightly wider group of your friends and family, for example, can get together to try out skills such as telepathy (conveying information from one mind to another), precognition or clairvoyance (guessing which card, for example, will be turned up next), or retrocognition (listing the order of an already shuffled pack of cards).

If you have a pack of ordinary playing cards, you can begin some simple tests. Get someone to spread out the playing cards face down on a table and shuffle them very thoroughly, and then give you the whole deck, face down. You then take this pack and, picking the cards up one at a time, still face down, try to guess, imagine or see what colour each one is. Place each card in turn, still face down, on one of two heaps, representing black and red. If you get stuck with some cards, make another heap and go back to them at the end. When you have reached the end of the pack, turn over the heaps and see what has happened. You might

be surprised how many you get right first go! Let a companion have a turn and see if they do better or worse.

ZENER CARDS

To test a psychic's powers of telepathy, a popular research tool used by parapsychologists is a pack of "zener cards". Designed in the 1920s by JB

Rhine, a Harvard biologist, each pack consists of 25 cards depicting five different symbols: a circle, a cross, a square, a five-pointed star and three wavy lines. Each symbol appears on five cards, and is boldly printed against a

Use packs of cards to work on your psychic skills. Innate powers of telepathy, precognition and retrocognition can all be improved on with practice and training.

white or plain-coloured background. In a typical experiment, the cards are shuffled and turned over one by one by a "sender", who then concentrates on the image for a minute or so while the "percipient" (the person who is trying to pick up the image telepathically) tries to identify each card by drawing or saying whichever image comes into his or her head. Sometimes the sender and the percipient are in separate buildings, and the test is repeated several times, with the deck shuffled each time, to reduce the possibility of a chance good result. If you come across zener cards you might like to try some experiments yourself; alternatively it would be relatively simple to make your own deck.

PSYCHIC TAROT

Another experiment, which may be more interesting to magicians, uses Tarot cards. There are layers of interpretation attached to every Tarot card, which may be contradictory, depending on which of the 500 or so Tarot decks you are using. In other words, your view of the cards may be linked to the symbolism of the card, or to your own or a more traditional interpretation.

Place a pack face down across the floor or a large table and stir them about. The experimenter then picks up a card and, without seeing the picture, tries to name it, or describe the feelings, symbols or meaning of the card to a partner. Then both of you look at the card and see if any of it fits. Often, because the

It is important to discuss your results together, as the images you receive telepathically might not always be identical to what was being transmitted.

experimenter gets immediate feedback, by seeing the card after they have guessed, they will get better, more accurate impressions. This "game" has the added advantage of helping you to form telepathic links with your partner, as well as possibly discovering deeper levels of meaning to the Tarot. You could also try this with runes.

TAKING YOUR SKILLS UP A LEVEL

Later on, you may be able to send each other messages at a distance. For instance, you could agree with a friend that at a certain time you will "send" them a thought form which they should try and "tune in" to. To begin with, think of something relatively straightforward, such as a colour, shape or number, or you could try a feeling, such as calm, upset, happy and so on. With practice, you might be able to make the information more complex. For instance, you could try sending a number and a suit of playing or Tarot cards that would include a message, derived from the interpretation of that card or cards.

Find out what sorts of information you can pass from mind to mind and use your imagination to invent experiments to try. Each will help awaken, strengthen and control your psychic faculties.

PICTURE POSTCARDS

Start making a collection of picture postcards that contain clear images or graphic designs that you can use for telepathic experiments. The sender picks a card and tries to convey the illustration to the receiver in another room, who will attempt to draw or describe what they see.

When you are receiving telepathically, you need to be able to enter a relaxed and meditative state, allowing your mind to empty, so that the message can be clearly seen on the "blank screen" of your mind. Although it is not easy to draw exactly the same picture, receptive people should get some aspect of the design, or indicate the feeling of the sender's mind. For example, if the card showed yachts sailing on a calm sea, with birds flying above, the receiver might draw triangles and say it felt windy, or sunny, or that there was a feeling of swaying, etc. Sometimes the emotion of a picture of lovers, or the scent of a flower, or the speed of racing cars can be sent more easily than the actual shapes, colours or minor details of the design. Another technique is to allow the receiver to try to recognize the target card from a selection of the cards. Record your results and see how you improve.

Psychic experiments

Parapsychologists, working in laboratories with carefully selected subjects and using well-tested methods under strictly controlled conditions, have found that new subjects often score higher than those who have tried, and become bored with, card guessing, or attempts at bending metal. It has also been found that a relaxed frame of mind is a help to 'remote viewing' (astral travel to the magician).

SENSING AURAS

An aura is an emanation of the subtle, non-physical energies that infuse and surround every living thing in creation. In magical thinking, this includes rocks and stones, as well as trees, plants, animals and human beings. An aura is like an invisible extension of the physical form and through psychic development it is possible to be able to see or to sense it. This ability can be used to "read" what is going on for a person on a mental, emotional and spiritual level, and for the purposes of healing and rebalancing energies.

Before you use a pendulum to discover a person's aura, make sure you have established your yes and no responses.

THE THREE LAYERS OF AN AURA

Auras are a form of radiant energy that we can learn to detect. Many psychics see them as a halo of energy that has three distinct layers. These layers extend for about 30 cm (1 ft) from the human body, although the greater a person's spiritual vitality, the bigger their auric field. The inner etheric is easily visible to ordinary eyesight in a dimly lit room as a smoky band outlining the figure, and is seen best against naked flesh. Beyond that is a wider band of the astral health region, seen as faint-coloured filaments, such as you sometimes see around power lines on misty days. Outside that is an even fainter layer, the very fine threads of the emotional aura, which connects to all the people, places and objects with which you have any link.

MEASURING AN AURA

One of the easiest ways of discovering the extent of a person's aura is with a pendulum. Start about 10 m (30 ft) away from them and walk towards them, stopping every pace and testing by asking the question "Does the aura reach here?" and waiting for the "yes/no" response. It is also possible to use your hands to sense an aura. Approach the person very slowly with your hands stretched out, and notice any changes to your body sensations. Your hands may become warm or tingle, or you may "feel" their energy field as a springy "ball" that you can push up against. You will have to trust your intuition.

SEEING AURAS

It is also useful to be able to see auras, and this is a skill that can be learned with patience. Ideally, you should have your subject standing in front of a plain, pale surface and ask them to sway slightly from side to side while you stand about 5 m (15 ft) away, looking at the body's

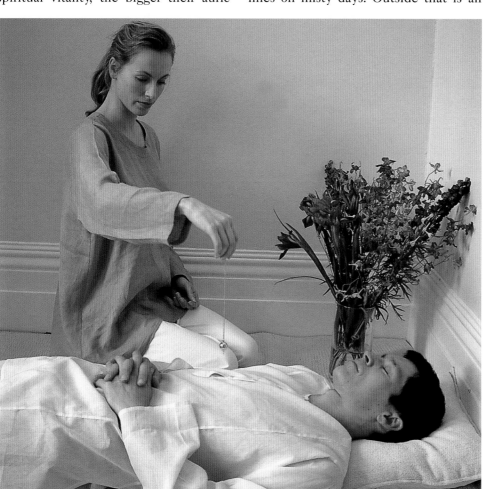

A pendulum is a useful tool to help you sense the condition of a person's aura. You can ask specific questions, as with other kinds of dowsing.

outline. After a while, you will see a light colour that moves as they do. With practice over a number of sessions, you will start to be aware of layers of lighter or deeper tone surrounding them. This is usually a series of bands, starting close to their body with the etheric, which is a dense, pale, smoke-coloured layer a few centimetres wide. Beyond that, stretching some distance, are a number of bands of what you will come to see as varied shades, going all around their outline, and in front of them too. You can try half-closing your eyes so that you are seeing through your eyelashes – some people find this helps. The aura is constructed of rays of light, to get an idea of what it looks like, try squinting at a candle flame. You may well see a kind of radiating rainbow of light around the centre. This is what an aura looks like, and it is a matter of time and practice before you can identify the bands, and eventually the separate colours. Some of these are beyond normal vision and may be hard to name or identify.

INTERPRETING AURAS

There are numerous books on interpreting the colours of auras, as to state of health, mood and so on, but remember that you are also looking through your own aura so the colours are a combination and may seem murky. You can see your own aura by standing naked in front of a mirror in a dimly lit room, and gazing softly at your reflection. The colours of the outer aura will be changing all the time, varying with emotion, hunger and temper, as well as our general state of health, and concentration on other people, which will brighten the filaments of auric material by which we are linked. Each individual's aura is different, and interpreting an aura's health is dependent upon the individual and the intuition of the viewer.

It may well be that it is along these delicate threads that the shared thoughts of telepathy flow; when you are psychometrizing an object (sensing its history), the impressions you receive are obtained from the same source.

SENSING CHAKRAS

Within everyone's aura are the chakras, a series of seven energy centres that run right through us. The base, or 1st, chakra is red and centred in the sexual region. It rules raw emotion. Next, is an orange sphere in the belly (the 2nd chakra), dealing with absorption and elimination, both physically and psychically. Above that at the solar plexus is a golden yellow chakra (3rd), our Sun and self centre. In the chest is the emerald green heart chakra (4th), for love and harmony. At the throat is a brilliant blue flower of living light (5th chakra), our power of communication and speech. At the forehead is a violet purple chakra (6th), linking to our intelligence and wisdom. At the top of the head is a brilliant white chakra of light (7th), which connects us to the Creative Spirit, through which spiritual feelings flow in and out.

You can use a pendulum on a partner to detect the vitality of each of their chakras; you can also tune in using your hands, in a similar way, to detecting the auric field.

Psychometry

Literally meaning 'soul measurement', psychometry involves holding a physical object, such as a ring, a sealed letter, or a piece of clothing, and attempting to 'pick up' something of its history and the emotions of those who have handled it (by psychic means). This is because everything we touch is linked to us through our auric field; by tuning in to this, it is possible to 'read' information that relates to an individual's life. One of the most renowned psychics of the twentieth century, Eileen Garrett (1893-1970), is reported to have used psychometry to trace the whereabouts of a missing man by holding a piece of his shirt and tuning in to her impressions.

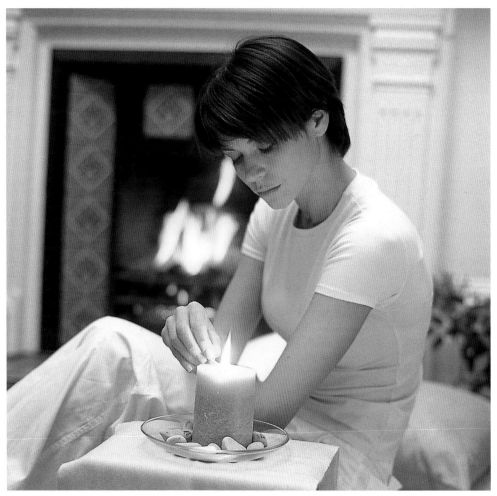

Meditating on a candle flame can help to open your inner vision and make it easier for you to see auras.

ASTRAL TRAVEL

The starry, or astral, plane is thought to be another layer of reality that is separate from the everyday world that we inhabit during our waking lives. Many people believe the astral plane is the realm of dreams, while the astral body, which includes your aura, is thought to be able to leave the physical body and visit other locations. Those who walk the paths of witchcraft and magic teach themselves consciously to enter the astral planes and bring back information or power. Although some dreams may be thought of as astral travel – particularly those that involve flying – being able to travel at will rather than by accident is a skill that can be learned through meditation and visualization. This is also known as astral projection.

It is possible to teach your mind to travel to other worlds, leaving your body behind.

LEAVING THE BODY

Meditation is a doorway to the inner landscapes and guided meditation, creative visualization and pathworking all teach the astral traveller how to shift from the outer, mundane level of awareness to the inner, and return safely with a full awareness of what has been observed. This does take practice, however, and you are unlikely to be able to travel if you do not have a regular meditation practice. Before attempting to travel, you need to get comfortable with moving in and out of your body.

As you enter meditation, visualize yourself splitting into two: in your mind's eye, see the physical you that is sitting in meditation, and your astral or auric body as a shadow or outline, separating from your physical body, but connected to it with an "umbilical cord" of white light. You may start to feel floaty or light-headed (this is why it is important to be well-grounded before attempting this sort of work); you may even find yourself being able to look down on or at your physical body and having what is known as an "out of body" experience.

LEARNING FROM A TEACHER

Out-of-body techniques are probably best learnt from someone who has a lot of experience of this work. Mastering the techniques can take years of practice and you have to have the passion to really want to do it. Some people don't like the feeling of loss of control that goes with out-of-body travel, so it is important to work within your own limits of what feels comfortable and safe for you.

Meditation is the doorway to astral travel. Burning incense will help you to achieve the mental state necessary for your journey.

Concentrating on the flame of a candle will help to focus your mind during meditation.

Flying witches

It is quite possible that the stereotype of a witch flying across the night sky on her broomstick actually came about as a result of reports of mind travel and out-of-body experiences. These in turn are linked with traditional shamanic practices such as shape-shifting and journeying between the worlds.

The inspiration for inner journeys can be provided by a magical companion, who can lead the traveller onwards, and then bring them safely back.

THE COLLECTIVE UNCONSCIOUS

Influenced by Jungian depth psychology, some estericists believe that the astral realms are not outside of us but lie deep within the collective unconscious, the primordial part of the mind that is universal and where archetypal themes and symbols reside. The astral plane, it is argued, is the realm of feelings and emotions and its forms reflect the beliefs of every human being who has ever lived. Hence it is a land of demons and angels, dragons and unicorns, and all the saints and sinners, heavens and hells, and gods and devils of myth and legend.

MAKING AN ASTRAL JOURNEY

Like many of the other aspects of magic, you will need a quiet time and place. If you are intent on going into the astral levels you will also need a companion for basic guidance to share your visions with and help clarify their meaning.

1 Clear a physical and mental space, set up a basic circle and sphere of light around yourself and, having chosen a simple aim, say:
I wish to travel to the astral realms in order to discover….

2 Sit with your companion nearby. Your friend could speak a narrative leading you to the kind of place in which you imagine what you seek would exist. You have to find the landscape, which really already exists on the astral plane. Look on it as another continent or a different dimension of space. Acknowledge that it is real, and that, unlike some images you make, you can't change what you see.

3 Once you have seen the surroundings, which may be sufficient for one day, come back to normal awareness, report to your friend, and close your circle.

4 A second attempt will require a different exercise. Here you need to create your protective circle, but instead of setting off into the other dimension, begin to construct an image of your own body, perhaps

Bilocation

The ability to be in two places at the same time is known as "bilocation". Essentially a double of you (the astral body) can go out into the world and allow you to see what is going on while you remain going about your daily affairs. To do this, you enter a state of deep meditation and envision a filmy image of yourself leaving your body behind. Bilocation is a very advanced technique and usually takes many years of practice before it can be mastered.

dressed in the costume of the astral realm, standing before you, but facing away. In other words, see your own back in front of you. Work on this until you are really able to see it.

5 Once you have built your own figure, you need to transfer your awareness to it, by a kind of mental leap. This immediately puts many people back to themselves, but with gentle effort you can succeed. You then need to transfer to your "astral self" and insert that self into the inner surroundings so that you can meet your hero or Goddess. For this you may need help from your companion, who will describe the setting when you have indicated that you are in your astral body. What you will experience there is completely real but it has a different look or feel to "real life". With practice over a number of short sessions, most people find that they can do this if they don't force it. A few short sessions of half an hour are far better than a prolonged attempt lasting hours.

DREAMWORLDS

To dream is to move beyond the bounds of everyday reality and to enter the dreamworlds. This is a place where anything can happen – a magical world of limitless possibilities, where the dreamer can fly, shape-shift, walk through solid objects or swim in the sun. And, especially while the dream is going on, it is every bit as real as the common reality that we all share in our day-to-day existence. Magical thinking recognizes the validity of these other worlds and even suggests that our everyday world could be the "dreamscape" of some other dimension of reality. Being able to work with dreams is an invaluable skill for workers of magic: it develops intuition, heightens sensitivity to otherworldly experiences, and increases self-awareness and personal power.

Dreamscapes have an otherworldly quality to them, with a special, magical atmosphere.

THE DREAMING TRADITION

Whether or not we can remember our dreams, dreaming is something that we all do every night. Through the ages, workers of magic have always valued dreams and taken them seriously. Dreams have been regarded as messages from the gods and used as oracles to predict the future. They have also been attributed with the power to solve problems, heal sickness and bring spiritual revelation, and shamans and priests, wise women and sages have all acted as dream interpreters.

In magic, a dream is often seen as a way for the spirit self to communicate with the physical body, relaying information in allegorical frames that relate to the dreamer's life and experiences. This has an analogy with modern depth psychology, where dreams are widely believed to contain messages from the unconscious mind; in this context, dreams can be used to work out personal problems as well as a tool for emotional and spiritual growth.

PREPARE TO DREAM

Throughout the ancient world, "dream incubation" was widely practised at holy sites and shrines, many of them dedicated to the gods and goddesses of sleep and dreaming. This was an

Herbs, incense and oils for dreaming

Certain plants are conducive to relaxation, dreams and visions. You can use them fresh or dried, burn them as incense, or vaporize them as essential oils. You could also try making a dream pillow, using a mix of some of your favourite ones.

- Frankincense
- Sandalwood
- Agarwood (aloes)
- Dream herb (zacatechichi)
- Nutmeg
- Valerian
- Hops
- Passion flower

We can nurture the dreaming process through using herbs and oils that prepare body and mind for a restful night's sleep.

intensely ritualistic procedure designed to encourage an especially informative dream from the gods on a variety of issues – from everyday matters to omens and portents for the future. When you want to "incubate" a dream, it is important to put yourself in the right frame of mind before you go to sleep. This means using the evening as a time to relax and let the cares of the day float away as you reconnect with your inner self. Taking a leisurely bath with oils and/or herbs, burning incense, and practising meditation before going to sleep are all helpful.

DREAM RECALL

By their very nature, dreams are elusive and have an annoying habit of slipping away from the wakening mind very easily. Keeping a dream diary is one of the best ways to help with dream recall. Dedicate a special book or folder as your dream journal – you could use your Book of Shadows if you wish – and get into the habit of recording your dreams. Dreams can offer valuable insights into life situations, and keeping a record not only gives you material to work with, but

Record your dreams in a dream diary. You will need to write them down as soon as you wake up, even if that is in the middle of the night.

sends a message to your subconscious mind that you are interested and wish to remember your dreams. Keep the book and a pen by your bed so that you can write the dreams down the moment you wake up, even if this is in the middle of the night. Don't worry about it making sense, and even if you can only remember a fragment, this can be enough to work with.

Dream catchers

The "dream catcher" charm is a traditional Native American Indian device for capturing good, wise dreams and for letting the bad ones pass through it and into the night. It has a single thread that is wound in a spiral from the outside to the centre, symbolizing the journey from the waking world to  the world of dreams. The native Americans believe that their dreaming selves pass through the heart of the dream catcher and return with knowledge of the dreams of their true selves.

Making a dream catcher

Dream catchers are available ready-made but it is also possible to make your own. A dream catcher is a very personal thing and making one gives you plenty of scope to design it in a way that says something about you.

You will need

a thin bendy stick about 60 cm (2 ft) long
twine, such as fishing line, or strong cotton thread
coloured ribbon
knife
beads
feathers

1 Curl the stick into a circle and fasten it with twine wrapped around. Some people like to cover the whole of the wood in ribbon before they start, but it is up to you. Cut off any sharp ends of wood at the join and wrap some ribbon around it.

2 Tie one end of a length of twine on to any point on the circle and thread it across $\frac{1}{4}$ of the

circle. Tie it onto the circle and cut off the long end.

3 Come back towards your starting point and tie another cross-twine across the circle. Repeat this four times until you have four lengths going around the circle.

4 From the centre of each of these tie one twine to each of the other three. This gives you a sort of "cat's cradle" effect. Experiment until you have a pleasing criss-cross of lines resembling a spider's web. An alternative way to do this is to use a single length of twine, but this might take some practice before you succeed.

5 Add a bead in the centre of the web to represent the spider.

6 Finish by decorating the dream catcher with some ribbons hanging from the bottom of the circle. Add some feathers and beads to these downward-hanging ribbons.

INTERPRETING DREAMS

There are many dream dictionaries and interpretative guides to dreams, yet ultimately the best expert on your dreams is you. One way of unlocking the meaning of a dream is to decode its symbolism. Traditionally, certain symbols (such as an animal, a building, fire and so on) are associated with certain meanings, but it is probably best to ask yourself what a particular symbol means for you: dreaming of water, for instance, may mean quite different things to two different people. Another way to start to understand your dreams is to ask yourself how you feel when you first wake up: are you happy or sad, angry or fearful? Notice if this feeling is connected with your dream. You could also ask questions of whoever or whatever is in the dream and let that "part" speak to you.

REPLAYING DREAMS

It is very useful to be able to replay your dream again later when you are relaxed and awake as you may gain fresh insights. You can also interact with dream characters and landscapes to try to find out more information; for instance, you could ask the characters and even the places involved: "Who are you? Why are you here? What are you telling me? Why am I here?" Go with the first answer that comes to mind but don't accept "No". A character may run away, or try to frighten you, but don't be intimidated, follow them – they will lead you to an answer.

Learning to lucid dream

The most important key to learning how to generate lucid dreams is your level of motivation. The second is being adept at recalling your dreams, which comes through practice. However, the following techniques may also be used to encourage lucidity.

pre-sleep suggestion: as you drift into sleep, repeat a request or statement in your mind about becoming lucid in your dreams.

periodic questioning: develop a "critical-reflective attitude" to your state of consciousness while awake, asking yourself "could I be dreaming now?" through the day.

rehearse dreaming: sit down and pretend that you are dreaming. Use your imagination to create a dream.

if this were a dream: several times a day, stop and ask yourself "if this experience were a dream, what would it mean?"

meditation: practice your ability to meditate; people who regularly practise meditation seem to have more lucid dreams.

dream groups: it is possible to join up with other people who are interested in exploring their dreams. People with a regular forum in which to discuss their dreams tend to become regular lucid dreamers.

CHANGING DREAMS

Because all worlds are dreamscapes, the ability to change or direct a dream means that we can decide how we would like events to turn out, rather than letting things "just happen" to us by chance. Usually, the dreams that we want to change are ones that cause fear, pain or anger, and by taking control over them in the dreamworld, we are affirming our strength here, in this physical world.

When changing a dream, don't try to force things to happen, just let your intuition flow and allow your creativity to

One way of becoming more at home in your dreamworld is to replay your dreams when you are awake.

Consider every aspect of your dream, noticing figures, landscapes and any symbols.

Your dreams are about you

Usually the main characters and events in a dream represent various aspects of yourself. For example, disturbing dreams – perhaps involving death or violence of some kind – are not necessarily portents that some harm is about to befall the characters involved. Rather, the injured parties represent aspects of yourself that are being harmed, perhaps by not being allowed their full expression in the waking world, and that harm has a detrimental influence on the whole. By questioning the characters in the dream you can determine what aspects of your personality are trying to communicate with you, such as the child-self or the male/female-self.

If you dream of falling, and wake up before impact, revisit the dream and control its ending.

Many people believe that when you dream, essentially you are dreaming about one person – and that is you.

come to the fore. Remember, anything can happen in a dream, so don't restrict yourself to the logical constraints of everyday life.

CHANGING WHAT OCCURS

To change a dream, you will need to replay it, looking out for where you want to make the changes. For instance, say you have a dream in which you feel powerless, perhaps chasing someone who eludes you. A way of changing that type of dream is actually to catch the person you are pursuing. They may continue to escape when you re-enter the dream, but be persistent and persevere until you reach your goal.

CHANGING YOUR RESPONSE

In a similar way to changing the events, changing your response is another method of taking control. Fear dreams are often recurrent, and many feature being chased or stalked by a menacing presence. This can cause a great deal of anxiety and the dreamer may wake up short of breath and with a pounding heart. A way of taking control in this situation would be to transmute the reaction; instead of being tense and afraid in the dream, be light-hearted and happy. This will help dispel anxiety.

EXTENDING A DREAM

Most of us have experienced dreams that end prematurely when we wake, usually with a fearful start. A good way of changing this type of dream is to allow it to continue and see where it goes. Simply recall the dream and, at the point where you woke up, carry it on using your creative intuition. A typical situation in this type of dream is that the dreamer is falling, which can signify a leap into the unknown. The dream usually ends abruptly just before impact with the ground – but who knows what might happen if the dream were allowed to continue? Perhaps the ground might open up to allow safe passage, or maybe it would be soft and resilient. One way to find out is to give your creative intuition free rein and take that leap.

LUCID DREAMING

The term "lucid dreaming" is used to describe the state of being aware that you are dreaming whilst you are in the dream state. Lucid dreams seem to introduce us to that part of ourselves that creates our dreams. Consequently, learning how to recognize and generate such dreams has enormous magical potential – once we can direct our dreams at will, we are in touch with powerful forces for changing our lives in accordance with our wishes.

JOURNEYING TO OTHER WORLDS

We all have the ability to journey to different worlds, and indeed do so when we dream. As we know from dreams, these otherworlds are places of limitless possibilities, where information is relayed in a format the traveller can relate to. Unlike dreams, however, the journey to another world is undertaken with conscious intent and with a specific goal in mind. You may like to light a candle and cast a magic circle around you before you begin.

PLANNING A JOURNEY

When journeying to another realm, it is important to be open to whatever may happen and to anything you might meet. Trust your intuition, because what first comes to you is the right thing, whatever it may be. Just go with the flow and don't try to force anything. Remember that you have control over what you can accomplish in this otherworld that you travel to and don't be inhibited by fear. Be creative in circumventing problems and challenges that may arise.

As with physical travel in this world, if you prepare yourself properly before a journey, things will go more smoothly and it will be a more fruitful experience.

PREPARING FOR A JOURNEY

This simple ritual helps to prepare you for any kind of journey by centring you and focusing your attention on the journey you are about to undertake.

1 Gather your tools together (these may include musical equipment and an appropriate piece of music, incenses, oils or candles) and create a

When you are preparing for a journey you need to focus your attention before you begin.

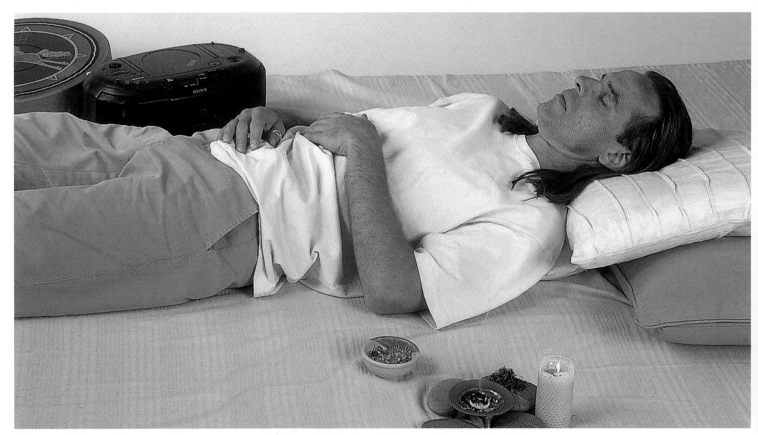

Before you begin your journey make sure you are comfortable and relaxed, and that you will not be disturbed.

comfortable place where you feel relaxed and safe from disturbance. Light a candle for inner illumination and contemplate it quietly for a while.

2 Smudge yourself, the tools and your surroundings. Make an offering to whichever spirits, gods or goddesses or angelic beings you are working with and voice your intent:
I call on (say the name) to assist me in this journey to (state reason of journey) and I make this offering in honour of you and in gratitude for your aid.

3 When you are ready, sit or lie comfortably and breathe deeply to get relaxed. Start the music if you are using it, and take some deep, regular breaths as your journey begins.

JOURNEY TO THE HALL OF THE GODS

Here is an inner journey to a place that is peaceful, powerful and magical, and where it is easy to sink into an altered state of awareness to commune with the gods. Make sure you will not be disturbed for about half an hour and get into a meditative frame of mind. If possible, record the narrative on tape, pausing after every sentence to allow the images to build up, or get a friend to read it to you, or go through it a number of times until you can recall the various stages. Allow the images to become as real as possible. You are creating the pictures partly from memory or imagination, and partly because they are real in another realm or dimension.

1 Sit upright, close your eyes and concentrate on your breathing. Allow it to slow down and become deeper.

2 Begin to build up a picture of an elaborate doorway; see the frame and the details of the closed door. What is it made of? What does it feel like? Does it open? This is the door from your world to the realm of the gods. There may be a guardian who is there to ask who you are and why you wish to go through, or ask for a password or token. You will have to find the answers.

You might like to perform your dream journeys within a magic circle, so that you benefit from the protective energy field that no hostile or negative forces can penetrate.

3 After a few moments, as you continue to relax and make the experience deeper, you will find that the door can be opened. At first a great light seems to be shining through the doorway, and you stand on the threshold while your inner vision adjusts.

4 The light dims so that you can look into the place beyond, and what you see is a glorious hall, built of golden stone. Upon the walls are paintings or hangings picked out in bright colours. You step forward on to a paved floor covered in mosaics.

5 Everything you see is on a grand scale. The ceiling is high above but that too is painted and gilded, and everything is beautiful. To one side of the room there is a platform reached by several

steps covered with marvellous brocade, and on the dais is a throne, carved and covered in gold. Upon it you start to make out a figure that is awe-inspiring but also approachable.

6 You move towards the steps and try to make out the face of the figure seated above you. This is the deity you have come to meet. Take as long as you need with them, and when you have had your audience, give thanks, even if the advice is not immediately clear, and act with respect.

7 Allow the image of the great hall to fade, so that you see again the door and threshold. The light dims and gently you return to your own place. Come back to normal awareness slowly, allowing yourself to recall every detail.

SHAMANIC JOURNEYING

The ability to journey to otherworlds is a traditional shamanic practice. It is a very powerful way to gain insights into problems, to look for healing, to seek allies or just to relax. When you journey, you enter a different world. It is essentially one that you create and guide yourself through, although your conscious self relinquishes control to your spirit. Before starting a journey, make sure you are in a place where you feel safe and won't be disturbed.

THE DRUM

Traditionally, a drum is used in shamanic journeying and it is good to have someone drum for you, as a regular rhythm of around 200 beats per minute helps you achieve the focus needed for the opening of a gateway. It is good to build up the rhythm gradually to allow the traveller to become acclimatized.

At first it is best to journey for a set time of around five minutes. At the end of this period the drummer can initiate the return with a call-back signal – say, four one-second beats followed by some very rapid drumming. With experience, the drummer will be able to use their intuition to tell when the journey is complete. Making a drum tape for journeying can also be very useful, as you can record several sessions of various lengths and incorporate your own call-back signal.

JOURNEY TO MEET A POWER ANIMAL

A power animal is your own personal spirit ally which takes the form of an animal. Meeting a power animal is a useful journey to start with because the animal can accompany you on future adventures and give you guidance, wisdom and protection. How to do this is described in the section on Animal Totems. This is not a deep journey but it does expand your awareness, taking you to the edge of your sacred space, where it borders the realms of other spirits. The

Entrances to the upperworld

The way into the upperworld could be:
- A gap in the sky which can be reached by flying or leaping
- A cave mouth high up a cliff that you need to scale
- A tall tree to climb
- A mountain that pierces a cloud
- A flight of stairs
- A ladder

animal you find could be anything, and it may not be what you were expecting, but once you have found each other you should spend some time together on subsequent journeys. Be aware of the love it has for you. Remember, the greater the detail the more real it will seem. If it feels appropriate, transform yourself into the same animal and run, fly or swim. Above all, have some fun.

When you have returned from your journey, go over it in your mind or, better still, write it down to help fix the details. This will aid you in future travels and make it easier to contact the animal.

JOURNEYING TO OTHERWORLDS

Deeper journeys to otherworlds require going beyond your sacred space. The otherworlds that shamans journey to are many and varied and can encompass any number of features, because each is a construct of the shaman who enters it. Essentially though, otherworlds are confined to two realms and when you journey from your sacred space you can travel downwards to the underworld or upwards to the upperworld.

The drum plays a very important part in Shamanic rituals. If you are working alone it is a good idea to make a drumming tape for your journeys.

Entrances to the underworld

The way into the underworld could be through any of the following openings:

- A cave or crevice in the side of a rockface
- A recess or a knothole in a tree
- An animal's burrow in a bank
- A wormhole
- A well
- A doorway or gate
- A waterfall or stream

When you are journeying for another person, spend some time tuning in to your partner's mind.

THE UNDERWORLD

Most shamanic journeys involve going to the underworld, which is not comparable with the hell of Christianity and other faiths, but represents the inner recesses of the traveller; you could also think of it as the deepest recesses of the unconscious mind. It is not a sinister place but a place of challenge and adventure. A shaman enters it to seek solutions and understanding. The challenges you might encounter are all manifestations of your own fears and problems. By confronting them and finding solutions in the underworld you are facing them within yourself and allowing your spirit to communicate the solutions to your conscious self. Because you are journeying deep within yourself, you are seeking an entrance that will lead downwards and in. Remember, to gain entry you can transform yourself to any size and shape required.

THE UPPERWORLD

Associated with the higher self or the soul, the upperworld is the place to go to for inspiration and communion with other spirits. Whereas the underworld is about confronting your inner fears, the upperworld is more concerned with seeking assistance from others, by meeting other spirits on an equal basis and sharing knowledge with them.

This realm is very light and tranquil, with a feeling of limitless space that stretches away forever. Because it is related to the higher self, it is reached by going upwards. As with a journey to the underworld, it is good to have some structure to follow to help maintain your focus. Because going upwards relates to the soul, a good focus to have is to connect with your higher self. This part of your being is calm and all-knowing. It is dissociated from the emotions that have such a strong influence on the physical, and can therefore give counsel with a dispassionate objectivity that will cut to the heart of a problem.

JOURNEYING FOR OTHERS

Sometimes a shaman may be required to journey to the upperworld or underworld on behalf of another, for purposes of healing or to seek the answer to a question. The principle is always the same: go with a specific aim in mind and be open to what befalls you on the way to your goal. The meaning of the tests and solutions might not be immediately apparent, but when you describe your experiences to your partner, they may understand the symbolism in ways that you did not.

Journeying on behalf of another person is mutually beneficial, and can form a close bond between the people involved. When you are doing this, take some time to develop a level of empathy with your partner by sitting quietly for ten minutes, holding hands and feeling each other's energy.

INNER GUIDES

The occult arts have always recognized the reality of the unseen forces that may help and heal, instruct and guide. Magicians and witches do not usually call up the spirits of the dead, accepting, on the whole, that the immortal human spirit needs to rest and assess its past life before being brought back into incarnation. Although there are discarnate sources of knowledge that may be contacted through magical applications of some of the spiritualists' methods, magicians and witches generally prefer to use their own ways to receive information from hidden masters or inner guides.

The one-eyed god Odin, leader of the Wild Hunt, had a central role in Nordic mythology.

MEETING INNER TEACHERS
Magicians and witches may have the ability to talk to teachers of wisdom from the past, or their own ancestors, or the people who founded their magical tradition. This can be done by creating an inner journey to the place in which these wise beings would dwell, and going there to hear what they have to say. Throughout, the modern magic worker is in control and able to terminate the experience if necessary.

INNER PLANE ADEPTI
Some schools of magic have named inner teachers who are known as the Inner Plane Adepti or Hidden Masters of Wisdom. These great instructors may once have been famous living people or they may be angels who have never lived on earth.

A well-established magical lodge will have one or more of these teachers, who are invited to witness the workings of the magical order and give guidance or instruction as necessary. If a group is fully aware of its Inner Plane Adept, they may see him or her during group meditations, or else one member of the group may have the skill to perceive this inner teacher and convey their words or philosophy to the other members. It requires a lot of faith and trust to enter a mind-to-mind contact with some unseen being, but those who are experienced in this method gain a great deal of genuine and original teaching material.

MYTHOLOGICAL HEROES
Legends and myths have given inspiration for guides and teachers to many traditions, in particular the Arthurian legends and Norse sagas. The Norse god Odin, leader of the Wild Hunt and giver of knowledge, is a complex figure who traded one of his eyes to drink in the underworld well of the wise god Mimir, and is therefore seen as a source of wisdom himself.

ANGELIC BEINGS
Among the other unseen beings who are often called on to help in magical work are the angels and archangels. They have many functions: as healers, teachers, protectors and illuminators of humanity.

Angels, whose name means "messenger" in Greek, are thought of as the active hands of the God or Goddess,

Egyptian temple pictures sometimes show deities and other celestial beings, as having wings. Here it is Isis who is shown as possessing angelic qualities.

Angels appear in many different spiritual traditions, acting as intermediaries and guides between this world and the next.

you see them as huge, delicate cloud formations like wings or feathers blown by the wind, and tipped with sunlight. They are always beautiful, and if you find yourself in their presence, it can be very moving and inspiring.

MEETING YOUR HIGHER SELF

Your higher self resides in the upperworld, or starry realm. It is the wisest and purest part of yourself that wants only what is best for your highest spiritual purpose – which is not necessarily the same as what your "lower" or everyday self desires.

To meet your higher self, you will need to journey to the upperworld (see Journeying to Other Worlds earlier in this chapter). Once there, pause and take a moment to observe your surroundings. Your higher self, or soul self, might be right there or you might have to go in search of it. When you meet your higher self, greet it with love. Pose any questions you may have and receive the answers gratefully. They might not be what your mortal self wants to hear but they will be honest. When it is time to return, thank your higher self for the meeting and slowly come back. Make a record of the events in a journal, because the meaning may not be immediately apparent and you may wish to read through the account again at a later date.

---

the source of all, or the One. They have no free will and travel between Earth and Heaven, bringing news or offering assistance. Working with angels is very popular because they appear to be benevolent beings of light, and are found in many religious philosophies. Pictures from ancient Egyptian temples show winged goddesses who seem to have many of the qualities of angels, and Christians, Muslims, Jews and many other faiths have accounts of angels in their religious texts.

Many different kinds of angels are particularly important to followers of the Hebrew mystical system of the Cabbala. The central glyph of this philosophy is the Tree of Life, which has ten spheres of creation. These are commonly linked to the powers of the planets, but each sphere also has an angel who rules over its working in the Earth plane.

MEETING ANGELS

Angels may be called upon by lighting a candle, relaxing and asking them to appear, or they might offer help unasked, if you genuinely need their assistance. They don't always look like we imagine them to be, as they can be vast in size, and as subtle as auric light. Sometimes

The planets and archangels

The Earth and seven "personal" planets are each associated with an angel, who rules over its working in the Earth plane.

Earth: Sandalphon
Moon: Gabriel
Mercury: Raphael
Venus: Anael
Sun: Michael
Mars: Zamael
Jupiter: Sachiel
Saturn: Cassiel

A word of warning

It is wisest not to attempt trances or try to contact discarnate spirits unless you have a reputable teacher, or expert help is at hand. Some people who have taken part in séances, played at "raising ghosts" or light-heartedly dabbled with Ouija boards have scared themselves. A few have opened doors to psychic perceptions that they did not know how to close, or have attracted the attention of entities they could not control. If you are aspiring to master the skills of magic, always work in the power of light, act sensibly and treat all beings – be they angels, gods, ghosts or elementals – with respect.

EXPLORING PAST LIVES

Natural magic honours the cycles of nature and its eternal round of birth, growth, death and rebirth. In human terms this is mirrored by a belief in reincarnation, which holds that each soul lives through many lifetimes, gradually gaining skills and strengthening its power to evolve. An aspect of this divine spark is within everyone – it is immortal and does not die when our bodies do. We recognize this eternal factor within us and probably think of it as our "inner self". Just as plants grow, blossom, fruit and die, so the human being grows, learns, reproduces, dies and is born again.

Trees "die" in winter and are "reborn" in spring, symbolizing the soul's eternal round.

THE SOUL

Throughout our time on the Earth plane, our soul gains new experiences and becomes more complete. When we die, it rests in a state that might be thought of as "heaven". Here it is not "judged" or made to account for "sins" but assesses its own progress and sees dispassionately how it has done in life. If a certain part of its development has been overlooked, it will reincarnate in another physical form to learn the lessons it needs to learn. The soul continues to reincarnate until its lessons on Earth are complete, when it transcends the birth, death, rebirth cycle by becoming one with the cosmic unity or the One.

KARMA

The theory of karma is central to the idea of past lives. Karma is a Sanskrit term to denote the concept of action and reaction, similar to the idea in Western thought of reaping what you sow. This means that every action has a consequence, and even if we may appear to "get away with it" this time around, our actions can return to haunt us in a future incarnation. Some people think that the qualities we are born with are the results of either "good" or "bad" karma, or that misfortune could be the results of karmic debts being paid off. Others believe that it is possible to choose to come to Earth in imperfect bodies in order to learn hard lessons quickly, and so evolve spiritually. It is impossible to agree on a precise doctrine,

Once the cycle of rebirth is over, and the soul has learned all it needs to know, it transcends birth and death to become one with the cosmic unity.

Discovering past lives

One way of discovering past lives is through hypnotic regression. This is not something that you can do by yourself and should only be undertaken with expert guidance. However, an effective way of finding out about past lives by yourself is to develop an inner journey to the Hall of Records where you can locate your own personal Book of Lives and look in that to see who you have been. It also avoids the emotional impact of re-living the past, which can be associated with regression techniques.

1 Sit in meditation and visualize yourself entering an old building and climbing a staircase to a great library. This is the Hall of Records and in it there are a great number of books of all ages, sizes and types. Explore the place fully using all your senses.

2 Librarians are available who can help you find your own records; you just need to ask for their help. The volume of your lives will have your current name on it and it can be taken to a quiet corner to study.

3 Continue to relax and allow whatever symbol of this personal record that arises to do so, rather than making it have a particular form. It could be a book, a stone tablet, or even a computer screen – there is no right form.

4 When you are focused, look at your personal record and you are sure to find something of interest. It could be a family tree, written words in familiar or ancient languages, pictures, or an image that is more like a window, through which you can pass to explore your own past.

5 Take your time and enter into the experience as deeply as possible, while making a mental note of everything that you find. You may experience life from the outside, merely witnessing domestic events as an onlooker, or you may find yourself viewing some past incarnation. What you get, and how deeply you are affected, will depend on how much you can go with the process.

6 Write up your experience in your Book of Shadows or other journal. You could also add drawings and anything else you gain from research later on.

Use the smoke from a snuffed candle to draw you into the meditation, and light it again afterwards to ground yourself.

but the idea of karma and its balance of good and bad deeds makes a worthwhile lesson. It is hard to get to the bottom of a single event, as every life is affected by complex patterns of action and reaction and it is the soul that chooses the conditions into which it will be born each time. No other being directs the pattern of reincarnation.

SOULMATES

It is possible that long-lasting relationships can continue from one life to the next. When people describe having a "soulmate", in the true sense of the word, they mean a lover with whom they have journeyed through many lives. This is because true love is eternal and its bonds outlive the grave.

PAST-LIFE RECALL

If you are interested in exploring your own past lives, go about it sensibly, because it can be an unsettling experience. It is vital to have a reliable companion, plenty of time, and to make detailed records. Do not take everything you learn for granted without checking the facts – there are plenty of accurate historical accounts of most times and places, and the research can help confirm whether what you recall is valid and "real". However, even if it is just fantasy, your imagination may have something valid to show you about yourself.

A mirror spell to see who you have been

This will allow you to get a small glimpse of the past, on which you can work to gain more details.

1 Make a magical circle of protection and calmness by sprinkling blessed water around you. Become relaxed and focused.

2 At night, place a mirror on a stand and a single lit white candle on a table so that the light shines on your face. Also take a sheet of writing paper and a pen. Write clearly the following words, then carefully burn the writing in the candle flame:

I wish to see who I have been in a past life, at a time when all was going well. Reveal to me in this shining glass, I summon old "me" by this spell.

3 Just focus your vision on your eyes reflected in the mirror and after a while you may see the image change and become another face. It can seem a bit weird at first, but if you are patient and certain it is what you want, it will happen.

4 When your face returns to normal, say:
Thank you, me, whoever you seem, perhaps we will meet again in dream.

MAGICAL CORRESPONDENCES

Magic is a vast and ancient subject and tables of correspondences have always been an important part of the magic-worker's tool kit. They provide a useful at-a-glance guide to some of the main properties of the various magical "ingredients" that are used in spells, ceremonies, rituals and all other kinds of magic. Once you start looking, you will find that there are literally hundreds of tables available – both ancient and modern – that can all be used to help you with your magical journey.

What is given here is a selection of some of the most useful correspondence charts to get you started, but as you become more experienced you will find the confidence to develop your own charts based on your own magical knowledge. This final chapter contains correspondence charts on the symbolism of crystals, birds and animals, trees, plants and herbs, incense and essential oils as well as colour. It also

contains tables of the elements, of planetary associations, and a guide to some of the main gods, angels and spirit beings in magical use today. Remember that such information is not intended as a substitute for in-depth knowledge, but as a quick reference tool to help you when selecting the appropriate ingredients for use in your magic.

The symbolism of crystals

Amber	Good luck stone, draws out disease and clears negativity and depression
Agate	For inspiration from the spiritual realm
Amethyst	Peace, protection and spirituality; healing; release from addiction, help with meditation and peaceful sleep, eases transition between life and death
Angelite	Heals anger, restores harmony; helpful in telepathic communication, connecting with angels and spirits
Aquamarine	Helps in the expression of spiritual truths; aids dreaming to increase psychic power
Aventurine	Healing at all levels, dissolves blockages, balances the emotions; green aventurine attracts good fortune and increases perception; pink aventurine heals relationships
Azurite	Mental clarity and renewal, releases painful ideas from the subconscious; also known as 'the stone of heaven', can help attunement to the psychic world
Beryl	Enhances psychic ability
Black onyx	Protects against negative energy, helps emotional stability, encourages connection with reality
Blue lace agate	Symbolizes health and long life, grounding, brings inspiration and facilitates self-expression
Calcite	Balances male and female energies; allays fears and stress, assists with astral travel; orange calcite is particularly useful for shock or trauma
Carnelian	Aids creative flow, grounds in the present, inspires confidence, courage and motivation
Celestite	To link with angels and spirit guides, a bright moontime crystal
Chrysocolla	Soothes and calms, eases fear and guilt, attracts luck
Chrysoprase	Emotionally uplifting, attracts abundance and success, spiritual energy
Citrine	Prevents nightmares, enhances self-esteem and responsible use of power, brings abundance and material wellbeing; a crystal of the sun
Clear quartz	Amplifies energy, spiritually and emotionally healing, aids meditation; a bright moontime crystal
Diamond	Symbolizes power, purity, strength, trust, commitment and love; instils wisdom and confidence
Emerald	Physically healing and protective; lends insight and security in love
Fluorite	Gathers together different energies and assists in focus and concentration; aids communication with higher self; yellow fluorite promotes self-confidence
Garnet	Stimulates energy, aids expression, strengthens love

Crystals are a powerful magical tool.

	and friendship
Haematite	Aids concentration, reasoning, memory and self-discipline; healing and protective; grounding
Herkimer diamond	Releases energy blockages, helps with dream recall
Jade	Clarity, justice and wisdom; balances the emotions, promotes peaceful sleep; attracts prosperity
Jasper	Often referred to as a talisman; one of the most powerful healing stones
Jet	Calms the subtle bodies, clears a heavy head and helps lift depression, useful for clearing negativity; a dark moontime crystal
Kunzite	Redresses compulsive tendencies and restores balance; opens up the heart and connection to higher self
Kyanite	Balances emotional disturbances, promotes inner peace; helps intuition
Labradorite	Develops psychic ability
Lapis lazuli	Strengthens will, awareness, integrity in relationships; aids the release of emotional wounds
Malachite	Healing, absorbs negativity, stimulates creativity
Moonstone	Wishes, intuition and new beginnings; restores harmony in relationships, calms emotions and induces lucid dreaming; a bright moontime crystal
Moss agate	Connects with earth spirits, brings abundance and self-confidence
Obsidian	Protective and grounding, reduces escapism and dissolves anger and fear; snowflake obsidian has a softer effect, restores balance and clarity
Opal	Visionary, attracts inspiration and insight
Pearl	Enhances purity, clarity and grace; balances emotions, increases confidence in inner wisdom
Pyrites	Harnesses creative thinking and practicality
Red jasper	Connects with earth energy, emotionally calming
Rhodonite	Fosters patience, selflessness
Rose quartz	Heals emotional wounds, restores love
Ruby	Amplifies emotions, releases and dissolves anger, attracts loyalty, awakens passion and beauty
Sapphire	Symbolizes peace, gives protection and wisdom
Selenite	Mental focus, clarity and clairvoyance
Smoky quartz	Lightly grounding and balancing; fosters self-acceptance; absorbs negative vibrations
Sodalite	Calms troubled mind and emotions; promotes inner peace
Sugilite	Aids physical healing and purification of all body systems; strengthens will; aid to meditation
Tiger's eye	Creates order and harmony; attracts beauty
Topaz	Symbolizes light and warmth, heals and absorbs tension, attracts love and creativity
Tourmaline	Grounding, healing and protective, absorbs negativity and brings discernment and vitality
Turquoise	Healing and protection; blessing and partnership

The symbolism of birds and animals

Alligator/ crocodile	Guardian and fierce protector; stealth, ferocity; primal power
Antelope	Vision and foresight, speed and quick action; gentleness
Armadillo	Armour, boundaries and protection
Badger	Strength and perseverance; fighting for what you want, tenacity; prophesy and divination
Bat	Death and rebirth; initiation, transition, change
Bear	Receptive female energy, earth wisdom, introspection; lunar energies
Beaver	Industrious; flexibility and creativity
Blackbird	Gatekeeper
Bison (buffalo)	Wisdom of the elders; provider and protector; fertility, sexual vigour, power
Bull	Male sexual potency, strength; war
Cat	Independence, intuition; sacred to the Goddess, female medicine
Cow	Fertility and prosperity; motherhood, family life
Coyote	Childlike trust, innocence and playfulness; a trickster figure, mischievous and exposes pretensions in others
Crow/raven	Change; foresight and prediction; shape shifting; good and bad luck; all aspects of witchcraft and magic
Deer	Security and protection; male and female sexuality; keeper of wisdom, storyteller
Dog	Friendship, kindness, loyalty and protection, guardian of ancient secrets
Dolphin/porpoise	Understanding, wisdom; unconditional love; laughter, harmony and healing
Dove	Peace and love; marriage, spiritual harmony; purity and clear vision
Dragon	Mythical beast, symbol of good luck; energetic, fun-loving, confident
Duck	Love and harmony, domesticity, abundance; motherhood and children; new beginnings
Eagle	Divine and earthly power; freedom, fearlessness striving for higher goals; clarity, clairvoyance
Fish	Mystery, the depths of the subconscious, emotions; lunar magic
Fox	Trickery and guile, secrets; protection, family, maternal instincts
Frog	Cleansing, emotional healing; fertility; change and transformation
Goat	Relaxed and happy-go-lucky; ability to live in the present; creative, friendly, ambitious
Goose	Storytelling; protection, fertility; rebirth; links with the Great Mother
Hare	Quickness of thought; intuition, sensitivity, creativity; associated with the moon goddess, fertility

Hawk	The gift of foresight, perception, psychic powers; messenger from spirit world bringing knowledge and wisdom

The proud eagle symbolizes freedom and fearlessness

Heron	Self-reliance
Horse	Freedom, swiftness, stamina and endurance; earthly and otherworldly power; strength and self-confidence
Jaguar (panther, leopard)	The gift of vision; prediction, prophesy and divination; intuition and psychic power
Lion	Strength, majesty; power and leadership
Lizard	Illusions, letting go; adaptability; change, transition
Magpie	Relationships
Moose (elk)	Strength and endurance; male and female sexuality; relationships
Monkey	Inquisitive, energetic, competitive; leadership; clever and sharp-witted
Mouse	Finely attuned sensitivity; messenger; abundance and fertility
Owl	Wisdom; understanding hidden truths; insight and telepathy; all forms of magic
Ox	Patience, kindness and responsibility; routine, order and discipline
Pig	Diplomacy, common sense; prone to greed
Pigeon	Messages
Rabbit	Fertility and love; fear and cowardice
Ram/sheep	Lust, fertility; action without forethought, youthful zest
Rat	Self-motivated, strong sense of self-preservation; cheerful, ability to bounce back
Robin	New beginnings; protection
Rooster	Flamboyant; a good communicator
Snake	Shedding of the old; transformation; philosophical, mysterious, shrewd, sensual; underworld guardian
Swan	Purity, serenity, peace; spirituality and dignity
Tiger	Rash, impulsive, dynamic; risk-taking, leadership
Turtle	Endurance; knowledge; Mother Earth, women
Wolf	Loyalty; freedom; independence; afterlife and rebirth; teacher
Woodpecker	Magic and prophecy; sacred cycles; rain, storms and thunder

Wren	Protection

The wolf symbolizes loyalty and freedom.

The symbolism of trees, plants and herbs

Angelica	Burn dried leaves for protection and healing
Anise	Keeps away nightmares
Apple	For love and friendship; youth, beauty, innocence
Ash	The world tree; purification and cleansing
Basil	Gives protection, repels negativity, brings wealth
Bay	Guardian of the house, protects against illness; burn leaves to produce visions
Beech	Stability, flow of energy; protector of written wisdom, guardian of knowledge
Blessed thistle	Brings spiritual and financial blessing; fresh plant brings strengthening energy to a sickroom
Cabbage	Brings good luck
Carrot seed	Illuminating; use for visions and vision quests, journeying
Catnip	Encourages a psychic bond with cats; attracts luck and happiness
Chamomile	For meditation and relaxation; use in prosperity charms to attract money
Chickweed	For attracting love or maintaining a relationship
Chilli	Assures fidelity and love
Cinnamon	Aphrodisiac; draws money, protection and success
Clove	Banishes hostile or negative forces and helps to gain what is sought; use in spells to stop gossip
Clover	For love and fidelity
Coltsfoot	Brings love, wealth and peace
Comfrey	For safety when travelling
Cyclamen	For love and truth
Dandelion	Enhances dreams and prophetic power
Dogwood	Charm and finesse
Elm	Love, light and purification; death and rebirth;
Fennel	Protects from curses
Gardenia	For peace and healing
Garlic	For magical healing, protection and exorcism
Ginger	For success and empowerment
Grape	For fertility and garden magic, attracts money
Hawthorn	Marriage, fertility, happiness, protection of children; gateway to the otherworld
Hazel	Wisdom and fertility; used for wands, divining
Hibiscus	Attracts love, aids divination and dreams
Honeysuckle	Strengthens the memory, helps in letting go of the past
Holly	Strongest protective tree; dream magic, wisdom and courage; healing of subtle bodies
Hops	Improves health and induces sleep; goddess energy
Hyacinth	For love and protection

Tobacco is a sacred herb in the Native American Indian tradition

Hyssop	Purification; dispel negativity
Jasmine	Induces lucid dreams; brings good fortune in love, friendship and wealth; raises self-esteem
Juniper	Calms and brings good health; berries ward off evil
Lavender	Purifying; brings peace and happiness, love; helps sweet dreams
Lemon	Attracts happiness, relieves stress
Lettuce	Induces sleep, assists in divination
Lily-of-the-valley	Brings peace, harmony and love
Lime	Increases energy, encourages loyalty
Lotus	Emblem of enlightenment, elevates and protects
Magnolia	Assures fidelity
Marigold	Enhances visions and dreams; renews energy
Mistletoe	For protection, love and visionary ability; hang on the bedpost for beautiful dreams
Mugwort	For clairvoyance, scrying and dream interpretation
Oak	Wisdom, strength and endurance; groves of oak trees associated with prophecy and divination;
Olive	Brings peace of mind and fidelity in love fruitfulness and security
Orange	Attracts peace, power and luck
Orris	Attracts love and romance
Passion flower	Fosters friendship, brings peace and understanding
Pennyroyal	Increases alertness, helps peace between partners
Pine	Grounding and cleansing, use for a fresh start; repels evil; cleansing and purifying
Rice	Attracts fertility and money
Rose	Blesses love, domestic peace, generosity and beauty
Rosemary	Protects the home, brings mental clarity and sharpens memory
Rowan	Protection against evil, enchantment and negative energies; development of psychic powers
Sage	Brings wisdom, fertility, healing and long life
Silver birch	New beginnings, healing; mysteries of the maiden
Strawberry	For love and luck
Sweet pea	For friendship and courage
Thyme	For courage and confidence
Tobacco	Introduces sacred spirit
Valerian	Brings love and harmony
Vervain	For inner strength and peace
Violet	Contentment and love
Willow	Love and regeneration; lunar and feminine rhythms; healing and to empower wishes
Yew	Immortality, transformation and inner wisdom

Clover is associated with love and fidelity.

The symbolism of incense and essential oils

Acacia (gum arabic) Protection; develops psychic awareness

Agarwood (aloes) Protection, consecration; prosperity and success; connection with the upperworld

Amber Love and healing

Benzoin Aid to meditation; grounding, helps reconnect with inner self

Bergamot Attracts success and prosperity; use in rituals of initiation

Camphor Guardian of rebirth; assists in change and transformation; used in moon magic

Cajeput Spiritual expansion and freedom

Cedar Associated with magical power, vitality and immortality

Chamomile Peace, tranquillity and emotional stability; aid to sleep and dreaming

Clary sage Aphrodisiac; stimulates vivid dreams and encourages dream recall

Clove Clears the mind and assists in past life recall

Copal Protection, purification and banishing negativity; a fragrance of the gods and angels

Dragon's blood Neutralizes negative energies; cleansing and protecting

Eucalyptus Healing and purifying; use in space clearing

Frankincense Calms and quietens the mind; an aid to meditation; use in rituals of initiation and rites of passage

Galbanum Spells for endings and letting go; clears negativity

Geranium Balancing and adjusting; assists with new projects

Helichrysum Opens channel for healing, dreams and visions; spells for inspiration

Jasmin Imagination

Juniper Clearing negative energies

Lavender Psychic balance; brings emotions under control

Lemon grass Cleansing and purifying; releasing the past, forgiveness

Mandarin Inspiration; aid to communication, useful for harmony with friends and family

Mimosa Opens up channel of communication with higher self, angels and spirit beings

Melissa Strengthens connection with cosmic energies; love, harmony and happiness

The smoke of any incense will add the Air element to your ritual.

Musk For love and sexual attraction

Myrrh Helps connect with True Will, courage to follow the soul's path

Myrtle For spiritual love and immortality of the soul

Neroli For love and fertility; use in wedding ceremonies

Niaouli Clearing negative thoughts, expanding consciousness

Nutmeg Stimulating aphrodisiac; clairvoyance and psychic development

Olibanum Similar to frankincense, but with a lighter, more delicate fragrance. An incense of the sun

Palmarosa For letting go of the past and spiritual illumination

Patchouli Relaxing aphrodisiac; grounding, helps connection with earth energies

Peppermint For clarity and courage; increases perception and awareness in the dream state

Ravensara For spontaneity and determination; deepens meditation

Rose To honour the Goddess and strengthen a connection with all aspects of the feminine force

Rosewood For space clearing

Sandalwood Aphrodisiac (especially for men); comforts the dying and helps ease transition between the worlds; opens the gates to spirit guides

Storax Ancient incense burning substance with long tradition of use in magic and sacred ceremony; calming and relaxing, helps the mind unburden

Tea tree For space clearing and purification; a light in the darkness

Tobacco Sacred to native Americans, usually used for making offerings

Vanilla Aphrodisiac (especially for women); attracts love and romance

Vetivert Protection against negative energies; for over sensitivity to psychic impressions

Ylang ylang For love and sensuality

All kinds of incense can be bought in stick, cone or resin form.

The symbolism of gods and angels

Agni	Hindu god of fire
Amaterasu	Shinto sun goddess
Anubis	Egyptian god of the underworld, depicted with a jackal's head
Aphrodite	Greek goddess of love and beauty; known as Venus to the Romans
Apollo	Greek god of the sun, medicine and music, patron of the Muses
Arianrhod	Celtic mother goddess and keeper of time and fate
Artemis	Greek goddess of the waxing moon, protector of women; known as Diana to the Romans
Athene	Greek goddess of war, wisdom and the arts; known as Minerva to the Romans
Uriel	Archangel, earth
Bast	Egyptian cat goddess of love and fertility
Brigid	Celtic triple goddess, fire deity and patron of the hearth, healing, prophecy and inspiration
Cassiel	Archangel who assists with overcoming obstacles
Ceridwen	Celtic goddess of wisdom and death; her cauldron contained the brew of inspiration
Cerunnos	The celtic horned god, like Pan he is a fertility god; god of the witches
Cybele	Phrygian dark moon goddess who governs nature, wild beasts and dark magic
Demeter	Greek goddess of the earth, corn and vegetation; represents abundance and unconditional love; known as Ceres to the Romans
Dhagda	Celtic father god
Dionysus	Greek god of wine and ecstasy; known as Bacchus to the Romans
Epona	Celtic horse-goddess of fertility, abundance and healing

Pan, half man half goat, is the Greek personification of the horned god.

Freya	Norse mother goddess of love, marriage and fertility
Gabriel	Archangel of the moon, associated with the west
Gaia	Primeval Greek earth deity, prophetess of Delphi, goddess of dreams
Ganesha	Elephant-headed Hindu god of wisdom and literature, son of Parvati and Shiva, patron of business
Hades	Greek god of the underworld; known as Pluto to the Romans
Anael	Archangel of divine love and harmony, beauty and the creative arts
Hathor	Egyptian sky-deity, goddess of love, joy and dance, usually represented as a cow
Hecate	Greek triple goddess, rules magic, sorcery, death and the underworld; associated with crossroads
Hermes	Greek messenger god; represents communication, transition and exchange; associated with magic, healing and thieves; known as Mercury to the Romans
Hestia	Greek goddess of the hearth and stability

The huntress goddess Artemis was known as Diana to the Romans.

Horus	Egyptian sun god, depicted with a falcon's head
Indra	Hindu god of war; associated with weather and fertility
Ishtar	Mesopotamian goddess of sexual love, fertility and war
Isis	Egyptian mother-goddess, wife of Osiris and mother of Horus; represents life, loyalty, fertility and magic
Ixchel	Mayan goddess of storms and protector of women in childbirth
Janus	Roman guardian of the entrance and god of transition
Jizo	Japanese protector of children and travellers
Kali	Destructive aspect of the Hindu mother goddess
Kuanyin	Chinese goddess of compassion
Kwannon	Japanese goddess of compassion
Lakshmi	Hindu goddess of abundance, wealth and harmony
Lugh	Celtic sky god, associated with skills and the arts
Luna	Roman goddess of the full moon
Maat	Egyptian goddess of truth, justice and order
Mars	Roman god of war, lover of Venus
Manjushri	Buddhist bodhisattva of wisdom
Michael	Archangel of the sun, associated with rulership, marriage, music
Minerva	Roman goddess of wisdom
Mithras	Roman god of light
Morrigan	Celtic goddess of battlefields and death
Nephthys	Sister of Isis, the Egyptian mother goddess, guardian of the dead Osiris
Neptune	Roman god of the sea; known as Poseidon to the Greeks
Odin	Norse sky-father god and Master of the Runes
Osiris	Egyptian god of vegetation and judge of the dead, brother and husband of Isis; symbolizes regenerative power of nature
Pan	Greek horned god of wild things, half man, half animal
Parvati	Hindu mother goddess, consort of Shiva
Persephne /Kore	Kore, Greek goddess of Spring was abducted by Hades and became Persephone, Queen of the underworld
Raphael	Archangel of the air element, associated with communication and business
Re	Egyptian sun god and creator
Sachiel	Archangel ruling justice and financial matters
Samael	Protective archangel, helps with matters that require courage or perseverance
Sekhmet	Egyptian goddess of destruction and healing, depicted with the head of a lioness
Selene	Greek goddess of the full moon
Shang Ti	Chinese supreme god
Shiva	Hindu creator god whose meditation sustains the world
Shu	Egyptian god of the air, creator of earth and sky

The majestic glory of archangels must be treated with the utmost respect.

Sif	Norse goddess of the grasslands, wife of Thor
Sophia	Greek goddess of divine knowledge and wisdom
Sul	Celtic goddess of healing
Sunna	Norse sun goddess
Surya	Hindu sun god
Tara	Tibetan goddess of wisdom and compassion
Thor	Norse god of thunder and industry, married to Sif
Thoth	Egyptian god of wisdom and the moon, scribe of Osiris
Tiamat	Mesopotamian creator goddess
Tsao-chun	Taoist kitchen god
Uriel	Archangel of high magic
Vesta	Roman goddess of the hearth
Vishnu	Hindu protector of the world
Zeus	Greek supreme god; known as Jupiter to the Romans

Table of the four elements

	Air	Fire	Water	Earth
Direction	East	South	West	North
Season	Spring	Summer	Autumn	Winter
Time of day	Dawn	Noon	Sunrise	Midnight
Moon phase	New	First quarter	Full	Dark
Planets	Sun, Mercury, Uranus	Mars, Pluto	Moon, Neptune, Venus	Earth, Saturn
Astrological signs	Gemini, Libra, Aquarius	Aries, Leo, Sagittarius	Cancer, Scorpio, Pisces	Taurus, Virgo, Capricorn
Magical tool	Dagger, athame, sword	Candles, lanterns, solar icons	Chalice, cauldron, mirror	Pentacle/stone, wand
Altar symbol	Incense	Lamp or candle	Chalice	Platter
Communion symbol	Scent	Heat	Wine/water	Bread/salt
Elemental symbol	△	△	▽	▽
Archangel	Raphael	Michael	Gabriel	Uriel
Polarity	Male positive	Male negative	Female negative	Female positive
Human sense	Hearing and smell	Sight	Taste	Touch
Art forms	Poetry/painting	Dance/drama	Music/song	Sculpture/embroidery
Creatures	Birds, bats, winged insects	Lizard, snake, lion, ram	Cat, frog, turtle, dolphin, whale, otter, seal, fish	Ox, dog, wolf, goat, stag
Elemental beings	Sylphs	Salamanders	Undines	Gnomes
Exhortation	To will	To dare	To know	To keep silent
Mythical beast	Winged horse	Dragon, phoenix	Sea serpent	Unicorn
Magical arts	Divinations	Ritual	Healing	Talismans
God forms	Sky/weather god	Sun/protector god	Moon/water goddess	Earth/underworld goddess
Meditation	Sky/clouds	Bonfires	The ocean/rivers	Fertile landscape
Colours	Yellow, blue, violet	Red and orange	Blue, turquoise, green	Russet, brown, black, olive-green, sometimes white
Instruments	Wind instruments/harp	Brass instruments	Strings/bells	Drums/percussion
Natural symbols	Feathers, incense smoke, fragrant flowers	Flame, lava	Shells, water, river plants, watercress	Fossils, stones, grains and seeds, salt, earth
Trees	Elder, eucalyptus	Oak, hawthorn	Willow, alder, ash	Cypress, pine
Herbs	Comfrey, lavender, mint	Basil, bay, garlic, hyssop, juniper, rosemary, rue	Chamomile, hops, lemon balm, orris, seaweeds, yarrow	Pennyroyal, lovage, sage
Incense	Sandalwood, lemon	Frankincense, cinnamon, basil	Jasmine, rose	Myrrh, patchouli
Minerals	Mercury, aventurine, topaz	Brass, gold, iron, fire opal, garnet, haematite, red jasper, sardonyx, flint, pearl, sapphire	Silver, copper, amethyst, aquamarine, turquoise, tourmaline, opal, jade, moonstone	Lead, emerald
Images and Themes	Mountain Tops, flying, sunrise, Wisdom and knowledge Sun at Noon	Flames, Volcanoes, walking through fire, Healing and calm	Lakes/pools, living under water, setting sun, night, Growth and life	Caves/rocks, growing organically, moon/stars/

Fire element can be added with heat and flame.

Use smoke in your magic to add the Air element.

A bowl of water will bring the Water element.

Table of planets

Planet	Moon	Mars	Mercury	Jupiter	Venus	Saturn	Sun	Earth
Day	Monday	Tuesday	Wednesday	Thursday	Friday	Saturday	Sunday	Any
Metal	Silver	Iron	Quicksilver	Tin	Copper	Lead	Gold	Any
Colours	White, silver, blue	Red	Yellow	Royal blue, violet, purple	Green	Black	Gold/orange	All, but especially earth shades (browns, russets)
Gemstones	Moonstone, pearl	Garnet, ruby, bloodstone, haematite	Opal, beryl, agate, carnelian	Amethyst, lapis lazuli, aquamarine	Emerald, peridot, jade	Jet, onyx, obsidian	Diamond, amber, topaz	Agate
Number	9	5	8	4	7	3	6	10
Angel	Gabriel	Zamael	Raphael	Sachiel	Anael	Cassiel	Michael	Sandalphon
Deities	Artemis, Luna, Selene	Mars, Samael, Anath	Hermes, Mercury, Athena	Zeus, Jupiter, Juno	Aphrodite, Venus	Cronos, Saturn, Kali	Helios, Sol Apollo, Re	Gaia, Ceres
Trees	Aspen, willow, lemon, eucalyptus	Larch, hawthorn, dogwood	Ash, hazel	Almond, horse chestnut, oak	Apple, fig, magnolia, pear, elder, damson	Alder, beech, holly, elm, yew	Acacia, bay, birch, cedar, walnut, lime, orange, rowan, juniper	All
Plants and herbs	Jasmine, poppy, white lily, all aquatic plants	Anemone, tobacco, coriander, garlic	Impatiens, caraway, lavender, marjoram, dill	Honeysuckle, nutmeg, sage, star anise, cloves	Heather, hyacinth, rose, love-in-a-mist, iris, vervain, myrtle, yarrow	Ivy, evergreens, asafoetida	Mistletoe, marigold, bay laurel, benzoin gum, angelica, cinnamon, bay leaves	All
Incenses	Jasmine, sandalwood	Tobacco, pine	Mastic, lavender	Cedar, honeysuckle	Rose	Myrrh, cypress	Frankincense	Dittany of Crete patchouli
Magic for	Increasing intuition, psychic ability, fertility and all female issues	Improving strength, power and authority; banishing conflicts	All forms of travel and communication, including writing, teaching, speaking, learning, studying	Luck and prosperity; employment opportunities, travel, money, justice and wealth	Love, friendship, marriage, beauty and harmony creativity, artistic endeavours	Clearing obstacles and restrictions; patience	Good fortune in all areas of life; health, success and prosperity	Connecting with the Earth's mysteries, and the underworld

Saturn's influence in magic helps clear obstacles and remove restriction.

Use the moon's influence in magic to increase psychic ability and intuition.

Index